DAY TRIPS FROM HOUSTON

"Take a break from the hectic pace of city life."
—*Texas Highways* magazine

"This guidebook details 22 one-day getaways, each two hours or less from Houston. There is even a bonus directory with other helpful information in the back."
—*Books of the Southwest*

"Barrington truly knows her ground. . . . With this guide, I guarantee, you'll never be stuck in Houston with nothing to do. It's one of the best!"
—*The Monitor* (McAllen, TX)

"Concentrates on unusual things to see and do, restaurants off the beaten path and outside of the humdrum chain eateries."
—*The Gazette-Enterprise,* Seguin, TX

"A well-organized guidebook . . . offers the visitor to the city a welcome break from the fast pace."
—*The Longview Morning Journal*

"Dedicated to those who love the history and backroads of Texas."
—*Lake Charles* (LA) *American Press*

GETAWAYS LESS THAN TWO HOURS AWAY

Shifra Stein's
Day Trips® from Houston

FOURTH EDITION

by **Carol Barrington**

A Voyager Book

The Globe Pequot Press

CHESTER, CONNECTICUT

Library of Congress Cataloging-in-Publication Data

Barrington, Carol
   Day trips from Houston: Getaways less than two hours away/by Carol Barrington. — 4th ed.
     p.   cm.
   "A Voyager Book."
   ISBN 0-87106-158-9
   1. Houston region (Tex.)—Description and travel—Guide-books.
I. Title.
F394.H83B37   1991
917.64'14110463–dc20   91-13113
                                                   CIP

Local maps by Kathy Kent
Cover design by Ken Compton

Manufactured in the United States of America
Fourth Edition/First Printing

CONTENTS

N O R T H W E S T

W E S T

S O U T H W E S T

N O R T H E A S T

E A S T

S O U T H E A S T

PREFACE

After coping with the race-pace of Houston, a getaway trip literally can be a lifesaver. But where to go with little time and even less money? The answer is to explore what lies just beyond that last subdivision and skyscraper on the city's ever-expanding horizon.

For the past three decades, Texas and its largest city have been El Dorados for those willing to trust and test their own abilities and take chances. It must be something in the air. The seeds of today's Houston were sown more than 150 years ago by risk-takers like Austin and Crockett, Houston and Travis—and chapters of their life stories can be found just beyond the city's doorstep.

But history isn't all. Within a two-hour drive you can canoe a primeval swamp, angle for a free crab dinner, or learn to sail. There are ferries to ride, beaches to comb, and quiet country roads to mosey along on bikes. Ever been to a horse farm or country racetrack? How about a cotton gin or cane syrup mill? With this book in hand, you'll find hundreds of things to do within a comfortable drive of home.

Take along a good Texas map. Using it with the "Wandering the Backroads" sections of this book will let you mix and match portions of adjacent trips to suit your personal interests and available time. Do call ahead if you are planning an important stop. Barrington's First Law states that facts tend to change the instant they appear in print. Also, many of the restaurants and special activities listed are individual enterprises and sometimes economically fragile. Call ahead to make sure hard times haven't claimed yet another victim.

One hint: In nearly two decades of exploring the backroads around Houston, I've learned to travel Lone Star-style, stopping to chat as I go—and so should you. Texans are among the world's most friendly folk. They have taken me to see wild ducks wing in on the sunrise and have taught me to seine shrimp from the surf and then cook them in salt water on the beach. All restaurants mentioned are local recommendations.

There are fresh adventures popping up all the time. If you find something new and enjoyable, please share it with me by writing to my publisher. Together, we can make future editions of this book even more fun.

Happy Day-Tripping!

Carol Barrington

USING THIS BOOK

In most cases, hours of operation are omitted because they are subject to frequent changes. Instead, telephone numbers are listed so you can call for specifics.

Restaurant prices are designated as $$$ (expensive, $17 or over) per meal; $$ (moderate, $7 to $17); $ (inexpensive, under $7).

Listings in the "What to Do" and "Where to Eat" sections generally are in alphabetical order.

The symbol (CC) denotes that at least one credit card is accepted.

Please note: No payment of any kind is either solicited or accepted to gain mention in this book.

MAP REFERENCES

Several maps in this book are meant to be used in conjunction with more than one day trip. The table below lists the pages on which these maps, and their accompanying day trips, appear.

State section	map page	Day trip # / page
Northwest	33	4 / 32
		5 / 38
West	56	1 / 57
		3 / 71
		4 / 79
		5 / 86
Northeast	130	2 / 129
		3 / 138
East	148	1 / 149
		2 / 154
		3 / 158
Southeast	166	1 / 167
		2 / 172

NORTHWEST

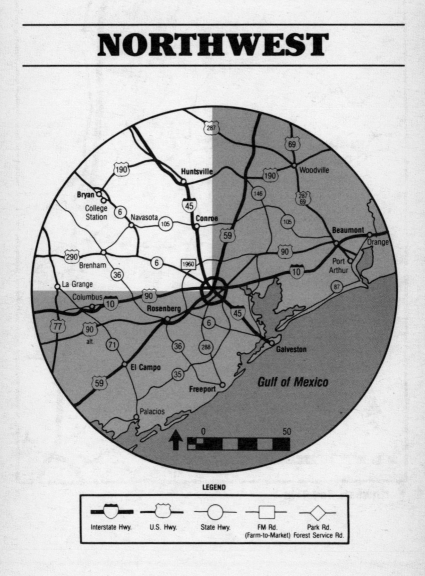

Huntsville
287
69
190
Woodville
Bryan
190
College
Station
146
287
69
6
Navasota
105
45
Conroe
105
Beaumont
59
Orange
290
Brenham
90
Port
6
1960
Arthur
36
10
La Grange
Columbus
90
87
10
Rosenberg
77
45
90
alt.
71
6
36
288
Galveston
El Campo
35
Gulf of Mexico
59
Freeport

Palacios

0   50

LEGEND

Interstate Hwy.   U.S. Hwy.   State Hwy.   FM Rd.   Park Rd.
                                           (Farm-to-Market) Forest Service Rd.

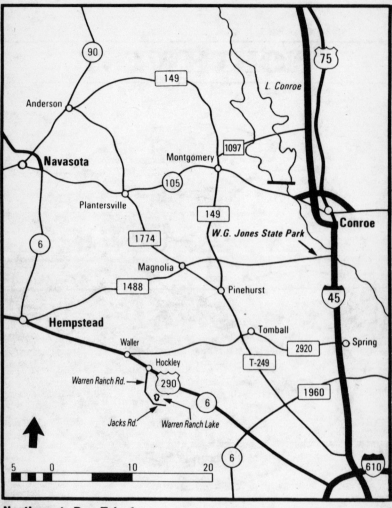

Northwest: Day Trip 1

Day Trip 1

TOMBALL
MAGNOLIA
MONTGOMERY
CONROE
SPRING

TOMBALL

One of the most scenic drives from Houston into the Brazos Valley or Lake Conroe areas begins by following T–249 north through rural woodlands and a series of small towns. You can shop as you go—on nice weather weekends, the shoulders of the road are lined with entrepreneurs selling everything from wind chimes to bonsai. Although none of the towns included in this day trip are of major interest in and of themselves, together they have enough interesting stops to make a great Sunday drive.

First up is the farming community of Tomball, named for turn-of-the-century congressman Thomas H. Ball. Turn east on Main Street at the T–249/FM–2920 intersection to find the old part of town. If you are headed for either the Merry Christmas Tree Farm or David Wayne Hooks Airport, continue east from town 2 miles on FM–2920.

WHAT TO DO

Flying High at David Wayne Hooks Airport. 20803 Steubner Airline at FM–2920, Tomball/Spring. The largest privately owned airport in Texas, this sprawling place offers numerous ways to get a bird's-eye view of Houston. Looking for an unusual birthday or anniversary present? Helicopters International (look for sign on large hangar) offers demonstration rides in a Robinson R–22 (twenty-minute introductory flight, $50; one hour, $190) or a pictorial look at Houston, including the Ship Channel and River Oaks, from 800 feet up in a Bell Jet Ranger (minimum one hour, $625). This is a federally licensed facility; all aircraft are maintained to federal standards. (713) 370–4354.

Hooks is home to numerous flight schools that offer sightseeing tours as well as discovery flights in which you can actually put hands on the controls. National Aviation, in the Mort Hall Aviation Building, offers hour-long discovery flights ($62) and pleasure flights for up to three people (one hour, $72); they welcome families and small groups for ground tours as well, (713) 370–5235. Horizon Aviation, in Hangar #15, has a twenty-minute introductory flight ($20–$25) and sightseeing tours ($60–$115), (713) 376–2932. Merriworth Aviation, in Hangar #6, offers thirty-minute discovery flights ($20–$25), (713) 376–0357. All are open sunrise to sunset daily. (CC). The airport's general telephone is (713) 376–5436.

Merry Christmas Tree Farm. 24950 Steubner Airline, Tomball/Spring. From Thanksgiving until Christmas you can select the one perfect tree from 25,000 that grow on this forty-two-acre farm. Call for directions and prices. (713) 351–5850 or 351–0818.

Spring Creek Park. One mile north of Tomball via T–249. On weekdays this oak-shaded park is a delightful place for a picnic. There's a large children's play area, plus an asphalt-banked ramp for skateboarders. Unfortunately, this park often is spoiled on weekends by rowdy crowds.

The Roy C. Hohl Nature Trail. On east side of T–249 at the Cypress Creek bridge, approx. 1 mile north of the FM–1960/T–249 intersection. This pocket of woods is a mini–Big Thicket, a roadside mix of botanical life zones worth exploring when the weather is nice. Good trails with picnic areas, and some catfish in the creek.

Willow Creek Fish Farm. 26925 T–249. This low–key place hides—watch for signs on the west side of the road about 2 miles south of Tomball. Best described as a shady picnic area with a three-quarter-acre pond, this fishing hole harbors rainbow trout December through February, catfish the rest of the year. At last notice, cane poles rented for $1, and bait was $2.25–$3.00. No license is required. The pond is stocked weekly on Thursday evenings, which makes Friday through Sunday morning the best times to fish. Although a few seven-to-eight-pound whoppers occasionally rise to the bait, the usual catch is two to three pounds. The only rule is that you must keep what you catch. There's no admission; you pay by the pound. No fish, no charge. (713) 351–5561.

Tomball Community Museum Center. North of Main Street at the end of Pine Street. Clustered on this cul-de-sac are some bits of the past collected by the Spring Creek Historical Society. The Trinity Evangelical Lutheran Church was a volunteer construction project of local German families in 1905, and all the furnishings and appointments are original to this white clapboard structure. Now often used for weddings and christenings, it also glows again with public services on Christmas Eve and at sunrise on Easter Sunday. Once each year a Lutheran service is conducted in both English and German.

The Griffin Memorial House is next door. Built in 1860 by one of Houston's earliest pioneers, Eugene Pillot, it stood at the intersection of Willow Creek and an early stage route known as the Atascosita Trail. Sam Houston frequently spent the night in this house waiting for the morning stage, and it was also a local gathering place and a school. The antique furnishings are of the later Victorian period and constitute, in themselves, the Magdalene Charlton Memorial Museum.

The Pioneer Country Doctor's Office and **Farm Museum** are across the way. The first is a turn-of-the-century doctor's office where Dr. William Ehrhardt practiced for more than fifty years. The museum contains early farm machinery, tools, etc., including a 100-year-old cotton gin from nearby Spring. Fee. This museum complex is open Thursday and Sunday; hours vary. Tours also by appointment. (713) 255–2148.

WHERE TO EAT

The Bake Shoppe. 22516 Tomball Parkway (T–249), in the Spring Cypress Village Shopping Center. This tidy, family-run place has breakfasts, lunches, and pastries like you wish Mom did make. The sandwiches come on homemade bread, and the cranberry chicken lunch entree is particularly good. Expect a line if you come between noon and 1 p.m.; the good food here is popular with executives from nearby Compaq. Open Monday–Friday. $. (713) 320–2253.

Mom's Pies—Just Like You Remember. 30006 Tomball Parkway (T–249), in the Sherwood Forest Center. Though she sometimes sells day-old pies by the slice, this tiny place specializes in whole pies to go, made that morning in the immaculate on-site kitchen. So put a cooler in the car and buy one for a feast either at home or on a picnic. If you call ahead, Mom will have your pie or cake waiting for you when you come by. She also bakes fresh strawberry, blackberry, and dewberry pies in season. Open Tuesday–Saturday. $. (713) 255–9779.

Goodson's Cafe. 27931 Tomball Parkway (T–249). Mrs. Goodson hung up her potholders and closed down her ramshackle but famous cafe on the outskirts of Tomball several years ago, and has since gone to her reward. But her recipe for hang-off-the-plate chicken-fried steak continues at this second-generation eatery. The menu also offers chicken, burgers, salads, and fish for lunch and dinner daily. $–$$; (CC). (713) 351–6490.

University Restaurant. 30522 Tomball Parkway (T–249). This pleasant place draws budget watchers with tasty all-you-can-eat specials (lunch, $2.99; dinner, $4.99) that include meat, veggies, potatoes, and a trip to a bountiful salad bar. At those prices you can't afford to eat at home. Open Tuesday–Saturday for breakfast, lunch, and dinner; Sunday and Monday until 3 p.m. $; (CC). (713) 351–9045.

The Viewpoint Restaurant. 29915 Tomball Parkway, (T–249). Country-style food in a casual setting. The chicken-fried steak and the salad bar are local favorites, along with the Sunday prime rib special. Cook/owners Ed and Carol Smith make their own muffins and yeast rolls, plus a memorable cabbage and Swiss cheese soup. Open daily for lunch and dinner. $–$$; (CC). (713) 351–0330.

MONTGOMERY and MAGNOLIA

From Tomball, drive north on T–249 to Pinehurst. Those brambles along the railroad tracks on your right are dewberry bushes, loaded in May and ripe for picking. Come prepared with a bucket, gloves, long-sleeved shirt, stout shoes, and a stick for scaring away snakes before you reach into the bushes.

At Pinehurst you must make a choice: Either continue straight north on FM–1774 to Magnolia and Plantersville or swing to the right, cross the railroad tracks, and follow FM–149 north to Montgomery. The first option, FM–1774, leads to a pick-your-own orchard during the summer months and to the sixteenth century in the fall; watch for longhorn cattle in the fields on the right and for beautiful horse farms on the left (such as the following).

WHAT TO DO

Arabians Internationale. 36441 FM–1774, one mile north of Pinehurst, on the left. Owned by Dan and Jamie McNaire, this 1,100-acre horse ranch welcomes visitors who have advance reservations. In addition to visiting the barns and paddocks (March through June is prime time to see new foals), you are welcome to watch both riding lessons and training sessions. Those who learn to ride here ultimately have access to trails throughout this beautiful ranch. No drop-ins, please. (713) 356–7094.

Hoffart's General Store. One mile south of T–105 on FM 1486 in Plantersville. The country equivalent of a Seven-Eleven, this is the kind of place that has homemade sausage in the meat case and free puppies and/or kittens in pens on the front porch. Open Monday–Saturday. (409) 597–5460.

The King's Orchard. Seven miles north of Magnolia on FM–1774 (1 mile north of the Renaissance Festival grounds). Although the apple, plum, and peach trees are a few years away from bearing crops, you can pick your pleasure of strawberries, blueberries, and blackberries at this thirty-two-acre farm. No chemicals are used in the growing process, and they'll call you when the fruit is ripe if you ask. (409) 894–2766.

The Relay Station. See "Where to Eat" section.

The Texas Renaissance Festival. Six miles north of Magnolia on FM–1774. For seven weekends starting around the beginning of October, the sights and sounds of merrie olde England brighten up this 247-acre woodland park. Visitors are encouraged to dress to the sixteenth-century theme and cavort with the jugglers, rope walkers, harpists, belly dancers, and jesters to their hearts' content. Fencers joust, Shakespeare struts upon the Globe Theatre stage, and King George and his royal court parade the grounds at high noon. Grand fun for the entire family, with horse and chariot races, assorted craftspersons, and food. Fee. Route 2, Box 650, Plantersville 77363. (713) 356–2178 (Houston); (409) 894–2516 (Plantersville).

Texas Opry Jamboree. 32243 Old Hempstead Road, Magnolia. Country music in a country setting, this tidy family-run operation puts on a lively two-hour music show featuring local entertainers every Saturday night, year-round. Expect singers, dancers, actors, and comedians at this mini Grand Ole Opry, all backed by the house band. Have you always had a hankering to be in show biz? Give them a call; they hold try-outs on a regular schedule. No alcohol is allowed or served, but the concession stand does a land office business in homemade cakes and brownies. Bring the kids. Fee. (713) 356–6779 (tape and ticket reservations from "Jake, the Janitor"); (713) 356–7355 (live information).

WHERE TO EAT

Henry's Hideout. Four miles north of Magnolia on FM–1774 (approximately 2 miles south of the Renaissance Festival grounds). Billing itself as the "Horniest Place in Texas" and "The Museum of 5,000 Horns," this surprisingly spiffy saloon is one of a kind. The walls are studded with hunting trophies, and the ceiling is a mass of deer horns. It seems that Henry started collecting horns in 1950 and can't stop; his place gets "horn-ier" by 100 or more sets of antlers every year. In addition to the friendly bar outlined with a world-class collection of neon beer signs, numerous pool tables are scattered around, and there's live music and dancing in the adjacent dance hall on Friday and Saturday nights. The menu runs from barbecue to pizza, tamales, and sausage-on-a-stick. $; (CC). (713) 356–8002.

The Relay Station. On T–105, 0.6 miles east of the FM–1774 intersection in Plantersville. Well known for its tasty steaks, hamburgers, and seafood, this Western-theme restaurant and saloon is a great family outing, particularly for kids who have never been on a horse. Every second and fourth Friday night is Children's Play-time, a pint-size rodeo competition in the big roping pen out back. There's a "community" horse for the use of those who don't have their own, and the six-and-unders compete on hobby (stick) horses in keyhole races, pole bending, straightaway and clover-leaf barrel races, etc. Holidays like Easter and the Fourth of July bring free, family-oriented parties, complete with wheelbarrow races and apple bobbing, to the restaurant's pavilion. Can't make any of those? Relay has the best roping pen in the area, and local cowboys often use it for some pick-up competition, so check what's going on out back when you are there. Open daily for lunch and dinner. $–$$; (CC). (409) 597–6320.

Turning right from T–249 at Pinehurst and continuing north on FM–149 takes you through rolling woodland to Montgomery. An Indian trading post later settled in 1837 by Stephen F. Austin's fourth and last colony, Montgomery prospered for half a century as a major center for mercantile activity in this farming region. Today, Montgomery is a tiny village with a six-block collection of old homes, most of them just north of T–105. Home tours in April and December give peeks behind some of those private doors. For local information, stop at the Country Store on FM–149, just north of the traffic light, or call the Montgomery Chamber of Commerce, (409) 597–4155. There are several low-key antique shops in this hamlet and an interesting graveyard at the old Methodist church. Fifteen other sites have historical markers.

WHAT TO DO

Christmas Tree Farms. There are numerous cut-your-own places in the Montgomery-Plantersville area. Call for directions: Buena Vista Christmas Tree Farm, (409) 597–6060; El Kay Christmas Tree Farm, (409) 597–6107 or (713) 899–2341; Hellard's Christmas Trees, (409) 265–1253; Loch Ness Farm, (409) 756–9557; and Whiteside Christmas Tree Farm, (713) 444–5531.

Landrum Creek Hunting Resort. Ten miles north of Pinehurst on FM–149 (1.5 miles south of Montgomery). This 850-acre, year-round shooting preserve has lakes full of bass and bream (catch and release on the bass), ideal for either spinning or fly fishing ($30). Bring your own bait, however, unless worms will do. The shooting season for quail, chukar, or pheasant is October through March on gamebird farms such as this one because the birds are farm-raised and released for a specific party of hunters. Hunts run about $106 per person for three hours with a guide and include twelve birds. (409) 597–4267.

Tom McNaire Internationale. 35526 FM–149, Pinehurst. Turn right onto FM–149 from T–249 at the blinking light in Pinehurst, cross the railroad tracks and watch for a sign at the third driveway on the right. This fifteen and a half acres of paddocks and stables is a blue-chip horse breeding and training facility, specializing in pure-bred Arabians. Owners Tom and Rhita McNaire together were named Horseman and Horsewoman of the Year in 1985 by the American Horse Shows Association, a unique and well–earned dual honor. In addition to boarding and training up to eighty horses, the McNaires also teach basic horsemanship and all major styles of riding. Film star Patrick Swayze and his wife, Lisa Niemi, keep eight horses here and often perform in the ranch's annual exhibition horse shows. Individual visitors and groups are welcome, but they must have advance appointments; drop-ins cannot be accommodated. (713) 356–4449.

WHERE TO EAT

Decker Prairie Cafe. 31910 T–249 in Decker Prairie. This is a "three pickup" cafe, with tasty home-cooking on the lunch steam table and chicken-fried steak and daily specials on the menu. Locals like this place for its affordable Texas-size breakfasts and homemade pies. Open daily for breakfast, lunch, and dinner; Sundays until 4 p.m. $. (713) 259–0511.

Heritage House. One mile west of FM–149 on T–105. A favorite stop on the Houston-to-College Station run, this antique-filled home is known for its country cooking, chicken-fried steak, and homemade pies and rolls. Open for lunch and dinner, Tuesday–Sunday. $–$$. (409) 597–6100.

WANDERING THE BACK ROADS

To continue this day trip from Montgomery to Conroe and Spring, travel east on T–105. A turn west on this same highway will connect you with Trips 3 through 6 in this sector.

As an alternative, you could continue north on FM–149 through Montgomery to Anderson (Trip 5, this sector). From Anderson, you can return to Houston via Navasota and Hempstead on T–90 and T–6.

How about heading east to New Waverly and Huntsville (Trip 2, this sector)? From FM–149 on the northern outskirts of Montgomery, turn northeast on FM–1097; this enjoyable road arcs east to Willis, crossing Lake Conroe in the process.

CONROE

In 1880 the Central and Montgomery Railroad had a line running from Navasota to Montgomery. With the extension of the track in 1885 to a small sawmill run by Isaac Conroe some 15 miles to the east, the town of Conroe came into being. Within five years Conroe was thriving with 300 citizens and aced Montgomery out of the county seat honor by some sixty-two votes. Always the center of a prosperous lumber industry, it hit the financial big time with George Strake's discovery of oil southeast of town in 1931.

Conroe today needs no introduction to Houstonians, as it is a prosperous business and bedroom satellite 39 miles north on I-45. Although little history has been preserved here, it's fun to visit the Creighton Theater (circa 1930) near the courthouse on North Main. Restored in vaudevillian style, it again hosts the performing arts. To day-trippers, however, Conroe primarily is the gateway to a forest and water playground.

WHAT TO DO

Albert Moorhead's Blueberry Farm. Who says you can't grow plump, luscious blueberries in Texas? Mr. Moorhead has fifteen acres of the high bush variety, and he welcomes guest pickers who call in advance for directions. Bring your own pail; at last notice, the fee was $1 per pound. The best picking times are in the early morning or late afternoon in June and July. His farm is deep in the woods between Conroe and Porter, and Mr. Moorhead will meet you and guide you in. (713) 572–1265.

Lake Conroe. Numerous points of access from I–45. The dam, several of the larger marinas, and the entrances to three major resorts are 5 miles west of Conroe via FM–105. One of the most beautiful lakes in the state, Lake Conroe is 15 miles long and covers 22,000 acres. A complete list of marinas, campgrounds, and public services is available from the Montgomery County Chamber of Commerce, P.O. Drawer 2347, Conroe 77305. (409) 756–6644.

Want an affordable weekend escape? Two private resorts welcome overnight guests with advance reservations: Walden, (713) 353–9737; (409) 582–6441; and April Sound, (713) 350–1173; (409) 588–1101. In addition, the Del Lago Resort Hotel & Conference Center has numerous package vacations, a long sand beach and lagoon, and a full-service marina offering guided fishing via pontoon boat as well as other types of watercraft rentals. (713) 350–5023; (800) 833–8389.

The Woodlands. Twenty-seven miles north of downtown Houston via I–45. Although its lakes and neighborhood parks are for residents only, this giant development offers several recreations to the general public. More than 50 miles of trails thread beautiful woods, just right for hiking, jogging, or biking (bring your own wheels and park by the Visitor Center). Visiting golfers are welcome on the Tournament Players Course (fee) of the Woodlands Country Club, (713) 367–7285, and with a current YMCA membership plus a small guest fee, visitors can enjoy the South Montgomery County YMCA's 28,000-square-foot, all-sport facility in the Village of Cochran's Crossing, (713) 367–9622.

Consider planning a trip around a performance in the Cynthia Woods Mitchell Pavilion, the Woodlands' beautiful outdoor performing arts center. Offerings range from bluegrass to ballet and Broadway shows, rock to Rachmaninoff, Gershwin to Willie Nelson, and the setting reminds of Tanglewood and Interlochen. Advance tickets are available from Ticketron and Foley's; day-of-performance tickets can be bought at the box office, or you can charge by phone, (713) 526–1709 or (800) 284–5780. Do inquire about parking fees, use of cameras and paging devices, and restrictions on lawn chairs, coolers, picnics, etc. (713) 363–3300.

If you want to make a weekend of it, check out the tennis, golf, and pampering packages at The Woodlands Inn. (CC). (713) 367–1100.

W. Goodrich Jones State Forest. Five miles southwest on I–45. Take the FM–1488 exit. Logged in 1892 and burned in 1923, this 1,725 acres is again a verdant wildlife refuge now under the watchful eye of the Texas Forest Service and part of the Texas A&M system. The Sweet Leaf Nature Trail is self-guided, and a small lake offers picnicking, fishing, and swimming. No admission fee.

Worldwide Safari, Inc. Six miles south of Conroe on the west side of I–45; use the FM–1488 exit and follow signs. This 255-acre open-air zoo has more than sixty different species of animals, many of them endangered exotics. Beyond the petting area, you travel 2.5 miles in your own car, windows down and buckets of feed (fee) at the ready. Ever met a giraffe or rhino face to face? You will here, so bring a camera. Hayrides can be arranged for groups of fifteen or more. Fee. Open daily (except major holidays) from 8 a.m. to dusk. (409) 273–5454.

WHERE TO EAT

Edie's Oasis. 7000 Kinston Cove Lane (at Seven Coves). Take the FM–830/Seven Coves exit from I–45, go west 5 miles, and turn in at the lighthouse. What could be nicer than dining on a deck overlooking Lake Conroe? When AC weather hits, you can reserve a window table inside to retain the view while enjoying Edie Parsley's good food. The menu offers most of the standards, from hamburgers to seafood. Wednesday night means prime rib ($8.95 and 9.95), and Thursday night is all-you-can-eat catfish ($7.95). $–$$; (CC). (409) 856–5635.

Marchione's Emporium and 1934 Tea Room. 118 W. Pauline, Conroe; take the T–105 east from I–45, turn north on Dallas, right on Thompson, and left on Pauline. Pronounced "Mar-*shones*" and housed in an oak-shaded Texas Historical Landmark home, this pleasant place has southern ambiance and primarily Northern Italian food, with lighter sandwiches and salads at lunch. $–$$$; (CC). (409) 539–3490.

Vernon's Kuntry Katfish. On the south side of T–105, 6.5 miles west of Conroe. Even if you don't like catfish, come here. Tasty choices run from frog legs to chicken-fried steak and burgers. Open for lunch and dinner daily. $–$$; (CC). (409) 760–3386.

From Conroe, Day Trip 1 swings south on I–45 to the Spring-Cypress Road exit. Turn left (east) under the freeway and follow Spring Cypress to the railroad tracks.

SPRING

Back in the late 1800s a community called Spring sprang up to serve the International and Great Northern Railroad as a switching station north of Houston. As the railroads prospered through the turn of the century, so did the town, and in 1902 the Wunche Brothers' Saloon was built within a toot of the roundhouse. It had eight rooms upstairs to house railroad personnel.

But we all know what happened to the railroads of America and to the many small towns that depended on them. By the 1920s the roundhouse had relocated to Houston, and the Texas Rangers had enforced the Prohibition laws by shooting every bottle in the saloon. Then came the depression of the 1930s, and when I–45 bypassed Spring in the 1960s, it was the final blow. The old town area lapsed into civic limbo as businesses began to thrive around the new freeway interchange 1 mile west.

So much for yesterday. Today, Old Town Spring is in its second bloom and is a great day-trip destination. Specialty shops, eateries, a few antique stores, flea markets, art galleries—all are right at home in the quaint old houses. In general, the shops are open Tuesday–Saturday and on Sunday afternoons. If you are coming north from Houston, take the 70A exit from I–45 and swing east (right) at the signal on Spring Cypress Road. When you see the Old Town Spring sign, you're there. Information: (713) 353–9310.

WHAT TO DO

Carter's Country. 6231 Treaschwig Rd.; take FM–1960 exit west from I–45, turn north on Aldine-Westfield Rd. to Treaschwig. Tucked away in the woods, this well-designed place offers pistol, rifle, trap, skeet, and country clay shooting at a variety of distances—your guns or theirs. Children can also shoot BB guns here if they have adult supervision. Open daily. Fee. (CC). (713) 443–8393.

Goodyear Blimp Base. 20201 I–45 north (Holzwarth Road exit). This giant hangar is home to the *America,* and although no public rides on the blimp are available, you are welcome to take a close look. An attendant explains the Super Skytacular, the computer-controlled night sign that flashes public service messages and Goodyear advertising in glowing lights along the sides of the blimp. Be aware that *America* travels to other parts of the country from early May until late October, and that when she is home, she flies over Harris County five days a week. Monday and Tuesday are good times to go, but check in advance. (713) 353–2401.

Mercer Arboretum. 22306 Aldine-Westfield Rd., north of FM–1960. This 214-acre county park is a sleeper, often overlooked by day-trippers. What they miss is an outstanding collection of native Texas plants, a series of self-guided nature trails, a bird sanctuary, special gardens (ferns, ginger, water lilies, azaleas, etc.), picnic areas, and educational programs, all along a wooded stretch of Cypress Creek. Free and open daily, except major holidays. (713) 443–8731.

Oasis Hobby Park. 4307 Treaschwig Rd.; take FM–1960 exit east from I–45, turn north on Aldine-Westfield Rd. to Treaschwig.

Love radio-controlled cars and boats? You can either bring your own or rent one at this park, which is devoted to the racing of both. Open Tuesday–Sunday. Fee. (713) 443–6003 or 529–6595.

Splashtown USA. 21300 I–45 North (exit 70A). When summer's heat hits, there's no better cooler than the thrill slides, raft rides, and wave pool at this large water park. This thirty acres of fun doesn't allow you to bring your own food and beverages inside the gates, but you are welcome to bring lunches, coolers, etc., for a family picnic on the grounds. Open daily from May through Labor Day, with live entertainment on weekends and special events during the off-season. Fee. (CC). (713) 350–4848.

WHERE TO EAT

British Trading Post. 26303 Hardy Road. Have a hankering for meat pies, mushy peas, or a shandy? This is the place. Lunch only, Tuesday–Saturday. $; (CC). (713) 350–5854.

My Secret Garden Cafe. 417–C Gentry. Soups, salads, sandwiches, special entrees, and luscious baked goodies are the rule in this charming spot run by a well-known local caterer. Lunch only, Tuesday–Saturday. $. (713) 288–4275.

Spring Cafe. 26608 Keith. Reinstalled in Old Town Spring just a block from its first site (where Wunche Brothers' Cafe is now), this local institution still brags that it has the best food and slowest service anywhere. The old Spring Cafe was widely known for its marvelous hamburgers, and the owners have salvaged the old grills, so the tradition continues, including the time-honored thirty- to sixty-minute wait. If that's too long, try the homemade veggie soup, chili, or burrito on a stick. Open for lunch and early dinner Tuesday–Saturday. $. (713) 350–8530.

Wunche Brothers' Cafe and Saloon. 103 Midway. Back again to its original name and character after a sojourn as the Spring Cafe, this historic landmark, circa 1902, is freshly renovated and offers some nifty live music (everything from progressive country to rock and roll) Tuesday–Sunday evenings. Lunch ranges from burgers to sandwiches and salads; a cowboy steak gets added at dinner. Save room for dessert—the chocolate whiskey cake is a house specialty. Open Tuesday–Sunday, lunch and dinner, till 2 a.m. on Friday and Saturday. $–$$; (CC). (713) 350–CAFE; (713) 353–2825 for performance information.

Day Trip 2

NEW WAVERLY
HUNTSVILLE
MADISONVILLE
CROCKETT

NEW WAVERLY

Begin this day trip by driving north on I–45 from Houston, turning east at the New Waverly exit.

Settled in the 1850s, the pioneer community of Waverly thrived for a time on a cotton and cattle economy. Fearing damage to their cattle, residents turned down the International and Great Northern Railroad Co.'s request in 1870 for a right-of-way through town, a fatal mistake. The tracks were laid 10 miles to the west, people began relocating around the station of "New" Waverly, and the original Waverly was doomed. Visitors to the latter now find only an old cemetery with interesting headstones and the visually charming Waverly Presbyterian Church, built around 1904 and still filled every Sunday. "Old" Waverly is 10 miles east of I–45 on T–105.

New Waverly had a heavy immigration of Poles between 1870 and 1902. After working in the fields to pay back the area's large landowners who had advanced their passage money, the Poles began their own businesses and left a strong ethnic stamp on this community. Stately, Gothic-styled St. Joseph's Catholic Church in the heart of town is one of their legacies. Built between 1905 and 1908, it is well worth a visit.

WHAT TO DO

Christmas Tree Farms. Call Iron Creek Farms for directions, (409) 767–4541.

Miss Robin's Buggy Shop. On the left as you enter New Waverly on FM–1375. This one-woman operation specializes in old-time wagons and buggies, and you are welcome to just stop in and see them—Miss Robin loves visitors. There usually are fifteen to

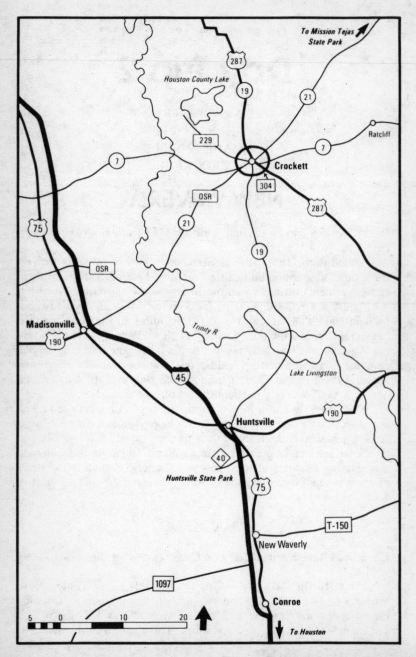

Northwest: Day Trip 2

twenty-five vehicles in the showroom at any one time, ranging from two-wheel carts, covered wagons, and carriages to fancy surreys and doctor's buggies. Miss Robin also trains driving horses and mules and specializes in draft horses—you'll find some of her "one-ton darlings" in the twenty-acre pasture across the street. She herself uses a cart and horse to run errands, including trips to the local bank's drive-through window. If time permits and you give her a call in advance, she'll give you a jog around town (fee). It's wise to call ahead whether you want a buggy ride or not; she often closes the shop at odd hours to work weddings, hayrides, and parades with her rig. Fun to know: Buggy driving is a major sport in these piney woods, with numerous weekend competitions and shows. Ask Miss Robin what's on when you plan on coming. (409) 344–2352.

WHERE TO EAT

Waverly House. At the intersection of FM–1375 and T–75 on the western edge of town. When a Houston newspaper asked its readers to vote for the best country cafes in Texas in 1989, this friendly place was in the top ten. Known for their homemade cream pies, they also dish out freshly baked dewberry cobbler year-round. Order the chicken-fried steak only if you're starving or willing to share; it laps over both sides of the plate. If you are in New Waverly on a week-day, don't pass up the workingman's steam table lunch. Open for lunch and dinner daily except major holidays. $–$$; (CC). (409) 344–2185.

From New Waverly, continue this day trip by driving north on I–45 to Huntsville.

HUNTSVILLE

In the early 1830s an adventurous frontiersman named Pleasant Gray thought this rolling, wooded wilderness looked like his former home in Huntsville, Alabama. Because there were good springs nearby, he settled in and established an Indian trading post. By 1836 the tiny settlement of Huntsville was thriving, and in 1847 Sam Houston built his family home and plantation, Woodlands, at the south edge of the city.

Sam's home now seems right downtown, across from the Sam Houston State University campus, and those old Indian trails long since have been formalized into highways. Today's visitors come via

I–45, taking the T–30 turnoff (which becomes Eleventh Street) and heading east to the center of town.

Tour booklets are available weekdays from the Huntsville Chamber of Commerce, 1327 Eleventh St., P.O. Box 538, Huntsville, 77342–0538; (409) 295–8113, (800) 289–0389. Area information is also available here at an outdoor Visitor Information area, convenient for weekend visitors. Expect numerous antique stores around the square and a 1890s-era motorized trolley that runs a regular route through downtown on weekdays and for special weekend events.

Want to overnight? Bed and breakfast now is offered at two vintage homes. In town, The Whistler is an 1859 Victorian that has been in the same family for six generations; (409) 295–2834, (713) 524–0011. Bluebonnet Bed and Breakfast is a 1912 beauty, recently moved from town to seven acres on FM–1374; (409) 291–5833.

WHAT TO DO

The Blue Lagoon. North of Huntsville off FM–247. Also known as Cozumel-in-the-Pines, this old rock quarry offers some exciting scuba territory to certified divers. There are two large lakes, both with 40-foot visibility underwater and sunken shipwrecks to explore. You must have your C-card with you to be admitted, and no children under fourteen, pets, or glass containers are allowed. Open Friday–Sunday in winter, daily in summer. Call for directions and further information. $$. (409) 291–6111.

Christmas Tree Farms. This also is prime tree-cutting territory. Call any of the following for directions: Big Bill's Christmas Trees, (409) 295–4824; Charlie's Christmas Trees, (409) 295–6531; Four Notch Christmas Tree Farm, (409) 295–4965; Mill Hollow Christmas Tree Farm, (713) 469–2981 or (409) 377–4044; PJ Christmas Tree Farm, (409) 295–2778; and Killian's Christmas Tree Farm, (409) 874–2293.

Gibbs Bros. Building. Eleventh Street and Avenue K (University Avenue). Started in 1841 as a store, the business evolved into the town's first bank because Thomas and Sanford Gibbs owned the only safe. Now under restoration after being disguised for decades by a modern brick front, this is the oldest business in Texas still on its original site and under the same family ownership.

The Gibbs-Powell Home. Eleventh Street and Avenue M. This excellent example of Greek Revival architecture was built in 1862 and can be toured Thursday–Sunday. Donations requested. (409) 295–2914.

Henry Opera House. Twelfth Street and Avenue K. Such elegance as this must have represented in the 1880s now is hard to visualize. Only the tall windows on the upper floor give a hint to the building's cultural past. Built as a Masonic Hall in 1880, it soon became the property of Major John Henry, who installed Huntsville's first department store on the first floor and converted the second floor into an opera house.

Texas Prison Museum. 1113 Twelfth Street, on the south side of the city square. Want to keep your kids on the straight and narrow? Bring them here for a look at a 9-by-6-foot cell. Guides also explain other exhibits, including Bonnie and Clyde's rifles and some blood-chilling photos of their area escapades; the actual electric chair used through 1964; rare ball and chains; and assorted contraband confiscated within the nearby prison. Housed in an old bank building, this interesting museum also can special-order any type of prisoner-made leather goods, from "Bubba" belts to snuff can holders. Prices are reasonable, and both quality and craftsmanship are excellent. Open daily except Monday, with flexible hours. Fee. (409) 295–2155.

Huntsville State Park. Eight miles south of Huntsville via I–45, then west on Park Road 40. Spanning more than 2,000 acres, this park centers on Lake Raven and offers swimming, canoeing, and limited sailing and motorboating. Hiking and birding are excellent, and the forest is dominated by loblolly and shortleaf pine, dogwood, sweet gum, sassafras, and assorted oaks. Good camping and picnicking.

Oakwood Cemetery. Two blocks north of Eleventh Street on Avenue I. (Those two blocks of Avenue I are T–1, the shortest official highway in the state). Sam Houston sleeps with good company in this historic cemetery. Deeded as a free burial place in 1847 by Huntsville's founder, Pleasant Gray, Oakwood has several tombstones carrying burial dates as early as 1834.

Sam Houston Memorial Park and Museum. Between Seventeenth and Nineteenth streets on Sam Houston Avenue. During a turbulent life that saw him the governor of Tennessee, a general in the Texas Army, the victor at the battle of San Jacinto, and the first president of the Republic of Texas, Sam Houston had many homes. None was as lovely or as beloved by him as Woodlands, built in 1847. Restored in 1981, this square log house with its white clapboard siding is just one of the pleasures in this shady park.

Start at the museum, touring the right wing first to keep the chronology straight, and then visit Woodlands, its separate kitchen, Houston's law office, and a blacksmith shop. Close by are the War and Peace House and the unusual Steamboat House where Houston died in 1863. The docents at both homes speak of Sam and his wife Margaret as if they might return at any moment. The park's small lake was a fresh, bubbling spring during Houston's residency here; today it is reshaped to resemble the state of Texas and is a pleasant spot for a picnic lunch. Spring visits get a bonus of flowering dogwood and azaleas. Sam Houston's grave is also of interest, across town in Oakwood Cemetery. The park and museum are open Tuesday–Sunday. (409) 294–1832.

Sam Houston State University. Five blocks south of the town square on Sam Houston Avenue (US–75). Founded in 1879 as a normal institute (teachers' college), SHSU had two buildings worth exploring until a disastrous fire in early 1982 destroyed a Gothic wonder known as Old Main (1889). Now only historic Austin Hall (1853) recalls the school's early days. The public is welcome on campus; to find out what's going on when you'll be in town, call the SHSU Public Information office, (409) 294–1111, ext. 1833. Guests can also attend slide/lecture programs given by the school's planetarium staff several times a month. Some outings allow viewing through the university's 16-inch telescope 12 miles north of Huntsville. For information on planetarium programs, call (409) 294–3664.

Texas Berry Farm. Take exit 113 from I–45, continue north on T–19, west on FM–2821, right on FM–247, and right again 7.5 miles on FM–980. Started in 1986 by expatriate Houstonians Barry and Debbie Teare, this 180–acre farm now has forty acres of luscious blueberries you can pick from about May 1 to mid-July, as well as a long list of vine-ripened vegetables that can be picked all summer. Buckets are provided—one pound of blueberries fills a pint ($1.25)—but you should bring shallow boxes to carry the fruit home. Groups also are welcome for parties and hayrides by advance arrangement. Bring a picnic for munching on the farm's lakeside deck. (409) 294–0416.

The Walls. Three short blocks east of the town square. This is the original main unit of the Huntsville State Prison.

WHERE TO EAT

The Junction Restaurant. 2641 Eleventh St. Just look for an 1849 plantation house with an old-fashioned buggy on the front porch. Inside, the house specialties are catfish, fresh seafood, steaks, and chicken, plus there are some light entrees for dieters. Local legend has it that the skylight (near the salad bar) was built to watch for Indian attacks. Open daily for lunch and dinner. $–$$; (CC). (409) 291–2183.

King's Candies & Ice Cream. 1112 Eleventh Street, on the Square. First cousin to King's Confectionery on The Strand in Galveston, this old-fashioned sweetshop makes traditional shakes, malts, and banana splits at its soda fountain, squeezes lemons for the lemonade, cooks its own candy, and serves Blue Bell ice cream. Good place for a lunch sandwich also. Open Monday–Saturday. $. (409) 291–6988.

MADISONVILLE

From Huntsville you can follow the old Dallas Highway (US–75) to Madisonville (30 miles) or zoom up I–45. Either way, you roll through pastureland studded with oaks, cattle, and horses, some of the prettiest country in the state. Madisonville is a quiet town of 3,000 that lost its historic soul in 1969 when its century-old courthouse burned. Another relic of the past, the old Woodbine Hotel at 109 Madison, was restored in 1981 and may now be rented for special events.

Unless you own cattle, don't wear cowboy boots in this town the last weekend in May through the first week of June. The local Sidewalk Cattlemen's Association sponsors an annual shindig of dances, rodeos, trail rides, horse shows, etc., and the ground rules are firm. If you own two head of cattle, you put your left pant leg in your boot; if you own three head of cattle you stuff the right pant leg; if you own four head, put both pant legs in your boots; and if you own six head or more, you are entitled to wear spurs. If you don't play by the rules, you'll get dunked in the horse trough on the town square.

WHAT TO DO

Christmas Tree Farms. Call Roman's Tree Farm for directions, (713) 554–7329.

Horizon Limousin Ranch. From I–45, take T–21 northeast 3 miles toward Crockett, turn right on FM–1428, and continue 5 miles to the ranch entrance (on the left). Look for a white pipe fence, cattle guard, and HLR sign. This 250-acre spread breeds champion limousin cattle, and visitors are welcome if they have made advance arrangements with manager Neil Scott. (409) 348–3503.

Madison County Lake. One-half mile west of I–45 on T–21. This small lake has good bass and perch fishing. Try your luck from the banks during a picnic.

Monterey Mushrooms. Five miles south of Madisonville on US–75. Open without charge and by advance arrangement only to groups of ten or more, this vast operation specializes in genetic engineering of mushrooms and is the largest producer in the southwest, shipping between 360,000 and 400,000 pounds of fresh mushrooms weekly. Visitors must wear flat, rubber-soled shoes; the tour requires extensive walking over wet concrete floors. (409) 348–3511.

WHERE TO EAT

Hilltop Lakes Resort. Take the OSR exit from I–45, go 10 miles west to Normangee, then 9 miles north on FM–3. This large and casual place serves everything from steaks to Mexican food, including a large noon buffet on Sundays. Open to the public Wednesday–Sunday for lunch and dinner; breakfast on weekends. Sorry, the other resort facilities are for homeowners only. $–$$; (CC). (409) 855–2222.

WANDERING THE BACKROADS

The OSR turnoff, 10 miles north of Madisonville on I–45, is a meandering country drive with more than a touch of history. The initials stand for the Old San Antonio Road, but it also is known as El Camino Real because it was created by the order of the King of Spain in 1691. The Spaniards, through their control of Mexico, claimed Texas from 1519 until 1821, but the French also coveted this rich, wild land, sending explorers into Texas in the late 1600s. To reinforce its claim, Spain created a series of missions in East Texas and blazed this road to bolster and serve those primitive outposts. Today, OSR follows, after a fashion, T–21 from San Marcos northeast to the Louisiana border, one portion linking the Madisonville area to Crockett.

Turning west on OSR from I–45 takes you through the tiny but historic community of Normangee en route to Bryan–College Station (Trip 3, this sector). As an alternate to Madisonville, consider a Huntsville–Crockett exploration, slightly outside our two-hour driving limit (117 miles) but rich enough in history to be worth the drive.

CROCKETT

Davy Crockett and two companions had to do some fast talking here. Local folks found Crockett's campsite near this area in 1836 (the trio was en route to their destinies at the Alamo) and nearly hanged them as horse thieves. The fifth oldest town in Texas, Crockett's history is easy to trace. Visitors should start at the traditional square in the heart of town and then go exploring. For advance information, contact either the Houston County Chamber of Commerce (700 East Houston, P.O. Box 307, Crockett 75835, 409–544–2359; or the Houston County Historical Commission, Houston County Courthouse, Third Floor, Crockett 75835, 409–544–3256).

WHERE TO GO

Davy Crockett Spring. West Goliad at the railroad underpass, west of the town square. The spring still flows and serves as a public drinking fountain at what is thought to have been Crockett's campsite.

Discover Houston County Visitor's Center–Museum. 303 South First Street. Although its historical displays are still being developed, this former railroad depot (circa 1909) is the starting point for guided tours of Indian massacre sites, early burial grounds and churches, Caddoan burial mounds, and the Mission Tejas Park. Open Monday–Friday afternoons, other times by appointment for groups. Advance arrangements are required for the guided tours. (409) 544–3269, evenings.

Downes-Aldrich Historical Home. 206 North Seventh Street. Listed in the National Register of Historic Places, this Victorian survivor is now the historical and cultural activities center for the town. Open Wednesday, Saturday, and Sunday afternoons, March–December. (409) 544–4804.

Monroe-Crook Home. 709 East Houston Avenue. Built in 1854 and also listed in the National Register, this Greek Revival home is open for public tours on Wednesday morning and weekend afternoons, March–December. Fee. (409) 544–5820.

WHERE TO EAT

Cattleman's Royal. 112 South Fifth Street, on the Square. The house specialty is chicken-fried steak. Open daily around the clock. $–$$; (CC). (409) 544–3863.

Crockett Inn. Loop 304 east. An excellent salad bar and homemade breads complete the steak/fish/chicken menu. Specials at lunch and at the Sunday buffet. Open daily. $–$$; (CC). (409) 544–5611.

King's Inn. Loop 304 east. The daily buffet features rib-stickin' cowboy country food, making this a good place for families and budget-watchers. Open daily. $; (CC). (409) 544–2294.

The Wooden Nickel. Loop 304 east. A jillion junk-tiques decorate the porch and walls of this zany restaurant, plus there's a library next door (bring a paperback to swap) and a very miniature golf course out back. The blackboard menu of down-home food ranges from Mexican to burgers to BBQ and back again, and there are steam table specials as well. Open for lunch and dinner Tuesday–Saturday, until 3 p.m. on Sunday. $–$$; (CC). (409) 544–8011.

WANDERING THE BACKROADS

If you feel like extending your drive well beyond the two-hour limit of this book, continue north on OSR (T–21) from Crockett through the Davy Crockett National Forest to the Mission Tejas State Historical Park. The Rice family log home here is special, built between 1828 and 1838 and used as a stage stop. Nearby is a commemorative log structure similar to the old Spanish mission established here in 1690 to serve the Tejas Indians, the first of its kind in Texas.

A second option follows T–7 some 20 miles east of Crockett to the Ratcliff Recreation Area, and a third suggestion is FM–229 northwest from Crockett to Houston County Lake. Locally, this is considered the best bass fishing in the state.

Following US–287 southeast from Crockett takes you through the Kickapoo Recreation Area near Groveton and hits the northern limit of the Livingston–Woodville day trip in the northeast sector of this book.

Day Trip 3

BRYAN–COLLEGE STATION
AND THE BRAZOS RIVER VALLEY

BRYAN–COLLEGE STATION

From Houston, follow T–6 and US–290 north to Hempstead and continue north on T–6 through Navasota into Bryan and College Station.

These joint communities tend to have a single connotation to Houstonians—Texas A&M University. And, while visitors to that sprawling campus find much of interest, there are several other things to do in the vicinity of Aggieland.

Bryan and College Station today flow together into a combined metropolitan area that ranked first in growth in the state and sixth in the entire country in the 1980 census. Not bad for a slow starter. This rich sliver of agricultural land bounded by the Brazos River on the west and the Navasota River on the east was sparsely settled until the advent of the Houston & Texas Central Railroad in 1866. The Reconstruction years after the Civil War were rough on the young town of Bryan, and it wasn't until the formal opening of Texas A&M College in 1876 that the area settled down to some semblance of respectability.

Some of the footnotes on Bryan's past are interesting. The original street grid inadvertently provided for today's traffic by making Main Street wide enough to turn a five-yoke oxen team; and the college was deliberately sited on the open prairie 5 miles south of town so as to be well removed from the influence of demon rum flowing freely in Bryan's saloons.

An information-loaded historic map covers Bryan's old commercial and residential districts as well as the remains of several small pre–Civil War settlements outside of town. This and other area guides are found at the Bryan–College Station Chamber of Commerce Convention and Visitor Bureau, 715 University Drive East, College Station 77840, (409) 260–9898. (Monday–Friday only; write in advance for maps and brochures if you intend to explore on a weekend.)

Leaving Texas A&M to its own section, which follows, here are some suggestions of what to see in Bryan and College Station.

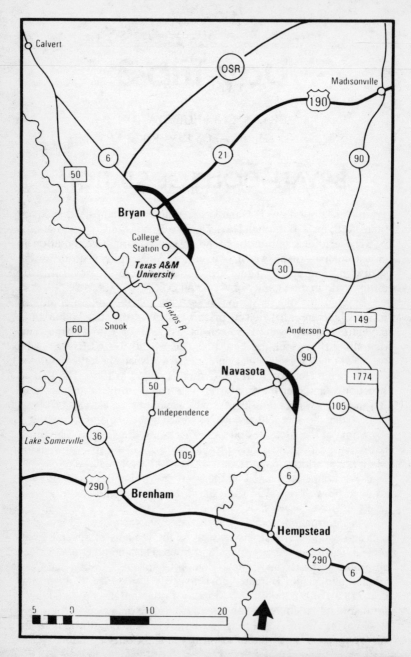

Calvert

OSR

Madisonville

190

21

90

6

50

Bryan

College
Station

30

*Texas A&M
University*

149

Brazos R.

Anderson

60

Snook

90

Navasota

1774

50

105

Independence

Lake Somerville

36

6

105

290

Brenham

Hempstead

290

6

5   0   10   20

Northwest: Day Trip 3

WHAT TO DO

Birding. The Brazos Valley is home to an enormous variety of bird life. A self-guided tour covering five areas and a list of birds common to the Brazos County Arboretum are available from the convention and visitor bureau previously mentioned.

Brazos Center. 3232 Briarcrest. Take the Briarcrest exit east from T–6 bypass. This is the special events place for the area, hosting giant weekend antique shows in March, July, and October. Year-round visitors can enjoy the Brazos Valley Museum of Natural Science and a small nature trail on the grounds. Free. Open Tuesday–Sunday. (409) 776–8338 (center); (409) 776–2195 (museum).

Canoeing on the Brazos River. First, so you'll sound like a native, it's pronounced "*Braa*-zas," not "*Bray*-zos as you might expect from the spelling. Although its water is muddy with sediment, the Brazos generally is quiet and otherwise scenic, a good one- or two-day float if you have your own canoe. As of this writing, there are no canoe rentals available in the Bryan–College Station area. You'll find float information in several river books available at major bookstores.

Christmas Tree Farms. Want to cut your own? Call either of the following for directions: Evergreen Farms, (409) 775–1717, or J. P. Seven Christmas Trees, (409) 846–7916.

Messina Hof Wine Cellar and Vineyard. Exit T–6 at Boonville Road; stay on access road going north; turn right on Old Reliance Road; winery is 3 miles east on the left. Paul and Merrill Bonarrigo began planting grapes in 1977; their successful vineyard now covers forty-six acres and produces about 50,000 gallons (250,000 bottles) annually. Using the classic European grape *Vitis vinifera* grafted onto Texas root stock, they bottle sixteen varieties of wine, including chardonnay, cabernet, port, red and white zinfandels, and champagne. Harvest time is July and August, and you can pick and stomp grapes yourself by signing up in advance for their Pickers' Club (free). The turn-of-the-century Howell manor house and gardens have been restored as the winery's retail sales and tasting room; it is open daily, plus there are winery tours at specific times. The Bonarrigos also invite the public for Springfest in April and a premier party for new wines and vintages in November. Other special events occur throughout the year (get on their mailing list), and there's a Vintner's Loft hideaway for couples seeking an overnight retreat (nonsmoking adults only). (409) 778–9463.

Texas World Speedway. Six miles south of College Station on T–6. Who needs Daytona or Indianapolis? Everything from Indy and

NASCAR racers to eighteen-wheelers test their times on this Texas oval, the world's fastest 2-mile track. Advance tickets usually can be bought in Houston during racing season; check Ticketron. Racing fans are welcome to camp on the infield. If you like racing, get on the mailing list: P.O. Box 11000, College Station 77842; (409) 690–2500.

EXPLORING TEXAS A&M UNIVERSITY

Even if you haven't a prospective student in tow, this handsome 5,250-acre campus has much to offer. Located in the heart of College Station, and hard to miss on the west side of T–6, Texas A&M was the first public institution of higher education in the state. Originally an all-male military college, A&M now has a co-ed enrollment in excess of 41,000 and is in the top ten schools nationally in funding for scientific research.

Aggie traditions are stories in themselves. Ask about the Elephant Walk, the Twelfth Man, and Silver Taps at the Visitor Information Center in Rudder Tower for an insight into what makes Aggies so loyal to their Alma Mater.

A book of suggested walking tours on campus can be bought in the student bookstore (409–845–8161), in the Memorial Student Center, or in advance from the Texas A&M University Press, (409) 845–1436. The following are among the things to see.

Rudder Tower. At University Center on Joe Routt Boulevard. The visitor information center in the lobby introduces you to the university with maps, an excellent booklet about the school, and campus guides. Visitor parking (fee) is adjacent to the building. Open daily; call for hours. (409) 845–5851.

Memorial Student Center (MSC). Also part of the University Center complex. Ask at the information center in Rudder Tower as to the current locations of the Buck Schiwetz paintings, the Metzger–Sanders Gun Collection (antique and historic firearms as well as the Sam Houston Sanders Commemorative Colt Collection), and the Texan Campaign Staffordshire China (circa 1850). Also of interest are the Centennial Wood Carvings in the corridor between the student lounge and the cafeteria (six walnut panels that trace the history of the school from 1876) and assorted art exhibits in several galleries. Don't miss shopping in the student bookstore.

The David G. Eller Building for Oceanography and Meteorology. Super view from the fifteenth floor. The "working collection" library in room 1103 of the Oceanography Department and the specimen room (706) are interesting and open to the public at specified times. Tours by advance reservation only. (409) 845–7211.

Nuclear Science Center. Off-campus, near the Easterwood Airport. This multimillion-dollar facility houses the largest nuclear reactor on any campus in the Southwest and produces radioactive isotopes for scientific research. Tours Monday–Friday. (409) 845–7553.

The Clayton W. Williams, Jr., Alumni Center. Corner of George Bush Drive and Houston Street. Displays include an Aggie ring collection. (409) 845–7514.

Floral Test Gardens. On Houston Street across from Moore Communications Center. Some 1,000 varieties of seeds and bulbs are grown here annually, part of the all-American seed-testing program across the country. You are welcome to look around on your own. Picnic areas and the floriculture greenhouses are nearby. Tours of the latter are easily arranged, (409) 845–8553. Questions about growing vegetables? Call Dr. Sam Cotner, (409) 845–7341. Want to know what's wrong with your flowers? Call Dr. William Welch at that same number.

Tours also can be arranged for the Cyclotron Institute, (409) 845–1411; Computing Services Center, (409) 845–4211; and the Veterinary Medicine College, (409) 845–5051.

WHERE TO EAT ON THE A&M CAMPUS

The Creamery. In the Meat Science and Technology Center, adjacent to the Kleberg Building. The best chocolate ice cream in the world is sold here, along with milk, butter, cheese, eggs, and meats produced on the university's farms. Open weekdays. $.

Memorial Student Center. Two choices here: the cafeteria (409–845–1118) and the new food court on the lower level. $.

WHERE TO EAT IN THE AREA

Black Forest Inn. On the north side of T–30, 20.8 miles east of Bryan–College Station toward Huntsville. Trudie Adams's skill with the classic bourgeois food of Europe as well as with our own fresh gulf seafood brings devotees from as far away as Austin and Dallas, just for a meal. Everything is fresh and made from scratch with no additives or preservatives, including Trudie's own salad dressings and mayonnaise. Should you have to wait for a table, feel free to select a record from the extensive classical music collection or a good book and settle down on a sofa in front of the fireplace. Reservations are a necessity, particularly for Sunday brunch or if your party numbers four or more. $$; (CC). Closed after brunch on Sunday and on Monday. (409) 874–2407.

Chicken Oil Company. 3600 South College, Bryan. This giant wooden building is filled with antiques and nostalgic memorabilia, and its hamburgers have been voted the best in town in local polls. Open for lunch and dinner daily. $. (409) 846–3306

Fajita Rita's. 4501 Texas Avenue South, Bryan. Great Tex-Mex and margaritas served in a bright cantina atmosphere. Open for lunch and dinner daily. $–$$; (CC). (409) 846–3696.

The Grapevine. 201 Live Oak (behind La Quinta Motel on Texas Avenue), College Station. The emphasis of this quiet bistro is on light foods that are tasty and good for you. Chef/owner Patsy Perry and her mother, Jo Dunn, do special things with fish and chicken, plus they have quite a following for their homemade soups, quiche, cheesecake, and mousse. Cheese and wine are also important here; there's a large selection of the latter by the bottle, and five house and two special selection wines are available by the glass. Open for lunch and dinner Monday–Saturday. $–$$; (CC). (409) 696–3411.

José's Restaurant. 4004 Harvey (T–30), College Station, 1.5 miles east of the T–6 bypass. Mix Mexican Colonial with English Tudor decor, top it off with classic Mexican food, and you have a nice place to eat. The chimichangas and green enchiladas are recommended, along with the tacos al carbon and fish Mexicana. Open for lunch and dinner, Tuesday–Sunday. $–$$; (CC). (409) 776–8979.

WANDERING THE BACKROADS

From College Station, turn west on FM–60 at the University Drive signal and follow the local folks some 15 miles to Snook (pronounced "Snuk"). The big attractions, especially on Saturday mornings, are oven-fresh breads, pies, and kolaches at the Snook Bakery (409–272–8501) and fresh sausage from Slovacek's, (409) 272–8625.

As an alternate to returning home from Snook through College Station, backtrack only as far as FM–50 and swing south to Independence and Brenham (Trip 6, this sector). Those fine fields you pass north of Independence are part of the Texas A&M Experimental Farms.

If wanderlust really takes over and you want to stretch the two-hour driving limit of this book, continue north on T–6 from Bryan some 60 miles to Calvert. Established in 1868, this nice old town is the unofficial antique center of Texas. There's a flea market the first Saturday of every month, plus you can tour some outstanding vintage homes during the Robertson County Pilgrimage in April and a

Christmas celebration in early December. Calvert's Main Street is a twelve-block collection of old brick and iron-front buildings, most of which now house antique shops that are open Wednesday–Sunday. For information on bed and breakfast accommodations in the area, call Front Porch Antiques (409) 364–2933. For information on Calvert, call the chamber of commerce (409–364–2559) on Tuesday or Friday.

You can return to Houston from Bryan–College Station one of three ways. The first is the simplest—just reverse the route you followed coming up.

The second is more scenic. Follow T–6 south to Navasota and swing east on T–105 toward Conroe. Turn south on FM–1774 for a forest drive through Plantersville and Magnolia before connecting with T–249 south at Pinehurst. Note: This route is to be avoided on weekends from October 1 through November 15 because of Renaissance Festival traffic. T–249 south from Pinehurst ultimately intersects I–45 north inside the Houston city limits.

If you feel like exploring further, go east on T–30 to Huntsville (Trip 2, this sector) and then scoot south on I–45 to home.

Day Trip 4

HOCKLEY and PRAIRIE VIEW
HEMPSTEAD

HOCKLEY and PRAIRIE VIEW

The primary path from Houston into this northwest sector is US–290, rambling its way through Cypress and a lot of interesting country en route to Austin and points west.

Cypress has rodeos on Friday evenings in summer, and Hockley is pure country—ranches, an old general store, and a great fishing hole. Prairie View today is home to Prairie View State University, but just over a century ago it was the site of the Kirby Plantation, known as Alta Vista. Deeded to the state in 1876 for use as a college for black youths, the old mansion was the school's first educational building. It is gone now, along with de facto segregation, but look for St. Francis Episcopal Church, a small frame building (1870) moved to the campus from Hempstead in 1958. The first Episcopal church north of Houston, it still has the original pews, handmade by its first congregation.

WHAT TO DO

Birdwatching at Warren Ranch Lake. In Hockley, turn left at the tallest rice dryer on your left and follow Warren Ranch Road 3.4 miles. The lake will be on your left. It is private and a protected refuge, but the viewing (with binoculars) is excellent from the shoulder of the road. The largest winter concentration of ducks and geese in North America is found in the rice fields of this area, and the fifty wild acres of this lake have been known to host as many as 20,000 ducks and geese at one time. With luck, you'll also spot some bald eagles, an endangered species and America's national bird. For information, call the Houston Audubon Society at (713) 932–1392.

Blueberry Picking. In summer, call Cook's Blueberry Farm. (409) 372–5338.

Boy's Country. Thirty miles northwest of Houston on US–290, then right 2 miles on Roberts Road. This working ranch provides a

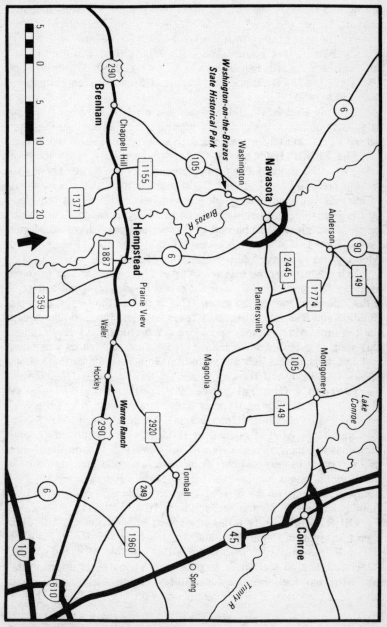

Northwest: Day Trips 4 and 5

stable, homelike environment for 120 boys. On weekdays during the spring and summer, the ranch's small but neat nursery sells hanging baskets, herbs, and perennials at excellent prices; call ahead if you want to shop the nursery on a weekend. (713) 351–4976.

Christmas Tree Farms. When it's cutting time, call the following for directions: Christmas Tree Land, (409) 372–2737; Smith Tree Farm, (713) 528–3787; and St. Nicholas Christmas Tree Plantation, (409) 372–3850.

Cy-Fair Rodeo. On Telge Road, just off US–290 west (Cy-Fair High School area). Every Friday night during the summer the high school's FFA club stages a fun rodeo. (Fee). (713) 897–4600 weekdays.

The Fishin' Hole. 14120 Cypress-Rosehill Rd., just north of US–290 and 2 short blocks from Juergen's General Store. These two fishing lakes are stocked with farm-raised catfish, and the motto is "Catch all you want—Keep all you catch." No license is required, bait is available, and fishing rigs can be rented at modest cost. Your catch is weighed and charged at $1.95 per pound live, $2.35 per pound fileted. If it's hot and sunny, bring your own shade. Closed Monday and Tuesday. Admission fee. (713) 373–0123.

Friendship Carriage Works. Take US–290 northwest through Hockley to the blinking light at Kickapoo Road. Turn right and go 8 miles; the road ends at the ranch. This is one of the largest carriage building and restoration works in Texas, an ideal place to take a step back in time. Although they specialize in museum-quality restorations, this shop also builds new carriages from scratch. Visitors welcome; just follow signs through the Friendship Ranch to the carriage shop. Closed on Sunday and Tuesday. (800) 235–0593 or (409) 372–2585.

Juergen's General Store. 26026 Hempstead Highway (US–290), at the Spring Cypress Road Intersection (6 miles northwest of FM–1960/US–290 intersection). A forerunner of today's convenience store when it opened in 1903, this old-fashioned general store hasn't changed much. It still sells everything from hardware and hip boots to beer and soft drinks and is a good place to pick up some picnic snacks and swap stories. Don't miss the collection of antiques and junk on the shelves above the old lunch counter. Closed Sunday and until 3:30 p.m. on Monday. (713) 373–0371.

Oil Ranch. Twenty miles northwest of Houston via US–290, then turn right on Hegar Road and right on Magnolia Road. Families are welcome to play "cowboy for a day" at this pleasant spread. Activities include pony rides in the corral, swinging on ropes in the hay barn, hayrides through the pastures, paddleboating on a small lake, and exploring a large maze inside Fort George Bush. There's also an Indian village, a petting zoo, a swimming pool, and a miniature golf course; plus kids can hand-feed the cattle and learn about the cattle industry. Special events include barn dances and free pumpkins around Halloween; there's even a Christmas tree farm where you can cut your own. Special activities for groups. Fee. Call for a free brochure and/or reservations. (713) 859–1616.

Vicker's Arabians. 17110 Cypress-Rosehill Road. (Turn north from US–290, 6 miles west of the FM–1960 intersection.) This fifty-five-acre ranch breeds, raises, and shows nationally ranked Arabian horses. Visitors are welcome if they call ahead. (713) 351–1391.

HEMPSTEAD

It's hard to believe that this quiet town once was known as Six-Shooter Junction and that for several decades after the Civil War it was a wild and woolly place. The rolling land south of Hempstead was settled as early as 1821, although only scattered historical markers tell the stories now.

The town was platted in 1856–57 as the terminus for the Houston and Texas Central Railroad, an early line that tooted over much of Waller County before expanding north to Bryan–College Station. During the Civil War, the railroad made Hempstead a major supply and troop depot for Confederate forces, and when the war ended, the defeated men began their long walks home from here.

Hempstead literally was the turning point in Texas's battle for independence from Mexico. Sam Houston and his retreating forces camped and regrouped here from March 31 to April 14, 1836, and then began their aggressive march to San Jacinto, site of their ultimate victory over Santa Anna and his Mexican army. A brief jaunt down FM–1887 today finds a historical marker about the Texian Army camp.

Hempstead slowly is reawakening to its heritage, but at present all vintage structures remain in private hands and are not open to the public. A windshield tour of the quiet residential streets on either side of US–290 offers such rewards as Coburn Cottage, 327 Twelfth Street; the Ahrenbeck-Urban Home, 1203 Bellville Highway; and the Houx House, on the corner of US–290 (also called T–6 locally) and New Orleans Street.

One good reason to stop in Hempstead is Dilorio's thriving produce market on US–290 at the southeastern edge of town. There is adequate off-street parking, but re-entering US–290 is very hazardous.

WHAT TO DO

Huisache Farm. Coming north on US–290, turn right at the third (and last) signal in Waller and go 7 miles to FM–1488; turn left for 200 yards and then turn right on FM–1736 and go 3 miles. Watch for black board fences and beige barns. This 502–acre ranch breeds and trains thoroughbred horses, and visitors with advance arrangements are welcome to tour the paddocks and barns. If you want to see foals, come in April or early May. (409) 826–3366.

   Liendo Plantation. From US–290 slightly south of Hempstead, turn northwest on FM–1488 and then right on Wyatt Chapel Road. Originally a Spanish land grant of 67,000 acres, Liendo was one of the earliest cotton plantations in Texas, and its large Greek Revival-style home was built by slave labor in 1853. During the Civil War, Liendo was a Union camp for Confederate prisoners, directed by George A. Custer, and from 1873 to 1911 it was the home of sculptress Elisabet Ney and her husband, Dr. Edmond Montgomery. Both are buried on the grounds. Now privately owned, this gracious old home has been restored and furnished as it would have been during its cotton-growing days. Liendo is both a Texas Historic Landmark and on the National Register of Historic Places. Docents give guided tours at specific times on the first Saturday of every month. Call for details. Fee. (409) 826–3126.

WHERE TO EAT

Dairy Palace. 240 Austin Street, (US–290/T–6). You'll find the best of Blue Bell ice cream here, along with sandwiches, burritos, hamburgers, and tacos. Open daily for lunch and dinner. $. (409) 826–2428.

   The Hempstead Inn. 435 Tenth Street, (US–290/T–6). This old railroad hotel was built in 1901, 100 yards closer to the train tracks than its present site. It closed in 1968, only to rise to useful life again in 1981. Lunch and dinner are served in boardinghouse style, and the simple food is like what Grandma used to fix—fresh vegetables from the local markets, fried catfish, pot roast, etc. Guests help themselves from never-empty bowls, so you can sample or take seconds of anything you wish. Open for lunch and dinner daily. $-$$. (409) 826-6379.

WANDERING THE BACKROADS

From Hempstead, you have several choices if you wish to journey on. The easiest is to continue on US–290 west to Chappell Hill and do all or part of Day Trip 5, this sector. Or you can swing southwest 16 miles on T–159 to Bellville and pick up Day Trip 5, West Sector. If you do the latter, plan a stop midway at the Cochran General Store. Run by an ex-Houstonian, it's a good place for a cold drink and some Texas-style chatting.

Day Trip 5

CHAPPELL HILL
WASHINGTON-ON-THE-BRAZOS
NAVASOTA
ANDERSON

CHAPPELL HILL

From Houston, this day trip follows US–290 northwest approximately 75 miles through Hempstead to the intersection of FM–1155. A short jog north takes you to the first stop, Chappell Hill.

This charming village just north of US–290 may be the Brigadoon of Texas, so true is it to its time. Settled in 1847 and named for early Texas hunter Robert W. Chappell, Chappell Hill thrived as a stage stop on the Houston-to-Austin/Waco run and became the cultural center of Washington County, the home of two four-year universities. But the fickle tides of progress soon moved on, and visitors today often feel they have stumbled on a quiet place left over from the 1880s.

The universities have long closed, their charters transferred to become the seeds of Southwestern University in Georgetown; Southern Methodist University in Dallas; and the University of Texas Medical Branch in Galveston. But the old Stagecoach Inn still is here, a private home restored to its antique glory, and the Farmer's State Bank, circa 1900, has its original brass teller's cage. Fun to know: This was the last bank in the region that registered its customers by name instead of magnetic codes and computers.

There's a latch-key library—local folks all have their own keys so they can come and go at will—and more than twenty-five historical medallions are scattered throughout this four-street settlement. Four treasured homes offer excellent bed and breakfast accommodations: The Mulberry House (circa 1855), (409) 830–1311 or (713) 461–1740; Lottie's Bed and Breakfast (circa 1850–70), (409) 836–9515; the Browning Plantation (circa 1850), (409) 836–6144 or (713) 627–8920; and the Stagecoach Inn (circa 1858), (409) 836–9515.

Buy an ice-cream cone at the old drugstore and then take a nostalgic walk through Lesser's Grocery, stocked with kerosene, seed spuds, local sausages, and jams just as it was in great-grandfather's day. Other parts of Main Street and seven additional local sites are on the National Register of Historic Places.

WHERE TO GO

Browning Plantation. One mile south of US–290, off FM–1371. Also listed in the national register, this three-story wood home was built as the heart of a 2,000-acre plantation in 1856 by Col. W. W. Browning, a loyal Confederate supporter and one of Chappell Hill's leading citizens. By the early 1980s, however, the house literally was a teetering ruin surrounded by 170 acres of wild country. Bought and restored in 1983 with love and megabucks by a Houston couple, this 6,000-square-foot house is once again an elegant charmer and filled with antiques. Tours are given by appointment, and four bedrooms are available for classy B&B. Don't miss the "before" photos in the downstairs parlor. Fee. (409) 836–6144 or (713) 627–8920.

Chappell Hill Historical Museum and Methodist Church. On Church Street, one long block east of Main. The museum is in the old school and is staffed on Sunday afternoons only. The church has stained-glass windows worth seeing and is open for Sunday services. Donations are appreciated.

Chappell Hill Sausage Co. On westbound side of US–290, 3.5 miles east of Chappell Hill. Six different kinds of sausage are made here, primarily for supermarkets around the state. You can watch the sausage-making process and buy your favorite to take home. Closed Sunday. $. (409) 836–5830.

Old Masonic Cemetery. Turn west at the blinking light at Main and Chestnut streets, then right on the first dirt road for one-half mile. At least twenty-four Confederate soldiers are buried here, along with assorted Crocketts and the son and daughter of William Barret Travis. The latter were longtime residents of Chappell Hill.

Cemetery lovers also will enjoy the old Atkinson Cemetery, south of town on County Road 87.

Rock Store Museum. East side of Main Street, near the bank. The prime display is the town's history, embroidered and appliquéd on two 30-foot-long cloth panels. Open weekend afternoons or whenever the local ladies feel like socializing. Donations are appreciated. Special appointments: (409) 836–9515.

Stagecoach Inn. Main and Chestnut streets. This is the public's best look at the past in all of Washington County. Listed in the National Register of Historic Places, this beautiful Greek Revival structure was built in 1850 and was a busy stage stop through the Civil War. Note the Lone Star and 1851 date inscribed on the downspout heads, the detail of the Greek-key frieze on the cornice that encircles the house, and the old-fashioned flower gardens. Groups of four or more can arrange guided tours (fee), plus this wonderful old place now is back in business as a bed and breakfast inn (409–836–9515). Through this number you also can arrange tours of other historic homes in the Chappell Hill area.

Owners Elizabeth and Harvin Moore also operate an antique shop in the historic Weems house behind the old inn, as well as Lottie's B&B, a two-bedroom cottage across Main Street from the inn.

Waverly Plantation. One-half mile east of Main Street on Chestnut (FM–2447). Watch for a one-story white plantation house with columns. This 1850s Greek Revival treasure is special for its original foundation, wood siding, kitchen, and beveled-glass front doors. The Waverly Shop sells antiques in the old kitchen, and tours of the house can be reserved in advance. Fee. (409) 836–5067.

WHERE TO EAT

Bever's County Cooking. Main Street in Chappell Hill. This combination house/real estate office/restaurant serves tasty salads and sandwiches, homemade soup and chili, and the best Mexican food in the county. Dinners also run to chicken-fried steak, hamburgers, and nightly specials. Open for lunch and dinner Monday–Saturday. $. (409) 836–4178.

Bluebonnet Hills Inn. On westbound side of US–290, between Chappell Hill and Brenham. Formerly chef at River Oaks Country Club and Sakowitz Post Oak, owner Henrique Valdovinos knows his way around both the kitchen and a Continental menu. He buys his veggies fresh from Dilorio's in Hempstead and guarantees that his chicken-fried veal cutlet is tender enough to cut with a fork. Open for dinner, Tuesday–Saturday. $$; (CC). (409) 836–4642.

Chappell Hill Restaurant. On eastbound side of US–290 at Chappell Hill (blinking light) intersection. New management has turned what was a forgettable eatery into one of the best country cafes in Texas. BLTs come on bread baked that morning, all veggies served have just been picked from the garden out back, and the fried chicken is better than Mom ever made. Menu also includes shrimp, fish, and steaks. Open breakfast through dinner, Tuesday–Sunday. $. (409) 836–0850.

(Nice to know: Floyd's Meat Market next door has outstanding Polish sausage, steaks, and home-cured bacon.)

WASHINGTON-ON-THE-BRAZOS

From Chappell Hill, continue north 18 miles on FM–1155 to Washington-on-the-Brazos. Early settlers used this same route.

This portion of Texas was crossed by countless trails that were the interstate highways of the seventeenth and eighteenth centuries, and numerous highway markers today comment on three major routes. The Old San Antonio Road ran to the Louisiana border and passed to the north of Bryan–College Station. The Coushatta Trail through Grimes County to the north of Washington was part of the Contraband Trace, used for smuggling goods from Louisiana into Spanish Texas. A third trail, La Bahia, went from Goliad to the lower Louisiana border, sometimes running in tandem with the Old San Antonio Road.

In 1821, one of Stephen F. Austin's first settlers started a small farm and ferry service where the busy La Bahia Trail forded the Brazos River. In 1835, the settlement was capitalized as the Washington Town Company, lots were auctioned, and the raw beginnings of an organized settlement began to emerge on the riverbank. It was to become a pivot point for history.

March of 1836 was a fateful month for Texas. While Santa Anna was devastating the Alamo, some fifty-nine men were creating the Republic of Texas at the constitutional convention at Washington-on-the-Brazos. Washington later served twice as the capital of Texas, but ultimately lost that honor to Austin. Bypassed by the railroads, the community faded into obscurity and then literally disappeared after the Civil War.

WHAT TO DO

Antique Co-op. Everything from dolls and quality Texas primitives to general junk is housed in or near the old schoolhouse behind the post office. Reba's dewberry jelly, fig preserves, and wild grape jam are known throughout Washington County; don't leave without buying at least one jar. Open Friday–Sunday in spring and summer, weekends only in fall and winter. (409) 878–2112.

Washington-on-the-Brazos State Historical Park. Today only a handful of relatively new wooden buildings and the park's special structures mark where the Republic of Texas began. Road signs clearly mark the route to the park headquarters. All of the following are within the park boundaries, charge no admission fee, and are open daily from March through Labor Day. Closed Monday and Tuesday, September–February.

Barrington. Built in 1844–45 and restored in 1968 and 1971, this was home to Anson Jones, the fourth and last president of the Texas Republic. Furnishings are from that period.

Independence Hall. This simple frame building is a reconstruction on the original site of the signing of the Texas Declaration of Independence. An audiovisual program comments on the 1836 convention.

Star of the Republic Museum. Start with the slide presentation for a good historical perspective, and then take the self-guided tour through a variety of displays that include a rare 1845 mail coach from Galveston. The museum also attracts excellent traveling exhibits and is noted for its reference collection of Texana material, including old maps, documents, letters, and rare books. Guided tours can be arranged in advance.

For more information on any of the above, contact Star of the Republic Museum, P.O. Box 305, Washington 77880, (409) 878–2214.

WANDERING THE BACKROADS

After exploring Washington, continue north on FM–1155 to the intersection at T–105. At this point you have a choice: Either continue this day trip by turning right (north) to Navasota or turn south on T–105 to Brenham and connect with Trip 6, this sector.

NAVASOTA

Settlers responding to Stephen F. Austin's advertisements for colonists founded this town in the 1820s. A generation later, cotton was king of the plantation economy here, thriving on the rich bottomland of the Brazos River.

The coming of the railroad in the 1850s brought even larger profits, and the wealthy farmers splurged on lavish town homes in Navasota, many of which remain in fine shape today. Some line Washington Avenue (T–105) as it flows through town, and others require short detours onto Johnson, Holland, and Brewer streets. All are private homes, a number of which open to the public during Navasota Nostalgia Days the first weekend of May. One Victorian mansion (circa 1893), The Castle Inn at 1403 E. Washington, welcomes bed and breakfast guests (409–825–8051). Another, LaSalle House at 412 E. Washington, is an 1897 Queen Anne Victorian that houses an antique co-op; house tours (fee) are available on weekends (409–825–3865). Antique lovers also should visit Past & Present, 716 E. Washington; closed on Monday and most Sundays (409–825–7545).

Not too surprisingly, Navasota stood heart and soul with the South during the Civil War, but unpaid Confederate soldiers angrily burned much of the town in 1865. A yellow fever epidemic two years later dealt the final economic blow. Today this quiet community of 5,000 snoozes in the heart of horse farm country, its grand past only a memory and its downtown a National Historic District.

Even fewer traces of the area's Indian and Mexican history survive, and visitors often are startled to find a statue of French explorer La Salle in the center of the main road. It memorializes his death nearby in 1687 at the hands of his own men.

Information as well as walking and driving tour brochures are available from the Grimes County Chamber of Commerce, 117 S. LaSalle (P.O. Box 530), Navasota 77868. (409) 825–6600.

WHAT TO DO

Bank of Navasota. 109 W. Washington Ave. This 1880s building has been restored to its original look and use. Open Monday–Friday and Saturday mornings.

Navasota Livestock Auction Co. Three miles east of Navasota on Highway 90. Ranchers from Grimes, Washington, and Brazos counties bring their livestock here for sale, making this auction the state champ in volume and dollars. Visitors are welcome to watch the action, but don't scratch your nose or tug on your ear—you may go home with a live calf as a souvenir. Saturday mornings only. (409) 825–6545.

The Peaceable Kingdom School. From Navasota, take T–105 south approximately 8 miles (just past the turn-off to Washington). Turn right on Washington County Road 96, also known as the Old River Road, and take the first right turn. Follow this dirt and gravel road 1.7 miles to a yellow cattleguard on the left, and you are at the Peaceable Kingdom. This residential craft community emphasizes holistic health and uses the environment as a teaching tool. Depending upon who is in residence and the time of year, you may find classes ranging from natural fiber dyeing or massage therapy to cultivated and native herbs. Founded by Libbie Winston in 1970, this small farm also has animals, organic gardens, a solar greenhouse, assorted workshops, and the Brazos River Outpost, a small shop that sells local crafts and live or dried herbs. The emphasis is on learning from the land. The public is welcome to visit, to bring their children to "A Child's Day with Nature," and to attend weekend crafts workshops as well as the Peaceable Kingdom School. Overnight accommodations are limited to primitive camping and three indoor units. Of interest: Libby Winston is a widely recognized authority on the native plants of Texas. Open Wednesday–Sunday. Box 313, Washington 77880. (409) 878–2353.

Rudolph's Treeland. To cut your own Christmas tree, go 7 miles south of Navasota on T–6, then 2 blocks east on FR–318. (409) 846–2604.

Schumacher Oil Mill. Two blocks north of Washington on North LaSalle. Built in 1866 along the banks of Cedar Creek, this cottonseed oil mill was the oldest in the world when it closed to the public. Now it is interesting just to drive around the massive old building and read the historical marker. Bring a picnic and have lunch in the new Cedar Creek Park, across from this old building on LaSalle Street.

WHERE TO EAT

The Golden Palace. 201 N. LaSalle. Locals say this Chinese food is worth the drive from Houston and that the daily lunch buffet is an excellent buy. Open Tuesday–Sunday for lunch and dinner. $–$$; (CC). (409) 825–8488.

Margarita's. 310 E. Washington. Tex-Mex in all its forms is the house specialty. Open for lunch and dinner daily. $. (409) 825–2284.

R & A's Country Kitchen. 121 E. Washington. Tasty homestyle lunches here. Open daily. $. (No phone at this time.)

Ruthie's Cafe. 905 W. Washington. This undistinguished-looking barbecue place is a Texas classic—six kinds of meat pit-smoked over oak and mesquite. Closed Wednesday. $–$$; (CC). (409) 825–2700.

From Navasota, this day trip continues to the tiny town of Anderson, 10 miles northeast via T–90.

ANDERSON

Time stopped here about 1932, and the entire town looks like a stage set for a Bonnie and Clyde movie. Fact is, one member of the Barrow gang was tried here in the old courthouse, a tidbit duly noted on the building's historical medallion. But Anderson's history reaches back much further than the 1930s.

Established in 1834 as a stage stop on the La Bahia Trail, the town became an important assembly point and arms depot during the Civil War. Those days of glory live again during the Anderson Trek each spring and Texian Days in late September when local folks don period costumes and open their homes to visitors. The entire town—everything you can see from the top of the courthouse—is listed in the National Register of Historic Places. For information on the town, call Historic Anderson, Inc., (409) 873–2662.

WHAT TO DO

Baptist Church. Left side of Main Street, 2 blocks south of FM–1774. Built of native rock by slaves in 1855, this handsome church still has regular Sunday services. LBJ's granddaddy was once Anderson's preacher.

Fanthorp Inn. Bottom of Main Street on the left. One of the first stage stops in Texas and the seed that started the town, this old inn was built in 1834 and led to Anderson's being, for a time, the fourth largest town in Texas. Owned by the Texas Parks and Wildlife Commission since 1977, the inn has been restored to a somewhat rumpled 1850s appearance; visitors have a sense that one stage has just departed and another is on its way. A barn of that period has been reconstructed with a stagecoach (reproduction) and exhibits that detail the early stage routes across Texas. The entire site is staffed with interpreters and is open Wednesday–Sunday (closed from 12 noon to 1 p.m.). Fee. (409) 873–2633.

Grimes County Courthouse. Top of Main Street. Built of hand-molded brick with native limestone trim, this oldy has its original vault. Note the handsome pressed-tin ceilings with rounded cove moldings in the main hall. Open weekdays during business hours.

Historic Anderson Park. South of the intersection of FM–1774 and T–90. Four architectural relics of Anderson's past are preserved here, including the Steinhagen Log Cabin, built by slaves in 1852 and notable because its walls are unspliced hand-hewn timbers; the Steinhagen Home, with a wing added to its 1850s period; and the Boggess Store, filled with turn-of-the-century merchandise. These old buildings can be toured only during special events or by prior arrangement. (409) 873–2662.

New York Row. Parallels Main Street, 1 block east. This lane is where the town swells lived during Anderson's heyday.

WHERE TO EAT

Kott's Cafe. On Main Street, next door to the post office. This clean and simple place looks like someone's house, complete with front porch. Open for lunch and dinner Monday–Saturday, it serves a great hamburger and country plate lunch. $. (409) 873–2022.

Clint's Supermarket. On Highway 90, across from the bank. The deli sells great barbeque and chicken, just right for a picnic on the grounds of the Fanthorp Inn. Open daily. $. (409) 873–2550.

WANDERING THE BACKROADS

For those who like country drives, getting home from Anderson via FM–1774 south is pure pleasure. While spring is prime because of the wildflowers, a fall season drive recalls the rolling hills of western Massachusetts. The oaks turn color with the first frost, and Anderson's lone church steeple pokes up through the landscape like a sentinel on a hill.

Day Trip 6

BRENHAM
DIME BOX
SOMERVILLE
INDEPENDENCE

BRENHAM

If it wasn't a 72-mile commute on US–290 each way, Brenham would be overrun with refugees from Houston. This thriving community of slightly more than 12,000 is close to the ideal American small town—old enough to be interesting but new enough to keep up with the times.

Shaded residential streets still sport a number of antebellum and Victorian homes, and many of the turn-of-the-century buildings downtown are spiffed up and in use. Just blocks away it's open country again—thousands of acres of beautiful farmland. In the spring the bluebonnets and other wildflowers are magnificent, a carpet of color rolling to all horizons.

Founded in 1844 and settled by German immigrants during the ensuing two decades, Brenham was occupied and partially burned by Federal troops during the Civil War. Most of the town's surviving history can be seen on a windshield tour, courtesy of a free map and visitor's guide available from the Washington County Chamber of Commerce, 314 So. Austin, Brenham 77833 (409–836–3695). Call in advance to arrange a very inexpensive guided tour of the downtown historic district. Groups should inquire about tours and use of the Citadel, a former country club (circa 1924) that has been restored to *Great Gatsby* elegance. Highly visible on the west-bound side of US–290, it looks like a massive plantation house sitting amid a young vineyard 3 miles east of town.

Should you enjoy Brenham too much to leave, there are a number of bed and breakfast establishments in town, among them: the James Walker Log Cabin, (409) 836–6717; Country Life, Ltd., (409) 830–0477; Secrets, (409) 836–4117; Captain Tacitus T. Clay House, (409) 836–1916 or (713) 622–6744; Depot Guest Cottage, (409) 836–6489; Heartland Country Inn, (409) 836–1864; and Vernon's Bed and Breakfast, (409) 836–6408.

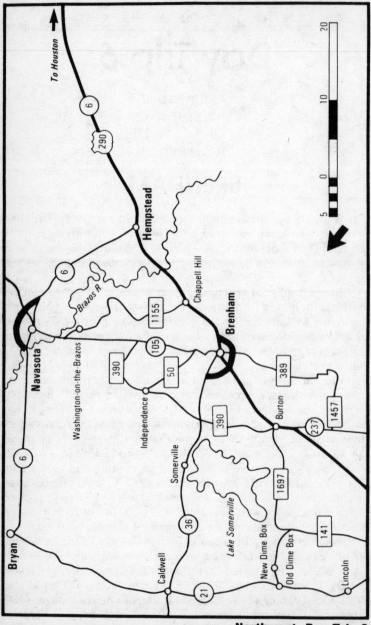

Northwest: Day Trip 6

Nearby Burton (see "Wandering the Backroads" section) is beginning to thrive again and now has three vintage B&Bs: Long Point Inn, (409) 289–3171; The Knittel Homestead, (409) 289–5102; and The Cottage at Cedar Creek, (409) 278–3770.

WHAT TO DO

Ant Street Historic District. This downtown section of Brenham has been undergoing a colorful renovation for several years and now sports fresh exteriors and several antique co-ops, one of which is in the newly refurbished train depot on Market Street. The historic district extends to the old Savitall Market at Commerce and Baylor streets, still open Monday–Saturday and worth a stop to see the grocery scene as it was before Randalls, Safeway, et al.

Bassett & Bassett Banking House. Corner of Market and Main streets. This vintage bank has been freshly restored as part of a Main Street revival program in Brenham. This is an ongoing business and open during normal business hours.

Blue Bell Creameries. Loop 577 (Horton Street). Free tours and tastes, but call ahead to confirm space. (409) 836–7977.

Christmas Tree Farm. Cut your own at Mockingbird Hill Farm, (409) 335–6386.

Ellison's Greenhouses. 2107 East Stone, three-quarters of a mile south of Blue Bell Creameries on Loop 577. Whatever the holiday, celebrate it early by touring this colorful wholesale nursery. Seasonally, the half-acre greenhouses are filled with poinsettias, tulips, Easter lilies, hydrangeas, etc. Tours by appointment Tuesday–Friday, but closed the days just prior to major holidays. (409) 836–6011 or (713) 463–0118.

Fireman's Park. 900 block of North Park Street. This shady city park has a fully restored Hershell-Spillman carousel, manufactured for carnival touring prior to 1910 and one of only twelve antique merry-go-rounds remaining in Texas today. Now visible behind protective glass panels, this wonderful antique operates whenever Brenham has a city-wide celebration.

Giddings-Stone Mansion. Near South Market and Stone streets. This twelve-room Greek Revival home with its imposing galleries was built in 1869 on a hill in what was then south of town. Now owned by the local heritage society, it is being restored as funds become available and is considered by architectural historians to be one of the ten most significant old homes in Texas. You may walk the grounds but not enter the house except during special events. Group tours can be arranged. (409) 836–3695.

Giddings-Wilkin House. 805 Crockett. Built in 1843, this is thought to be the oldest house still standing in Brenham. Now the property of the Heritage Society, it sometimes is open as a museum and can be toured by appointment. (409) 836–3695.

Miniature Horses at the Monastery of St. Clare. Nine miles northeast of Brenham via T–105 and FM–2193 east. The breeding, training, and sale of miniature horses is one of the self-support ventures of this cloistered order, the Franciscan Poor Clares, and three of the nuns are permitted to show the public around this outstanding ninety-eight-acre facility. Although the convent is open from 2 to 4 p.m. daily, visitors have a good chance of seeing the training process on Monday, Wednesday, and Friday. Spring visitors see twenty to thirty foals, each about eighteen inches tall, cavorting in fields filled with wildflowers; there are public shows in May and September. Individuals and families are welcome year-round, bus tours only by advance reservation from mid-March through mid-October. There's also a gift shop and picnic area, and the monastery chapel is open to the public. Fee for guided tours; self-guided tours are free. (409) 836–9652.

Ross-Carroll-Bennett House. 515 Main Street. This private residence typifies the fanciful fretwork of the Victorian era (circa 1893). What looks like blocks of stone on the exterior actually is cypress in disguise. The house is privately owned; please do not trespass.

Schaper Family Dairy. South of Brenham on County Road 35. Established in 1886 by German immigrant August Carl Schaper, this large facility still is operated by the same family. Tours are available to groups of twenty or more. Fee. (409) 836–0861.

WHERE TO EAT

The Great Ant Street Restaurant. 205 South Baylor in the Ant Street Historic District of downtown Brenham. If you have only one meal to eat in Brenham, eat it here—and you might consider getting a little gussied up for the occasion. From the time it opened in late November 1990, this handsome eatery won local hearts with its delicious food and 1970s prices. The lunch menu runs from hamburgers and oyster po-boys to soups, salads, and a daily special that includes a choice of two meats, four veggies, and dessert. Dinner is more classic; the prime rib is outstanding. House specials include an unusual cucumber salad dressing and giant biscuits served with crocks of butter and honey. Open Tuesday–Friday for lunch, Tuesday–Sunday for dinner. $–$$; (CC). (409) 830–9060.

The Burton Cafe. On FM–390, behind the post office in Burton. Homespun vittles and charm carry the day at this friendly place, considered by many to be one of the best country cafes in the state. The roast beef platters are great, the homemade bread and veggies are locally produced and the breakfasts are humongous. Want to know what's going on in the Brenham-Burton neighborhood? Just sit a spell and listen; you'll know as much as the locals. Open Monday–Saturday for breakfast, lunch, and dinner; closes at 3 p.m. on Tuesday and Wednesday. $. (409) 298–3849.

The Ice Cream Shoppe. Four Corners Shopping Center (US–290 and TX–36) in Brenham. Because of its easy access, this is a good and quick stop for sandwiches and Blue Bell ice cream if you are just passing through. Open daily. $. (409) 836–5301.

The Fluff Top Roll Restaurant. 210 East Alamo in downtown Brenham. The staff at this gingham-decked cafe bakes fresh yeast rolls daily, and the blue-plate specials are substantial and popular with the downtown Brenham business community. Open for breakfast and lunch Monday–Saturday; dinner on Friday and Saturday. $–$$. (409) 836–9441.

Must Be Heaven Ice Cream and Sweet Shop. 113 West Alamo in downtown Brenham. These folks have a strong local following for their tasty kolaches and other pastries. There's Blue Bell ice cream, along with soups, salads, sandwiches, and quiche. Open Monday–Saturday. $. (409) 830–8536.

WANDERING THE BACKROADS

Continue west on US–290 to visit the reviving small town of Burton (pop. 325). One of the few vintage cotton gins in Texas is under slow restoration here as a national historic landmark, plus there's an interesting old shoe shop next door. Tours of both are available by appointment Wednesday–Sunday (donation) and during Burton's annual Cotton Gin Festival every April. For information, call (409) 289–2863 or (409) 289–5102.

From Burton you can swing northwest on FM–1697 and FM–141 to Dime Box and some areas of Lake Somerville.

An alternate follows T–105 northeast from Brenham to Navasota (Trip 5, this sector) or you can jog south from Brenham on FM–389 (Trips 4 and 5, West Sector).

DIME BOX—OLD AND NEW

The name alone of these two separate communities brings some explorers. Perhaps this explanation will save some time, gasoline, and tempers.

Old Dime Box is on T–21, sort of around the corner a few miles from new Dime Box on FM–141. Of visitor interest in both places are the historical plaques explaining that the town name comes from the old custom of leaving dimes in the community mailbox on the Old San Antonio Road (T–21) in return for items brought by rural delivery from Giddings.

If you do explore in and around Dime Box, you can get back on your original day-trip route by following T–21 northwest to Caldwell and then T–36 south to Somerville. Continuing on T–21 northeast from Caldwell brings you to College Station, Trip 3 of this sector.

SOMERVILLE

Who would think that three little creeks could combine to form a 24,000-acre lake? Dammed in the early 1960s as a flood control and water conservation project, Lake Somerville has become a favorite water playground 88 miles northwest of Houston on T–36.

The town itself serves only as a gas and grocery supply depot—the lake is the big attraction. Popular with boaters, there are seven campgrounds around the lake, two of which are state parks. Fishing is good for largemouth and white bass, white crappie, and channel catfish. Deer abound, particularly on the islands within the lake.

The wild birds are varied enough to warrant a folder and field checklists, available free from the Texas Parks and Wildlife Department, Resource Management Section, 4200 Smith School Road, Austin 78744; (800) 792–1112.

Your day trip continues south on T–36 from Somerville to FM–390. Turn northeast (left) to Independence.

INDEPENDENCE

As far as Washington County is concerned, Independence is where it all started. Originally called Coles' Settlement for its first pioneer John P. Coles, the town's name was changed in 1836 to celebrate

Texas's independence from Mexico. Coles was a member of Stephen F. Austin's original 300 families, and his cedar log-and-frame cabin, built in 1824, stands just east of town at the entrance to Old Baylor Park. The town's interesting cemetery is equally old, about 2 miles north of the park entrance on County Road 60.

When Brenham won election as the county seat by two votes, Independence began a century-long slide into obscurity. Today, it is a mecca for Texana lovers because of its old stone church and historic ruins.

WHAT TO DO

LaCroix Limited. From Independence on T–50 south, turn west on County Road 68 (at Westerfeld Garage) and right again on County Road 60. One of the most beautiful horse farms in the state, this rolling, 168-acre spread specializes in breeding and training Polish and Polish-Cross Arabians. If you have made advance arrangements, guides are delighted to show you around, and if you are lucky, you'll catch a training session in the ranch's indoor arena. Bring your camera. This is the country-club life for horses—vast meadows, individual stalls outfitted with ceiling fans above and a deep carpet of cedar shavings under hoof, plus lots of TLC. (409) 830–1421.

The Antique Rose Emporium. One-half mile south of the T–390 intersection on T–50. More than 200 varieties of old garden roses, documented to have grown in Texas during its years as a republic, thrive here on the site of the Hairston-McKnight Homestead, which was settled in the 1840s. The remains of an old stone kitchen (circa 1855) have been restored as the center of a typical cottage garden of those times, a converted barn is now the office and bookstore, and an old corncrib has become a gift shop featuring rose-related items. There's also a selection of native Texas trees, shrubs, vines, wildflower seed, and other plant species appropriate to the climate and locale. Open daily. A catalog ($3) is also available; Route 5, Box 143, Brenham 77833; (409) 836–9051 (weekday catalog sales); (409) 836–5548 (retail).

Independence Baptist Church. At the intersection of FM–50 and FM–390. Organized in 1839, the church's present stone building was finished in 1872 and still has services every Sunday. Sam Houston saw the light here and was baptized in nearby Rocky Creek. (409) 836–5117.

The Mrs. Sam Houston House. On the south side of FM–390, the second house east of the T–50 intersection. Built in 1863, this was Mrs. Houston's last home, and the crape myrtles she planted still bloom by the front door. Now restored and occupied by a Houston couple, it is open by appointment. Fee. (409) 830–1959.

A second Sam Houston homesite has a granite marker across from Old Baylor Park.

Old Baylor Park and Ruins of Old Baylor University. One-half mile west of the church on FM–390. This birth site of Baylor University now is marked only by a few ghostly columns and some old oaks and is a good place to enjoy a picnic. The Coles cabin has been relocated here and can be toured either by appointment or on weekend afternoons in March and April. Contact the local chamber of commerce at (409) 836–3695. Donation.

Texas Baptist Historical Center. Adjacent to the Independence Baptist Church, this museum houses pre-Civil War artifacts as well as old church and family records. Mrs. Sam Houston (*née* Margaret Moffet Lea) and her mother are buried in a somewhat unlovely site across the street. Open Wednesday–Saturday; Sunday afternoon by reservation. Free. (409) 836–5117.

WANDERING THE BACKROADS

Independence is the last stop on this day trip, but you can easily extend your travels. Following FM–390 east brings you to T–105. Turn northeast (left) and you can tour Washington-on-the-Brazos, Navasota, and Anderson (Trip 5, this sector). An alternative is to continue south from Independence on FM–50 to T–105 and Brenham, connecting there with either FM–389 and Trips 4 and 5 in the West Sector, or with T–36 south to Bellville and home.

WEST

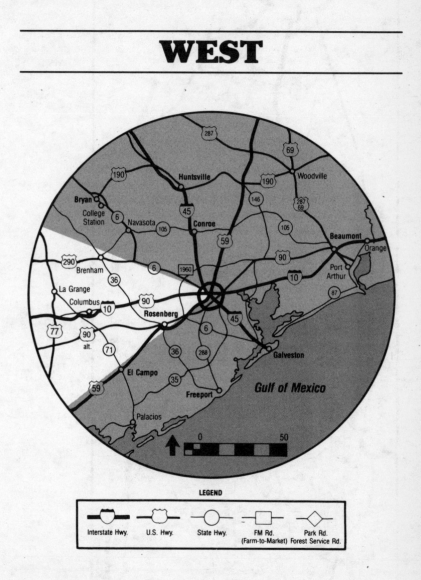

LEGEND

Interstate Hwy.   U.S. Hwy.   State Hwy.   FM Rd. (Farm-to-Market)   Park Rd. Forest Service Rd.

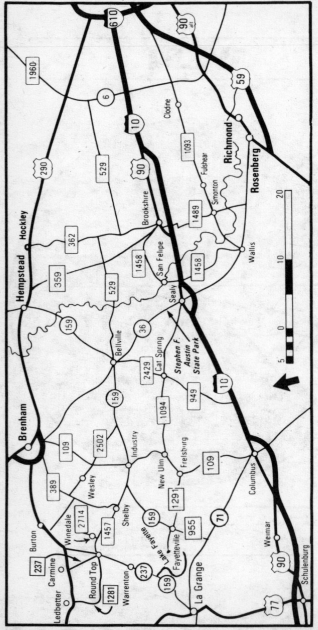

West: Day Trips 1, 3, 4, and 5

Day Trip 1

WEST HOUSTON
BROOKSHIRE
SAN FELIPE
SEALY
CAT SPRING

WEST HOUSTON

Because this day trip begins with a drive west on I–10, consider stopping on the western outskirts of town for one of the following activities.

Albert Alkek Velodrome. 19008 Saums Road in Cullen Park. Take the Barker-Cypress exit from I–10 and go north 1 mile to the park. Built for the 1986 United States Olympic Festival, this is one of only seven Olympic-quality velodromes in the U.S. and the site of the 1991 Junior National biking championships. The overall program includes general riding sessions, developmental cycling classes for beginners, races for graduates of that program, and a Friday-night racing series open only to USCF-licensed riders. Spectating is free, and helmets and track bikes can be rented on site. For a brochure and seasonal schedule, either call the track, (713) 578–0858, or write Alkek Velodrome, Houston Parks and Recreation Department, 2999 South Wayside, Houston 77023.

Great Southwest Equestrian Center. 2501 South Mason Rd., Katy. Three miles south on Mason Road from I–10. This 107-acre, multimillion-dollar facility welcomes visitors as well as dedicated horse lovers. In addition to local and national horse shows nearly every weekend (most are free; public welcome), they host horse sales and auctions and offer equestrian training and lessons. An observation deck overlooks both the lesson practice arena and the show complex. Call to get on the mailing list for their quarterly schedule. (713) 578–PONY (7669).

Flying at West Houston Airport. 18000 Groeschke Road. Take Barker-Cypress exit from I–10 and follow the airport signs north to Groeschke Road. You too can discover the wonder of flying in a two- or four-seat Cessna. Discovery flights (thirty minutes) are $25 and $37.50 respectively in these high-winged planes. Sightseeing and photography flights also can be reserved, starting at $77 per hour in the four-seater. Reservations required. (713) 492–2130.

Green Meadows Farm. Formerly in rural Brookshire, now at 19008 Saums Road in Cullen Park. Popular as a field trip with area school districts, this recreation/education farm experience specializes in allowing children close-up encounters with domestic animals. Activities include pony rides, egg gathering, a milking demonstration, and hayrides; visitors can also go into the animal pens to feed sheep and hold baby pigs, chicks, and ducks. In October, pumpkins are laid out in a field for easy pickin's. Absolutely no pets are allowed. Open daily from spring through midsummer and in the fall. Fee. (713) 391–7995.

Hot Air Ballooning. Several companies will take you silently floating over Houston for sixty to ninety minutes in a three-man basket suspended below a giant hot air balloon. Most lift-offs are at sunrise to take advantage of the still air, and costs are in the $200–$225-per-couple range (champagne is included at the end of the trip). Get the particulars from Above It All Balloons, (713) 277–1788; Air Ad-Ventures International, (713) 747–3242 or 956–9195; Better Way to Fly, (713) 493–2048; Pretty Balloons Unlimited, (713) 463–0080; and Rainbow's End Balloon Port, (713) 466–1927.

To continue this day trip, take I–10 west to the Brookshire exit.

BROOKSHIRE

Brookshire's history is brief. This small community was established in the early 1880s by the MKT Railroad to serve a rich agricultural area. Its ethnic past ranges from Polish to German, Greek to Czech, Swiss to Armenian. The Waller County Festival, held in October, is an energetic melding of these cultures.

WHERE TO GO

Blue Barn Fun Farm. On FM–1458 near Pattison; approximately three-quarters of a mile west of FM–359. Formerly named BMW Farm, this ten-acre country learning experience is run with loving care by long-time farmers Clyde and Maudine Brubaker to educate children about country life. Following a basic program set up with the assistance of Texas A&M, the pint-sized visitors learn how a machine milks a cow and get to try the hands-on method themselves. They also pet calves, baby chicks, and a baby (10-inch) alligator; jig for crawfish; and get up close to doves, bullfrogs, pigs, guinea pigs, deer, geese, ducks, bobwhite quail, turkeys, guineas hens, ring-necked and golden pheasants, rabbits, goats, chickens, and turkeys. A tractor-drawn hayride then hauls everyone to a picnic area shaded by 200 oaks, so pack a hamper when you come; cold drinks are sold on premises. October visitors receive free pumpkins; August visitors get stone-ground corn meal and a recipe for corn bread; July visitors are given free watermelon; and December visitors go home with candy canes. Cost is $5 per person in groups of twenty or more; $6.25 per person (including children) for individuals. Open weekdays only; advance reservations required. Closed September and Christmas–February. (713) 375–6669.

The Brookwood Community. 1752 FM–1489, in rural Brookshire, 1 mile south of I–10 (signs). This handsome 475-acre country facility is a privately funded, self-supporting community for functionally disabled adults (mentally and/or physically handicapped), aided in part by a volunteer staff made up largely of retirees. However, institutional gloom is not to be found here. Brookwood looks like a country club, feels like the home most people only dream about, and functions like a successful company. Last year the seventy handicapped adults in the program produced $500,000 worth of products in their horticultural and crafts industries. Their production of bedding, potted plants, and trees, as well as their artwork, is sold both on the premises and also through many Houston gift shops and nurseries. Tours are given the first Wednesday of every month or by appointment if you call in advance. Currently, visitors to Brookwood can purchase original ceramics, garden sculptures, silk-screened notes and cards, plants, and trees at the gift shop on weekdays only, 8 a.m. to 5 p.m. The nursery is also open Saturday, 10 a.m. to 3 p.m. (713) 391–9100.

Christmas Tree Cutting. Call Dry Branch Ranch, near Pattison, for directions. (713) 934–8937.

Lilipons Water Gardens. Just south of I–10 on FM–1489. Where else in Houston do you find acres of exotic goldfish amid blooming lotus and water lilies? The shop sells everything needed to create your own water garden, but visitors are welcome to just browse among the twenty-five production ponds out back. These folks also publish a large color catalog (fee) and even mail goldfish. Open daily in summer; Monday–Saturday in winter. (CC). (713) 934–8525.

The Waller County Historical Museum. 4026 Fifth Street at Cooper in Brookshire. Built in 1910, this nice old home contains period furnishings, historic artifacts and documents, and some interesting old photos. Free, but donations are welcome. Open Wednesday, Friday, and Saturday; call for hours. (713) 934–2826.

WHERE TO EAT

The City Cafe. Front Street at Velasco, Brookshire. You won't go away hungry here. A great favorite with locals, this tidy place offers up to four meats and six vegetables in its lunch specials, and the desserts are outstanding. Open Monday–Saturday for breakfast and lunch. $. (713) 934–8204.

 The Cotton Gin. 907 Bains Street, at the intersection of US–90 and FM–359. Fine food is reason enough to come to this restaurant, but the building itself is worth a look. Built in 1936, this cotton gin hummed with activity for a decade before closing down in 1946 due to a decline in area cotton production. Much of the equipment had come from an earlier Brookshire gin built in the 1920s. Today, that old equipment is part of the restaurant's authentic decor. Expect outstanding steaks, seafood, and chicken entrees, created by chef/owner Klaus Elfeldt with his wife Sara. Open Tuesday–Friday for lunch, Tuesday–Sunday for dinner; plus there's an extensive Sunday buffet. $–$$; (CC). (713) 391–4034.

WANDERING THE BACKROADS

If you are coming from the FM–1960/T–6 area of Houston and prefer backroads, swing west on FM–529 and then south on FM–362 to Brookshire. Going home, just reverse those directions to miss the traffic crunch on T–6 near Bear Creek.

 If you love country drives, save some time for wandering south of I–10 on FM–1489. This is horse and cotton-growing country, and the ranches and farms are beautiful. This road passes through the small communities of Simonton, Wallis, and East Bernard, an excellent route into the southwestern sections of this book.

 To continue this day trip to San Felipe, either drive west from Brookshire on I–10 for 8 miles and watch for the exit signs to Stephen F. Austin State Park, or follow the country route via FM–359 northwest to Pattison and then west on FM–1458. The latter is a great country ramble along the route of the pioneers.

SAN FELIPE

Alas, how fleeting fame. From 1823 to 1836, San Felipe collected a string of firsts that earned ·it a secure niche in Texas history. Then known as San Felipe de Austin, it was the original settlement and capital of Stephen F. Austin's first colony. It also was the site of the first Anglo newspaper and postal system in the territory and the founding spot of the Texas Rangers. The town was burned in 1836 to prevent its use by the advancing Mexican Army. Although rebuilt later in that decade, it never regained its original momentum.

In addition to visiting the oldest post office in Texas, visitors today find some pieces of San Felipe's past in and around the state park. Stop first at the small historical park where FM–1458 crosses the Brazos and search for the still visible traces of wagon ruts that lead to the old ferry crossing. A dog-trot log cabin replicates Austin's headquarters, and the J. J. Josey Store, built in 1847, has been restored as a museum. Unfortunately, both are rarely open. Bring a lunch; there's a nice picnic area along the river on the other side of the road.

Stephen F. Austin State Park is nearby and open daily, year-round; watch for the Park Road 38 turnoff from FM–1458. There's an outstanding eighteen-hole golf course, plus picnicking, camping, swimming, and numerous other family activities. This oak-shaded retreat is wonderful in warm weather. Fee. (409) 885–3613.

After enjoying the park, resist the temptation to take backroads to Sealy; the route that forks to the right immediately outside the park gate is frustrating and not scenic. Instead, return to I–10 and continue west to the Sealy exit.

SEALY

San Felipe sold a portion of its original 22,000-acre township to the Gulf, Colorado, and Santa Fe Railroad in the 1870s to create the town of Sealy in 1879. That town now bills itself as the "best little hometown in Texas" and collects a few more refugee Houstonians every month.

Is there any connection with the Sealy mattress? Yes indeed. A Sealy businessman named Haynes made the first tufted mattress early in this century, and folks referred to it as "that mattress from Sealy." Haynes later sold the patent and the name, but his factory, with its original equipment, is still intact, awaiting refurbishment as a museum sometime in the future.

Visitors enjoy a drive down Sealy's oak-shaded Fifth Street with its turn-of-the-century homes and a walk around the downtown sector which is being restored to its original appearance. There are numerous antique shops, most of which have free walking-tour maps of town. Time your trip to take in the First Saturday Trades Day, held every month.

April brings the Airing of the Quilts Festival; on July 4 there's a "Sealy-bration" in the Lion's Club City Park; and the first Saturday of December is a Christmas Market and Festival of Lights parade; the town and park continue to sparkle nightly for the entire month. The nearby Czech community of Frydek (pop. 150) celebrates its ethnic heritage every spring, and early summer brings the Polka Fest to Sealy, complete with cloggers, square dancers, and oompah bands.

For information on Sealy, San Felipe, or Frydek, contact the Sealy Chamber of Commerce, 311 Fowlkes Street, Sealy 77474. (409) 885–3222.

WHAT TO DO

Christmas Tree Farms. Call the following for directions: Santa's Christmas Forest, (409) 885–7896; Hilltop Christmas Tree Farm, (409) 865–3049.

Port City Stockyards. North of Sealy on T–36. This is one of the largest cattle auction operations in America, and visitors are welcome. Hogs are auctioned on Monday mornings and cattle on Wednesday mornings, year-round. (409) 885–3526.

Rabbit Hutch Ranch. 505 Cottonwood Court. From I–10 west, take the Mlcak exit just past the Brazos River Bridge, circle right under the freeway, follow the frontage road west to Chew Road, and turn left; go 1.2 miles and turn left; at Pecan Grove Road, turn left again, and watch for a blue-roofed home on ten acres. No, this isn't a rabbit farm. Bunny and Eloise Pearl raise and sell miniature horses, and they welcome visitors and groups who call in advance for an appointment. The Pearls explain about raising and showing these 18-inch-high wonders, and you'll be able to pet two Shetland ponies and a few African pygmy goats as well. This is a great experience for children. Open year-round. (409) 885–4640, (713) 346–1468.

Santa Fe Park Museum. On Main Street. Artifacts from the early days of Sealy and Austin County are displayed here. Just look for the small tin building with bright flowers, a flag pole, and a grader in the front yard. Open only on the first Saturday afternoon of every month or by special arrangement. (409) 885–3571 or 885–3222.

Sealy News. 111 Main Street. The type for this newspaper now is set by computer, but the Linotype machines and other archaic equipment from the days of "hot" type can be viewed on Thursdays and Fridays. (409) 885–3562.

WHERE TO EAT

Brazos Mill Restaurant. 210 Gebhardt Road, Sealy. This is a good place for families. In addition to a varied menu, there are three or four lunch specials. Open daily. $–$$; (CC). (409) 885–7077.

Villa Fuentes. 2104 T–36 north, across from the stockyards. Don't pass by this nondescript cafe. It serves some of the best Mexican food in the region. Open Tuesday–Saturday for lunch and dinner; Sunday until 3 p.m. $–$$; (CC). (409) 885–4654.

J. W.'s Crosstie. 955 Frydek Road, Sealy. Ever eaten a flat car? A caboose? Those are just a few of the specialty hot sandwiches offered here, or you can build your own po-boy if you prefer. The German potato soup is a local favorite. Open Monday–Saturday. $. (409) 885–4722.

CAT SPRING

When the wildflowers bloom in late March and early April, this tidy crossroads community looks like a calendar picture. From Sealy, take FM–1094 north toward New Ulm. Just past the intersection at FM–949 (to Columbus), watch for an unusual eight-sided building on a rise to your right. This is the Cat Spring Agricultural Society Hall, built in 1902 and still the heart of community activities today.

The Cat Spring Agricultural Society was founded in 1856 and is considered the forerunner to the modern Texas Agricultural Extension Service. Early German and Czech farmers pooled their knowledge through this society, keeping detailed planting and production records of their small cotton and grain farms in a central book. All entries were written in German until America entered the First World War. The practice was then deemed unwise, and all records thereafter were written in English. They are used even today as a reference by local farmers.

This still-German community knows how to make other good things last, as well. The queen of Cat Spring's annual June Feast (held on the first Sunday of that month) reigns for 25 years! The next royal election will be in the year 2006.

WANDERING THE BACKROADS

From Cat Spring, you have several choices. A turn southwest on FM–949 at its intersection with FM–1094 will scoot you through pretty country to I–10. A turn west then takes you to Columbus; a turn east returns you to Houston.

An alternate route takes you northwest to New Ulm on FM–1094 and then southwest into Frelsburg via FM–109. From Frelsburg, you can either continue south on FM–109 to Columbus (Trip 3, this sector), or you can go northwest on FM–1291 to Fayetteville (Trip 4, this sector).

If you haven't yet explored to the north, consider taking FM–949 and FM–2429 from Cat Spring northeast to Bellville (Trip 5, this sector). Continue north on T–36 to Brenham (Trip 6, Northwest Sector).

The entire area around Cat Spring is threaded with small country roads, and rambling is a joy. Be sure, however, that you have a good state highway map in hand if you really care where you end up.

Day Trip 2

FULSHEAR
SIMONTON
EAGLE LAKE

FULSHEAR

This short day trip on I–10 west is ideal if you enjoy beautiful country, the rodeo, good hunting, and meat—not necessarily in that order. The first stop is the crossroads town of Fulshear, and you have a choice of two routes. From I–10 west, take FM–359 south about seven miles, or from west Houston, you can continue out Westheimer to Fulshear and turn right at the blinking light that marks the FM–359 intersection.

Folks come to Fulshear for one reason—good barbecue at Dozier's. You can buy it either by the pound or as a sandwich to go, and Mr. Dozier will be glad to take you out back and show you how they make sausage and smoke their meats. Lest you should think this place is just another BBQ joint, be aware that they sell more than 3,000 pounds of brisket, 300 pounds of sausage, and 500 pounds of pork ribs every week. Closed Monday. $. (713) 346–1411.

WHERE TO EAT

Womack House. 29706 FM–1093, 15 miles west of T–6 on Westheimer. This homey-looking place is known far and wide for its down-home dinners served family-style. You get your choice of twelve entrees, plus a kettle of homemade soup, cream gravy, biscuits, and hot corn bread. In addition to the menu, there are four nightly specials. Good news for those with no children in tow: There's a special adults-only dining room with lacey place mats, antique furniture, and an oak bar console that came from an old drugstore in Columbus. Open for dinner Wednesday–Saturday, lunch and dinner on Sunday. $$; (CC). (713) 346–1478.

The Shade Tree Country Restaurant. 11511 FM–1464, Clodine. From T–6, take Westheimer 3.6 miles, then left 4.5 miles on FM–1464. This candy shop/restaurant usually has a passel of cats on the front porch, so if you are allergic to same, go elsewhere. That would be a shame, though; the food here is tasty, and the shady back-

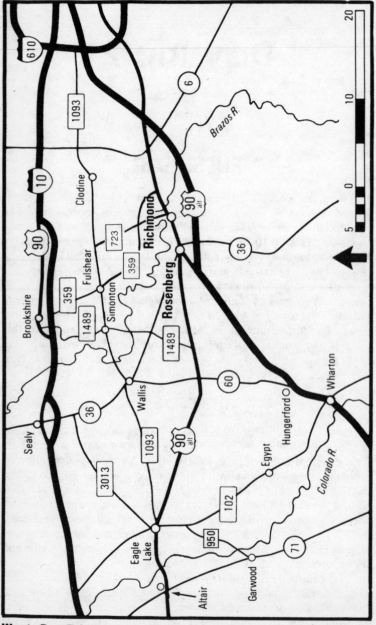

West: Day Trip 2

yard is a delightful place to eat on a nice day. In the mood for Mexican? The enchiladas are made from scratch. Do you love vegetables? You'll munch on ten different kinds in the giant Shade Tree salad. There's always a good variety of entrees on the menu as well. No smoking, except out back. Open for lunch and dinner Wednesday–Sunday. $–$$; (CC). (713) 277–1331.

SIMONTON

The big attraction here is the Roundup Rodeo, where anyone with the entry money can compete in anything from bareback riding and barrel racing to roping and bulldogging. There's a calf-and-goat scramble for the kids, and a dance polishes off every Saturday night. Alas, the barbecue dinner they once served prior to the rodeo is no longer available. (CC). (713) 346–1534. From Fulshear, continue west 5 miles on FM–1093 to Simonton. From I–10 west, take the FM–1489 exit in Brookshire south for 10 miles to Simonton. Turn right on FM–1093 (blinking light) to the arena.

EAGLE LAKE

Continuing west from Simonton on FM–1093 about 27 miles brings you to Eagle Lake. As to how this community got its name, you can go Gothic or plain vanilla. The Gothic version says that a Karankawa Indian maiden named Prairie Flower had two suitors, Light Foot and Leap High. Unable to decide between them, she challenged them to bring down a young eaglet from a nest in a cottonwood tree by a natural lake. Light Foot did and won the fair maiden's hand, whereupon poor Leap High decamped in high dudgeon to the nearby Colorado River.

The less romantic tale is that two of Austin's first settlers shot an eagle on the shores of this lake in 1823, and it was thereafter known as Eagle Lake. Whatever, the lake still is the main feature of this small town. Unfortunately, it is private, and only hunters on guided trips can see or use it.

The Eagle Lake community was settled in 1851 and today thrives as the "Goose Hunting Capital of the World." Day-trippers can arrange hunts through a number of guides; a list is available from the Eagle Lake Chamber of Commerce, P.O. Box 216, Eagle Lake 77434, (409) 234–2780. That mailing address translates to the old train depot next to the Prairie Edge Museum (see below) if you already are in town; the chamber office is open weekdays only.

There is some good fishing in assorted gravel pits around Eagle Lake, but most are on private property and hard to find. Permits to fish in one of the largest pits are available Monday–Saturday at Johnny's Sport Shop, 101 Booth Drive, Eagle Lake 77434, (409) 234–3516. Overnight guests at River Lake Farm, outside of town, can fish for bass, perch, and catfish in two lakes. (409) 234–2492.

If you love wildflowers, don't miss a spring trip to Eagle Lake. Thousands of acres west and south of town—the world's largest wildflower production fields—are color blankets of bluebonnets, Indian paintbrush, phlox, corn poppies, etc., the commercial crops of a very successful local industry called Wildseed, Inc. Guided wagon tours (fee) roll through the growing fields, usually mid-March through April; you can also pick up a map noting "best color" driving tours at the Prairie Edge Museum.

WHAT TO DO

Attwater Prairie Chicken National Wildlife Refuge. Six miles northeast of Eagle Lake, on the west side of FM–3013. This 8,000-acre refuge is the happy "booming" grounds for this nearly extinct bird, and day visitors can drive 12 miles of road through the prairie preserve. Best time to go is during the booming season, mid-February through April. Each male prairie chicken has his own domain and protects it with a war dance. Reservations are needed to use the photo blinds, and both long lenses and binoculars are highly desirable. To find the best observation spot, stop at the main office just inside the entrance to the refuge and ask directions. Open year-round. Visitors are encouraged to call in advance for advice. P.O. Box 518, Eagle Lake 77434. (409) 234–3021.

Blue Goose Hunting Club. (See "Where to Eat" section.)

Prairie Edge Museum. 408 East Main Street. A large collection of antiques and mementos having to do with the development of Colorado County are housed in the spacious quarters of an old motor-car company. Check out the 1924 Star, a four-cylinder Continental automobile in nearly mint condition. If you want to know what's going on in town, this is a good place to ask. Open Saturday and Sunday afternoons. Donation requested. (409) 234–7442.

WHERE TO EAT

Anna Lee's Kitchen. 112 West State Street. This charming home is a super spot for lunch if you've been smart and made advance reservations. The only time walk-ins are welcome is on Friday and Saturday during the November–December hunting season and daily during the wildflower tour season. Lunch only; groups with reservations are welcome. $–$$. (409) 234–2259.

Blue Goose Restaurant and Hunting Club. At the intersection of T–71 and Alternate US–90, 26 miles west of Eagle Lake. Expect outstanding game dinners in this restaurant as well as a varied menu that may include beef, frog legs, and soft-shell crab in season. Open for lunch and dinner daily during hunting season, for dinner only Wednesday–Saturday the rest of the year. $$; (CC). (409) 234–3597. Bonus here: the dining room's large dioramas filled with a rich variety of beautiful trophy birds, all locally caught. Owner John Fields also offers outstanding day hunts on private lands stretching from Richmond to Victoria from November through mid-February and sporting-clay shooting at his own range near Eagle Lake year-round. (409) 234–3597.

The Farris 1912. 201 North McCarty at Post Office Street. Constructed as the Hotel Dallas in 1912, this building flourished until the Depression and then floundered into disrepair and virtual abandonment. Thanks to the restoration efforts of Bill and Helyn Farris who bought it in 1974, this former flophouse is now a pleasant hotel and restaurant catering primarily to groups and hunters. Opened for guests again in 1977, it remains clean, spacious, and comfortable, with twenty-four bedrooms, a huge second-floor sitting room/mezzanine, and assorted public parlors. Stop in for a look or a meal, even if you can't stay.

Lunch is served during the wildflower weeks (mid-March through April), and the dining room opens again for breakfast, lunch, and dinner daily during goose hunting season (November–January). This is an all-you-can-eat operation. $–$$$; (CC). February through October, the hotel's antique and gift shop remains open weekdays, but meals are served only to tour groups, clubs, and private parties. Nice to know: There is no tipping ever at either the restaurant or the hotel. The Farris family also owns eight acres on the eastern shore of Eagle Lake which they make available to guests for bird watching and sunset appreciation. More than 260 species of birds are found in the Eagle Lake area, and guided birding trips are available through the hotel. Fee. (409) 234–2546.

The Sportsman's Restaurant. 201 Boothe Street (US–90A). Don't be put off by the mountain lion in the entry—he's an import from Laredo. The rest of the menagerie is local stuff. This busy place has the atmosphere of a hunting lodge and the menu of a cafeteria—more than sixty items ranging from steaks to Mexican and Cajun. Open for breakfast, lunch, and dinner Monday–Saturday, and breakfast and lunch on Sunday. $–$$; (CC). (409) 234–3071.

WANDERING THE BACKROADS

From Eagle Lake you can return to Houston by reversing your entry route: FM–1093 east to home. Alternates: Take FM–102 north to I–10 and jog west a few miles to Columbus (Trip 3, this sector) or take FM–102 south to Wharton (Trip 1, Southwest Sector) and turn north on US–59 to Richmond and Rosenberg (Trip 2, Southwest Sector).

Day Trip 3

COLUMBUS
FRELSBURG
NEW ULM

COLUMBUS

Some 56 miles west of Houston's city limits via I–10, Columbus is in one of the oldest inhabited areas of the state. The early Spanish maps of Texas marked this as a sizable Indian village known as Montezuma, and Stephen F. Austin's first colonists called it Beason's Ferry. Today, as Columbus (pop. 4,800), it is one of the prettiest and most historic towns in Texas. As you stroll through the shady town square, it's hard to believe that the busy interstate zips by less than 1 mile to the south.

Back in 1823 Stephen F. Austin brought a survey party to this fertile land looped by the Colorado River, thinking it would make a fine headquarters and capital for his first settlement. The river was deep enough for commerce, and the busy Atascosito Trail crossed the river nearby. But this was also the territory of the Karankawa, a fierce Indian tribe labeled by history as cannibals, and the threat made the existing settlement in San Felipe a better choice.

Some of Austin's colony did settle here, however, and a tiny village named Columbus was laid out in 1835. Its life was brief. In March of 1836, Gen. Sam Houston and his Texian forces retreated from Gonzales and camped in Columbus on the east bank of the Colorado River. The pursuing Mexican Army settled in on the west bank where it soon was reinforced by additional troops.

Knowing his position was weak and that an attack on the Mexicans would be suicide for both his men and Texas's independence, Houston elected to retreat further. Moving on to Hempstead (Trip 4, Northwest Sector), he ordered all the buildings in and around Columbus burned so that they would be of no use to the Mexicans. Caught in the middle, the local residents fled east to safety, a migration termed by history as "the Runaway Scrape."

Houston's strategy was vindicated by his victory over Santa Anna and the Mexican Army at San Jacinto the following month, and slowly, Columbus began to build again. Today it is a delightful small town full of live oak and magnolia trees. Thanks to its large natural deposits of sand and gravel, Columbus literally is "where Houston comes from." Approximately 90 percent of the aggregate used to construct Houston's skyscrapers was excavated nearby.

The town's mainstay always has been the river at its doorstep. Early settlers floated their construction lumber downstream from pine forests near Bastrop, and by the mid-nineteenth century, paddle-wheelers were making regular runs between Columbus, Austin, and Matagorda. Dressed up with names like the *Moccasin Belle, Flying Jenny,* and the *Kate Ward,* these flat-bottom boats also carried cotton from large plantations south of town to the shipping docks at Matagorda Bay (Trip 1, Southwest Sector).

The river continues to figure in the town's life, but with a lighter touch. Columbus children grow up "floating around the bend," and local high school seniors traditionally celebrate graduation with all-night float trips. The most popular stretch for recreation runs from the North River Bridge (T–71 north) to the East River Bridge (US–90), a distance of about one-half mile by land and 7 miles (about four hours) by water. Canoe rentals and livery service come and go in Columbus; check with the chamber of commerce for current status. You may need your own canoe and two cars, one of which should be parked at the East River Bridge take-out.

Wide and smooth (and usually opaque with sediment), with only a few small rapids, the Colorado River at Columbus is relatively safe for novice canoeists. The numerous long sandbars make night floats a timeless experience. Moonlight glows from these freshwater beaches, and the wildlife show is fascinating as the river comes alive with beaver, deer, and raccoon.

Exploring Columbus is easy with the Historical Trailguide published by the chamber of commerce. It is available weekdays at the chamber offices on the ground floor of the Stafford Opera House (435 Spring Street, across from Courthouse Square) or by mail: P.O. Box 343, Columbus 78934. (409) 732–5881 or 732–3864. The chamber also conducts guided walking tours of the town and many historic private homes on the first and third Thursdays of every month (fee). On those same days, local ladies set up mini-shops selling arts, crafts, antiques, and baked goods in a downtown building known as Thursday's Treasures. For information, call (409) 732–5881.

Another good time to come is the weekend closest to Columbus Day when the town celebrates its German and Czech heritage with performances in the opera house, a biergarten in the town square, and various other live entertainment.

There are more than sixty historical medallions and four Texas Centennial markers in town. Although the vast majority are on private residences that are open to the public only on the first and third Thursdays of the month, these homes may also be visited during the Magnolia Homes Tour in May and as part of other special events. Among the best candidates for a driving tour are the Tate-Senftenberg-Brandon House and Museum (1860s), 616 Walnut; Raumonda (1887), 1100 Bowie; the Alley Log Cabin (1836), 1230 Bowie; Dilue Harris House (1860), 602 Washington; the Youens-Hopkins House (1860), 617 Milam; the Gant House (1870), 936 Bowie; and the Montgomery House (1876), 1416 Milam. Four of the above offer B&B accommodations that include access to a private swimming pool, as well as swimming, golf, and horseback riding at The Falls Resort and Country Club in nearby Frelsburg. For information, call (409) 732–5135 or 732–2190.

WHAT TO DO

Christmas Tree Cutting. Call Raondo Christmas Tree Farm for directions. (713) 392–7198.

Colorado County Courthouse. Bounded by Spring, Milam, Walnut, and Travis streets on Courthouse Square. Built in 1890–91, this is the third courthouse on the same site and still is the county seat. The four-faced clock is original, but its steeple fell in a 1909 hurricane and was replaced by a Neoclassic dome. A full restoration completed in 1980 uncovered a handsome stained-glass dome above the district courtroom, hidden for generations under a false ceiling. The courthouse is open Monday–Friday.

Take special note of the stump of the famous Courthouse Oak, 2,000 years old and the site of the first district court held in 1837. At that time, the first courthouse on this site had already been burned by Houston's forces and the second was yet to be built. Judge R. M. Williamson, known as "three-legged Willie" because of his wooden leg, elected to hear cases under this tree.

Columbus State Bank. Across the street from the courthouse. A collection of early Texas maps and Republic of Texas money is on display during business hours.

Confederate Memorial Hall Museum. On the southwest corner of Courthouse Square. This old water tower was built 400,000 bricks strong in 1883. Dynamite didn't dent it in a later demolition attempt, so the United Daughters of the Confederacy decided it was a safe repository for their treasures. The exhibits feature clothing, small possessions, articles, documents, and pictures of early Columbus, including artifacts from the "Old Three Hundred," as Stephen F. Austin's first colony was known. Donations are appreciated; open by appointment and during the first and third Thursday tours. (409) 732–2571 or 732–5269.

Fishing. There are bass and catfish awaiting in the Colorado River. Andy's Drive-in Grocery and Sporting Goods at the intersection of highways 71 and 90 is a good source of information and bait, and there's a public boat ramp at the North River Bridge.

Grave of the Infidel. Odd Fellows Cemetery on Montezuma Street. Like all frontiers, the Columbus area attracted characters. Back in the 1890s, Ike Towell made a name for himself as an outspoken atheist. The town marshal, he also was instrumental in the establishment of the "Jim Crow" laws in the area. He wrote his own funeral service, and his tombstone reads HERE LIES IKE TOWELL, AN INFIDEL, WHO HAD NO HOPE OF HEAVEN OR FEAR OF HELL.

Hunting. Colorado County is happy hunting grounds for deer, quail, dove, and geese. Every winter it becomes the goose capital of the world because of its location on the Mississippi flyway. In addition to the Blue Goose Hunting Club (Day Trip 2, this sector), arrangements to hunt can be made through the following: Clifton Tyler (goose and wild duck guide; day and season hunting), 1139 Fannin Street, Columbus 78934, (409) 732–8014; and Francis Truchard (year-round hunting and fishing access to nineteen farms and ranches in the Sealy-Columbus corridor along I–10; day dove and day deer hunting in season), R.R. Box 2014, Columbus 78934, (409) 732–6849.

Live Oak Arts Center. 1014 Milam. Housed in a historic building, this gallery's exhibits change monthly and feature both local and internationally known artists. Open weekdays until 4 p.m., weekends by appointment.

Nesbitt Memorial Library. 529 Washington. Root-tracers prize this library's new archives room for its regional genealogical information; children and collectors love it for its antique doll collection. (409) 732–3392.

Preston Kyle Shatto Wildlife Museum. 1000 block of Milam. Animal trophies from around the world are shown here in simple dioramas. Open on first and third Thursdays.

Stafford Bank and Opera House. On Spring Street, across from Courthouse Square. Built by millionaire cattleman R. E. Stafford in 1886 for a reputed $50,000, this elegant old building originally housed Stafford's bank on the first floor and a 1,000-seat theater upstairs, where performed such headliners as Lillian Russell and Al

Jolson. Today the show-biz names may not be so grand, but the theater is, thanks to an eighteen-year, $1.5 million restoration financed entirely by local residents. The original 15-foot chandelier shines in the lobby, the theater's first elaborate stage curtain has been reproduced, and a variety of entertainments once again bring up the footlights. Don't miss either the museum in the basement or the unusual marble cornerstone. Open on the first and third Thursdays and during the Magnolia Homes Tour.

Texas Opera Jamboree. Oaks Theater, 715 Walnut (T–90). A little bit of Nashville in the heart of Texas, this family entertainment showcases outstanding local and regional C&W talent and regularly draws professional scouts. There's lots of audience-performer interaction and a wholesome, no-alcohol environment. $; kiddies under ten are free. (409) 732–5093 or 234–3765.

WHERE TO EAT

City Cafe. 424 Walnut. Grandma David turns out the best homemade kolaches in town nearly every morning. Open for breakfast and lunch daily. $. (409) 732–8009.

Dairy Bar. 1221 Fannin (T–71). Not much to look at, but this small place serves great hamburgers, chalupas, barbecue, and shrimp plates. Closed Sunday. $. (409) 732–2359.

Hackemack's Hofbrau Haus. On FM–109, 11 miles north of Columbus and 1 mile south of Frelsburg. You can't miss this place—it's a Bavarian chalet in the middle of a small pasture, surrounded by flying flags. And you shouldn't miss it, because the German food is great (as are the steaks and hamburgers), and there's lots of live oompah-pah when a local homemade band tunes up a wash tub, rake, accordion, and musical saw for a go at C&W and old German tunes on Friday and Saturday nights. Call to see what's going on fun-wise if you are coming this way on a weekend. Open for dinner Thursday-Saturday; lunch and dinner on Sunday. $–$$; (CC). (409) 732–6321.

Mikeska's Bar-B-Q. 519 Walnut. Known as the BBQ king of the southwest to local folks, Mikeska's is open Monday–Saturday for lunch and dinner. $. (409) 732–3101.

The Montgomery House. 1419 Milam. It's lunch only Tuesday–Friday at this classy tea room and restaurant housed in an 1876 Greek Revival home. Unusual soups, gourmet salads, and casseroles with flair are the entrees, and the desserts are yummy. Expect an overflow crowd on the first and third Thursday of the month. $. (409) 732–2666.

Schobel's Restaurant. 2020 Milam. Convenient from I–10, this family restaurant cuts its own steaks, grinds its own hamburger meat, and makes its own pies. The menu also includes seafood and Mexican dishes, and there's a large buffet for daily lunch and again on Friday night. $–$$; (CC). (409) 732–2385.

Stockman's Market. 1538 Fannin. This simple place is a local favorite for all kinds of barbecue; the pork ribs are highly recommended, along with the homemade pies and cakes. Open Monday–Saturday. $. (409) 732–2170.

Weimar County Inn. On the corner of Center and Jackson streets in Weimar, a fifteen-minute drive west from Columbus via I–10. This restored old hotel not only will put you up for the night in antique style, it also serves some of the best food and drink in south Texas. Chef Rickey Paige trained at NY's famed Culinary Institute and bakes his own bread and pastries. Open for dinner Thursday–Saturday and on Sunday for a midday buffet. The dining room is a charmer with its pressed-tin ceiling, and there's a park back for children to romp in when they get restless. $–$$; (CC). (409) 725–8888.

WANDERING THE BACKROADS

Columbus is the gateway to all of Austin and Fayette counties, rolling farmland that still looks much as it did when it was settled by Polish, German, and Czech immigrants in the 1800s. FM–949 north continues this day trip to the small German communities of Frelsburg and New Ulm.

FRELSBURG

When you stop to chat in this region, don't be surprised to hear strong German accents. The ethnic heritage of this community, 12 miles north of Columbus via FM–109, runs deep. The town is named for John and William Frels who settled here in the 1830s.

You'll see SS. Peter and Paul Catholic Church on a hill as you approach on FM–109. Although this particular Catholic sanctuary was built in 1927, the parish it serves was organized in 1847 and is the oldest in Texas. Visitors are welcome, either to celebrate Mass or to view the three carved wood altars. Nearby and a bit more humble in its architecture, St. John's Lutheran Church (1855–56) and its churchyard look as if they were transplanted from New England.

Heinsohen's General Store has served this area for generations. If you stop in to buy a cool drink, you'll find it stocks everything from the latest in electronic games to pegged pants. Don't leave without buying some of their home-done pickles for your poke.

The big doin's in Frelsburg is the annual Fireman's Picnic on the second weekend in June. A fund-raiser, it also is an enjoyable look at a small, still very German community in the heart of Texas.

WHAT TO DO

The Falls Resort and Country Club. Three miles east of FM–109 via Dr. Neal Road, between Frelsburg and New Ulm; watch for signs. The golf course of this large real estate development is ranked fifth in Texas among golf pros, a demanding eighteen holes designed by Jay Riviere and Dave Marr. The development's handsome equestrian center also is open to the public and offers wrangler-led horseback rides of varying distances as well as lessons and boarding facilities. Many of the rides include all-you-can-eat meals (sometimes steak and champagne!) and entertainment. After golf or horseback riding, drop in to this residential resort's restaurant ($–$$) to rejuvenate yourself for the trip back home. Sorry, that beautiful swimming pool is for members and residents only. Costs for both golf and horseback riding vary, and reservations are strongly recommended for both. Golfers should call for tee times five days in advance if possible. (CC). (409) 992–3124, (713) 578–5550, (800) 843–2557.

From Frelsburg, continue north on FM–109 to the more sizable community of New Ulm (pop. 650).

NEW ULM

Also founded by Germans, Czechs, and Poles in the early 1800s, New Ulm soon may be in for its second golden age. Back in the 1940s the entrepreneurial Glenn McCarthy made some Texas-size bucks in the nearby Frelsburg oil field and brought lots of his Hollywood friends to the quiet streets of New Ulm. Lately, new wells are hinting at another wave of prosperity sometime in the future. In the meantime, enjoy the simplicity and old-time rural architecture of this crossroads settlement as part of a country drive.

WHERE TO EAT

Big A's Parlour. Front Street. They serve a good steak, but the house specialties are fresh seafood and homemade desserts. Setups and six kinds of draft beer are sold at this former funeral parlour, and you'll be bellying up to an antique marble bar. Saturday night here means dancing to live bands playing everything from bluegrass and Dixieland to C&W. This is one of the oldest buildings (1893) still in use in Austin County, and don't worry about finding it. Painted a brilliant yellow with red trim, it probably even glows in the dark. Open for lunch Tuesday–Sunday, dinner nightly. $–$$; (CC). (409) 992–3499.

WANDERING THE BACKROADS

To reach Houston from New Ulm, go east 23 miles on FM–1094 to Sealy (Trip 1, this sector) and then east on I–10 to home.

If you want to extend this day trip, you have several choices. From New Ulm, take FM–109 north to Industry and its intersection with T–159. A turn west (left) and then a jog northwest on FM–1457 takes you to Round Top (Trip 5, this sector). A turn east (right) on T–159 brings you to Bellville (also Trip 5, this sector).

Day Trip 4

SCHULENBURG
LA GRANGE
FAYETTEVILLE

SCHULENBURG

Begin this trip by driving due west from Houston on I–10 to the Schulenburg exit and turning south on T–77.

Like Sealy, this is another railroad town, created in 1873 when the fledgling Galveston, Harrisburg, and San Antonio Railroad purchased a right-of-way across Louis Schulenburg's farm and built a station. Folks living in nearby High Hill used log rollers pulled by oxen to move their homes and businesses 3 miles south to the new town site, and Schulenburg began to thrive.

Today, local residents still tell time by train whistles, and day-trippers find an architecturally interesting Main Street, numerous historic sites and a string of "painted churches," the latter beautifully representative of the area's strong Czech, Austrian, and German heritages. Other ethnic traditions make the Schulenburg Festival a big event the first full weekend in August. For information, contact the Schulenburg Chamber of Commerce, 1107 Hillje (P.O. Box 65), Schulenburg 78956. (409) 743–3023.

WHAT TO DO

The Old Anderson Place. 510 South Main Street. Built before 1857, and later the home of Louis Schulenburg, this is thought to be the oldest occupied house in the area. Privately owned, it is not open for tours.

Painted Church Driving Tour. An interesting map to the rural countryside around Schulenburg is available from the chamber of commerce. It will lead you to the tiny Czech settlement of Dubina and its beautifully frescoed Sts. Cyril and Methodius Catholic Church; to Ammannsville and the unusual stenciled Gothic interior of St. John the Baptist Catholic Church; to Praha and the painted murals of The Blessed Virgin Mary Catholic Church; and to High Hill and the painted murals of St. Mary's Catholic Church. Worth seeing en route are a Russian-style house, a 100-year-old iron bridge over the Navidad River, Tietjen's Store and Dance Hall (where singer B. J. Thomas got his start), and the nation's first cottonseed-oil mill. Most of the churches are still in use and may or may not be open; best consult in advance with the Schulenburg C of C. (409) 743–3023.

Schulenburg Historical Museum. 631 North Main. Visiting this old store-turned-museum is wonderful on Sunday afternoons. There are no cars around, and the atmosphere is that of a quieter time. Lots of old stuff here, and it's fun to poke around. Donations welcome.

WANDERING THE BACKROADS

If you want to explore further, consider deviating briefly from the itinerary to visit Flatonia, 27 miles west and well beyond the 110–mile limit of this book. While I–10 and US–90 are hardly backroads, they are timesavers and the most direct route. Another railroad town, Flatonia was established in 1875 and is where many of Houston's eggs come from. Special walking tours on the first and third Fridays of every month take you to a historical museum and livery stable, an 1886 mercantile, and the oldest operating newspaper (since 1875) in the county. For information, call (512) 865–3720, 865–3368, or 865–3643.

LA GRANGE

There are two ways to get to La Grange from Houston, but they both follow I–10 west some 56 miles to Columbus. There you can either take T–71 northwest 26 miles to La Grange, or continue on the interstate another 21 miles to the US–77 exit, then north 16 miles to your destination.

Long before the flamboyant reporter Marvin Zindler focused the bright lights of TV publicity and traditional morality on Miss Mona and her Chicken Ranch on the outskirts of town ("Best Little Whorehouse in Texas") a few years ago, La Grange had a colorful personality. A bear of a man known as Strap Buckner was running an Indian trading post here by 1819, and local legend says he cleared the site of La Grange in a wild wrestling match with Satan.

Whatever the truth, a small community began about 1831 where the La Bahia Trail crossed the Colorado River, and some of Stephen F. Austin's first colony helped tame the land. By 1837 the town known as La Grange was the seat of government for Fayette County.

Today the courthouse, built in the 1890s, stands in the town square, and its original clock still chimes on the hour.

Pause for a moment under Muster Oak on the square's northeast corner. Through six conflicts starting with the Mexican attack of 1842, La Grange's able-bodied men have gathered here with their families before leaving for battle. The tradition was updated when Iraq invaded Kuwait; when area Army Reserve units came through La Grange, they found Muster Oak wrapped with a giant yellow bow.

La Grange is a nerve center for wildflower tours in the spring, and the local chamber of commerce will help you plan a driving route. For information on La Grange, contact them at 129 North Main (on the square), (409) 968–5756. If you like rummage sales, come on the second weekend of the month for La Grange Lions Market Days.

WHAT TO DO

N. W. Faison Home and Museum. 822 South Jefferson Street. The nucleus of this gracious frontier home is a two-room pine cabin built around 1845. Purchased in 1866 by N. W. Faison, a Fayette County clerk and land surveyor who survived the Dawson Massacre, the home remained in the Faison family until 1960. Open only for group tours by prior arrangement. Fee. (409) 968–5756.

Fayette County Heritage Museum and Library. 855 South Jefferson, across from the Faison home. A local Bicentennial project, the museum has special humidified archives to preserve historic documents. Open Tuesday–Sunday, but hours vary. (409) 968–6418.

Hermes Drug Store. 148 Washington, across from the courthouse. Established in 1856, this is the oldest drugstore in continuous operation in Texas. Visitors expecting a vintage sight will be disappointed, however; although many of the original fixtures and beveled mirrors remain, the interior is otherwise very much of our times. Open Monday–Friday; Saturday until noon. (409) 968–3357.

Holy Rosary Catholic Church in Hostyn. From La Grange, take US–77 south approximately 5 miles, then turn west on FM–2436 for 1 mile. Even non-Catholics enjoy strolling this hilltop, noted for its large stations of the cross, grottos, shrines, Civil War cannon, and replica of the first log church on this site.

Monument Hill State Historic Site/Kreische Brewery Historic Site. Two miles south of town off US–77. Even after the Texians' historic victory over the Mexican forces at San Jacinto, the Mexican Army continued to raid this portion of Texas through the following decade. The tragic 1842 Dawson Massacre near San Antonio and the ill-fated Mier Expedition are the focus of this memorial. Both are lesser known but interesting chapters of Lone Star history. This popular picnic site, high on a bluff overlooking the Colorado River, features a nature walk through the woods and has one trail specifically designed for the handicapped. The view north from the overlook takes in the old La Bahia Trail crossing on the river.

In 1978, the adjacent Kreische Brewery and homesite were added to the facility and subsequently restored. Kreische was a skilled stonemason and brewer from Europe who, between 1860 and 1870, established this first brewery in Texas below his home on what is now Monument Hill. Ultimately it became the third-largest brewery in the state, and his product, a dark beer called Frisch Auf, was sold at his beer garden. The restoration has cleaned out the springs that provided water for the brewery and stabilized the old buildings. Guided tours of the brewery are given on weekends. Open daily. Fee. (409) 968–5658.

St. James Episcopal Church. 156 North Monroe. Built in 1885, this small church, which is still painted its original rust and cream, uses the original furnishings that were handmade by the first rector and his congregation. All are welcome at the 10 A.M. Sunday service. (409) 968–3910.

WHERE TO EAT

La Grange is the baked-goods capital of central Texas, a good place to fill your freezer. Among the favorite sources are:

Bon Ton Convenience Store and Bakery. T–71 west. Also a deli, the Bon Ton is known for sandwiches, cookies, pigs-in-a-blanket, etc. Open daily. $; (CC). (409) 968–9413.

Lukas Bakery. 135 North Main, on the square. One of the best places to go for pigs-in-a-blanket, homemade breads, cookies, etc. $. Closed on Sunday. (409) 968–3052.

The following offer a variety of other foods:

The Bon Ton Restaurant. T–71 east. What started as a good but small cafe on La Grange's Courthouse Square is now a good and large family restaurant on the main road into town. There are daily specials and a buffet, plus a regular menu that ranges through the seafood/chicken/steak standards. Emphasis is on down-home German and American food. $–$$; (CC). Open daily. (409) 968–5863.

La Cabana. T–77 south. Ever had a Greek taco? You can here, along with a wide selection of Mexican favorites. Open daily for lunch and dinner. $–$$; (CC). (409) 968–6612.

Prause's Market. 253 West Travis, on the square. Fresh and smoked meats here, plus barbecue to eat on-site or take out. Open Monday–Friday and on Saturday morning. $. (409) 968–3259.

WANDERING THE BACKROADS

Your next stop on this day trip is Fayetteville. From La Grange, follow T–159 northeast 15 miles on its zigzag course through the countryside. Bass fishermen may want to detour east on County Road 196 to Lake Fayette, the 2400-acre cooling pond for the Fayette Power Project. Open year-round, it offers fishing, camping, swimming, and power boating. Fee. (409) 249–5208.

FAYETTEVILLE

If you like the big time and bright lights, move on. This small town, tucked away in the rolling farmland northeast of La Grange, keeps a low profile. If too many folks fall in love with it, it's bound to change, and that would be a pity.

Some of Austin's first colony were sharp enough to settle here in the early 1820s, and by 1833 the tiny community was a stage station on the old San Felipe Trail, with service to Austin via Round Top and Bastrop. The town was officially mapped in 1847, and the next decade saw extensive German and Czech immigration, an ethnic blend that continues here today.

In the town's settlement days free food was served to all comers, but occasionally the vittles would run out before the customers did. Late arrivals were told to "lick the skillet," and as a result Fayetteville also became known as Lickskillet. Today the town celebrates the Lickskillet Festival the third weekend of October with parades, fun, and a big meal in the town square.

Fayetteville looks much as it did at the end of the last century: a series of two- and three-block streets in a grid around a central square. The town's heart and pride is the rare Victorian precinct courthouse in the center of that square, a small wooden structure built in 1880 for the heady sum of $800. The four-faced clock in the steeple resulted from a ten-year fund-raising effort by the "Do Your Duty Club" and was installed with much civic horn-tooting in 1934.

City folks cherish this small town as a wind-down place. The best way to get on Fayetteville time is to pick up a walking map from one of the stores and take a slow stroll around town. There's a small museum on the square, some tree-shaded benches around the courthouse, ice cream at Schramm's, and an artist's retreat or two—but nothing much to raise your pulse rate or open your pocketbook. Call the local chamber of commerce in advance (409–378–2231) for copies of a walking tour and several interesting itineraries in the surrounding countryside.

WHAT TO DO

Chovaneks. Corner of Live Oak and Fayette streets, on the square. In what must be termed a Gargantuan case of overstocking, this old store still has dry goods typical of the 1940s and 1950s. Incidentally, the name is pronounced "Ko-*van*-itz." Open Monday–Saturday.

Fayetteville Emporium and the Fayetteville Workshop. Washington Street, on the square. You'll find stained glass, pottery, paintings, and photography on exhibit and for sale in this combination gift shop/atelier/gallery.

Hoot Owl Hill. On FM–159, 4.5 miles west of the Fayetteville city limits and 2.5 miles east of the FM–237 intersection. Visitors are welcome but appointments are necessary to visit this 300-acre racehorse breeding and training ranch. What you see depends on the time of year and can range from the collecting of stallion sperm for the artificial insemination program to the actual breeding of the mares or the birth of a foal. At any one time, from 100 to 400 thoroughbreds and quarter horses are bred and trained here, made fit for the yearling sales, and managed on national race tracks. Catering is available for large groups. (409) 249–3082.

Two-Creek Ranch. Six miles east of Fayetteville on T–159; turn north on County Road 270 (sign). This multimillion dollar, 680-acre spread looks like it could be in the heart of Kentucky's famous bluegrass country—vast fenced meadows, beautiful thoroughbred horses, swanky training barns, etc. Their business is training major thoroughbred racehorses for owners throughout the world. Visitors are welcome, but they must have advance appointments and report to the office upon arrival. (409) 249–3154.

WHERE TO EAT

Orsak's Cafe. On the square in Fayetteville. There's nothing fancy about this clean and basic cafe, but the food is nourishing and affordable. In addition to daily lunch specials, Wednesday night brings fried chicken and the Friday-night menu is seafood. You'll want to linger long enough to chat with local residents; nearly everyone who comes to town drops in to have a cup of coffee, pick up messages, etc. Open daily; until 2 p.m. on Monday. $–$$; (CC). (409) 378–2719.

WANDERING THE BACKROADS

After touring Fayetteville, you can continue east on T–159 to Bellville and then home (Trip 5, this sector). Or you can reverse the order, touring Fayetteville first and then continuing on to La Grange. See the map with this section for your route options. Either way, you easily can connect with tours of Round Top and Winedale (Trip 5, this sector) or Brenham (Trip 6, Northwest Sector).

If you are traveling any of this territory from late March through May, contact the La Grange Chamber of Commerce in advance. They scout the best routes for color during the wildflower season. Information: P.O. Box 70, La Grange 78945. (409) 968–5756.

Day Trip 5

LEDBETTER
ROUND TOP
WINEDALE
BELLVILLE

LEDBETTER

Begin this day trip by driving northwest from Houston on US–290 to Ledbetter, 25 miles west of Brenham. Enroute, antiques shoppers will want to spend some time in the whistle-stop town of Carmine, a few miles east of Ledbetter.

Both Carmine and Ledbetter are railroad towns, the latter platted in 1870 by the Texas and New Orleans Railroad. They anticipated big things—those old plats show a big depot from which wide streets with pretty names stretched in all directions. The depot did become a reality, the first and largest in Fayette County. The town, however, maxed out at about 1,000 residents in 1900 and began a steady decline after World War II. The last passenger train whistled through in 1952, the last freight in 1979. Now even the tracks are gone, and Ledbetter has a permanent population of approximately 100 souls. Perhaps the town is best defined by what it doesn't have: gas stations, fast food franchises, grocery stores, traffic lights, noise, or crowds—in short, Ledbetter is a perfect pause, en route to somewhere else.

WHERE TO GO

Stuermer's General Store and Working Museum. In Ledbetter at the intersection of US–290 and FM–1291 (blinking light). No one knows exactly when this old place was built, but the two antique bars (one dated 1836 on the back) were part of a saloon established here by the owner's great-grandfather in 1890. Today Chris Jervis and her mother, Lillian Stuermer Dyer, sell sandwiches and Blue Bell ice cream from those bars, and the rest of the two-story store is filled with memorabilia and antiques (not for sale), along with those sundry items no one can do without. Kids love this place; the juke box, pool table, and pinball machines are free. This is the oldest flag stop on the Kerrville bus route, and when the shutters are closed, the store is closed (usually Sunday except during wild-flower season); when the shutters are open, come on in.

Jay and Chris Jervis also have six B&B lodgings, one in a charming 1880s country cottage known as Grandma's House, the others in a refurbished 1860s hotel on the north side of the highway; all the units have private baths and include full country breakfasts in their basic $55–$65 nightly rate. Guests also have access to a party house, complete with indoor swimming pool and numerous free mechanical and electronic games. (409) 249–3330.

Ledbetter Buggy Shop. Two doors down from the general store on US–290. Jay Jervis sells traditional Amish buggies here, and with his wife, offers horse-drawn chuckwagon cookouts to a nearby ranch throughout the year. (409) 249–3066 or 249–3330.

Alice Darnell Studio. Between the buggy shop and general store. This artist specializes in spinning local wool into thread on antique equipment and then hand-looming that thread into handsome cloth. Open by appointment. (409) 249–3330.

To continue on to Round Top, take either FM–1291 south from Ledbetter or FM–237 south from Carmine.

ROUND TOP

When it comes to vintage Texas villages that have retained the essence of their past, Round Top is the champ. Officially founded in 1835 by settlers from Stephen F. Austin's second colony, it was originally called Jones Post Office and then Townsend, after the five Townsend families who established plantations in the area. The name Round Top came from a stage stop 2 miles north, a landmark by 1847 because it had a house with a round top. When the stage line between Houston and Austin moved its route slightly south, the town and the name followed.

Driving into Round Top is like passing through an invisible time warp. A small white meetinghouse in the middle of the village green is part of the town's charm. In fact, Round Top is so small, so compact and neat, that visitors often feel like giants abroad in Lilliput land.

Those first Anglo settlers were followed by Germans, many of whom were intellectuals oppressed in their native country. Others were skilled carpenters and stonemasons whose craftsmanship distinguishes numerous existing area buildings. A drive on the lanes around Round Top is a lesson in enduring architecture.

Nice to know: Two nineteenth-century cottages have been refurbished into duplex accommodations and are available through the

Texas Pioneer Arts Foundation (Henkel Square), (409) 249–3308. Furnished with early Texas antiques, they also come with a coffee pot and fruit bowl; the rest of breakfast is up to you.

With its current population of 87, Round Top holds two distinctions. Not only is it the smallest incorporated town in the state, but it has what many think is the oldest Fourth of July celebration west of the Mississippi. Local folks have been kicking up their heels on Independence Day since 1826, and the annual tradition now runs to orations, barbecues, a trail ride, and the firing of the cannon in the town square.

Whenever you visit, just park your car near the square and walk around. Round Top folks welcome visitors and have lots of tales to tell, so stop and chat as you explore. Need to make a telephone call? The red-white-and-blue phone booth on the town square is still only a dime!

WHAT TO DO

Bethlehem Lutheran Church. Up the hill from Moore's Fort and 1 block southwest. This sturdy stone church was dedicated in 1866 and is in use still. The front door is usually unlocked, so enter and climb the narrow wood stairs to the loft. Not only will you get a strong sense of the simplicity of the old days, you'll see an unusual cedar pipe organ, one of several built by local craftsman Johann Traugott Wantke in the 1860s for area churches. The old churchyard cemetery, charming and ageless, is enclosed by a dry-set stone wall reminiscent of New England.

Festival Hill. One-half mile north of the town square on T–237. What once was open rolling pasture graced only by bird-song is now a mecca for music lovers throughout the world. Back in 1968, noted pianist James Dick performed near Round Top and fell victim to its bucolic charm. Returning in 1971, he held the first of his musical festival-institutes in a small school building, a venture that has grown into permanent quarters on Festival Hill. Every summer sixty music students attend master classes taught by a professional guest faculty and perform with internationally known musicians in a series of public concerts.

Two handsome old homes have been moved onto the Festival Hill grounds. The William Lockhart Clayton House, built in 1870 in La Grange, is now staff living quarters, and the C. A. Menke House, originally an old ranch house in Hempstead, is used as a conference center. Limited overnight accommodations are available by advance reservation from August through April.

An early June weekend gala opens the summer concert series in the new (air-conditioned) Festival Hall, and many weekend performances are offered from August to April. Tickets can either be ordered in advance or purchased at the box office prior to curtain. There usually is a free concert for children in mid-June.

Picnic facilities are free for the summer concerts, and gourmet dinners ($$$) are served by reservation only on Saturday nights during the August-through-April series. Information: Festival Hill, P.O. Box 89, Round Top 78954. (409) 249–3129.

Henkel Square. On the square. Back in 1852, a German immigrant named Edward A. Henkel bought twenty-five acres in Round Top to establish a mercantile store. The following year he built a two-story home that is now the keystone of Henkel Square, an open-air museum operated by the Texas Pioneer Arts Foundation.

Dedicated to preserving the history of this region, Henkel Square is a collection of sixteen historically important structures scattered across eight acres of pasture in the heart of town. The docents are local ladies who explain each home and building, its furnishings, and how it fit into early Texas life. Don't miss the old Lutheran church, which doubled formerly as a school. Its painted motto translates from the German as: "I call the living to my church and the dead to their graves"—a reference to its two-clapper bell. One rings, the other tolls.

Five of the buildings were moved to Henkel Square from surrounding communities, and the lumber needed for restorations was cut in the local woods, just as it was in pioneer times. Using period tools and techniques, today's craftsmen have kept each structure faithful to its time, with attention to authenticity that has won Henkel Square awards for restoration excellence. Several of the homes have outstanding wall stenciling and period furniture.

The entrance is through the Victorian building that once housed Round Top's apothecary. Open afternoons year-round, except for major holidays. Fee. (409) 249–3308.

Moore's Fort. Across T–237 from the square. That double log cabin with an open dog-trot center was the frontier home of John Henry Moore. Built about 1828 near the Colorado River in La Grange, it was used primarily as a defense against Indians.

Round Top General Store. On the T–237 side of the town square. Not every hardware store serves beer, but this one does! That's what comes of being the gathering place for a predominately German community since 1847. Open Wednesday–Sunday, but hours are "very uncertain," according to owner Betty Schatte. (409) 249–3600.

WHERE TO EAT

The Round Top Cafe. On the north side of the square. This may be the only eatery in the world that has dime-store variety reading glasses at each table, the better to help folks through the witty, tightly written menu. As *Country Living* magazine put it, this small place features "the kind of food you come to the country for." Owners Bud and Karen Royer offer memorable sandwiches on homemade bread, a tasty chicken salad, and a full range of entrees that include fresh veggies, and homemade rolls topped with either herb butter or homemade applesauce butter. Don't dismiss the chicken fingers as preprocessed food. Karen cuts and breads them herself and makes the accompanying honey mustard sauce, a memorable meal. Frills run to Blue Bell ice-cream cones (vanilla only) and homemade desserts. Real apples and pumpkins go into the pies—no canned fillings are used—and if you are lucky, it will be dewberry cobbler day. Open for lunch and dinner Wednesday–Saturday, plus lunch on Sunday; expect to wait a spell on the front porch. $–$$; (CC). (409) 249–3611.

The Royers also offer Christian counseling seminars and B&B lodgings in a retreat atmosphere at Heritage Farm, 10 miles east of town. (409) 357–2838.

WANDERING THE BACKROADS

To continue this day trip to Winedale, take FM–1457 north 4 miles to FM–2714 and turn northwest.

If you have lingered too long in Round Top and now must head home, why not take the scenic route? T–237 south to La Grange (Trip 4, this sector) is one of the nicest country rambles in the state. Take a few minutes to travel east or west of the highway on the many graded county roads. You'll pass gracious old homes, log cabins, churches flanked by tiny cemeteries, and numerous historical landmarks. As you enter Warrenton on T–237 south, watch for a large two-story stone house on the west side of the road. This is the Neece House, built in 1869 and currently being restored as a private residence. You'll also pass St. Martin's, locally called the smallest Catholic church in the world because it can hold only twelve persons.

From La Grange, follow T–71 southeast to Columbus (Trip 3, this sector) and I–10 east to Houston.

WINEDALE

This is another look at yesterday's Texas. The settlement is blink-small: a gas station, a combination store and cafe, and a few homes, all tucked into a valley threaded by Jack's Creek. That old-style split rail fence on the right, however, encircles one of the most ambitious restoration projects in the state, the Winedale Historical Center.

Administered by the University of Texas, this 190-acre outdoor museum covers many pages of the past. The basic farmstead was part of a Mexican land grant to William S. Townsend, one of Austin's second colony, who built a small house on the land about 1834. In 1848, he sold the farm to Samuel Lewis, who expanded the home and plantation, and by the mid-1850s the Lewis farmhouse was a stage stop on the main road between Brenham and La Grange.

Winedale tours should start at a simple 1855 farm building known as Hazel's Lone Oak Cottage. The next stop is the focal point of the entire museum complex, the Sam Lewis House. This two-story farmhouse is notable for its authentic Texas primitive furnishings and beautiful wall and ceiling frescoes painted by a local German artist of the time, Rudolph Melchoir. Other rare examples of Melchoir's art can be seen in several of the Henkel Square houses in Round Top.

The Winedale complex has assorted dependencies such as a smokehouse and pioneer kitchen and two other major structures. The old barn, built in 1894 from cedar beams salvaged from an early cotton gin, now rings with the ageless words of Shakespeare every August, courtesy of University of Texas English students. The performances are Thursday–Sunday evenings; seats must be reserved in advance ($), and an inexpensive hunter's stew is served before the Saturday-evening show. You also are welcome to bring a picnic basket and feast in the field.

A ten-minute trek through the back pastures of Winedale leads to the McGregor-Grimm House, a two-story Greek Revival farmhouse built in 1861 and moved to Winedale from Wesley in 1967. As the Lewis House represents the earlier, rather simple plantation home of the area, the McGregor-Grimm House is more gracious and elaborate, typical of pre-Civil War cotton-boom wealth.

The Winedale Historical Center is open only on weekends (fee). The shady grounds and picnic area are open daily at no charge. (409) 278–3530.

WANDERING THE BACKROADS

From Winedale, turn southeast (left) on FM–1457 and go approximately 9 miles to the intersection with T–159. Turn east (left), and it's 19 miles to Bellville—beautiful country all the way.

If you have time to spare, follow FM–1457 only as far as the tiny town of Shelby, and swing north (left) on FM–389. At the intersection with FM–2502, turn right to Wesley. This was an early Czech-Moravian settlement and has the first church of the Czech Brethren faith built in North America (1866). The stone foundation is original and utilizes a huge oak log to support the center of the building. The interior has some unusual hand-painted decorations more than a century old.

From Wesley, continue south on FM–2502 to T–159 and turn east (left) to Bellville. Should you prefer to explore part of the northwest sector from Wesley, turn north on FM–2502 and then northeast on FM–389 into Brenham (Trip 6, Northwest Sector). From here, it's US–290 east back to Houston.

BELLVILLE

Settled in 1848 and the Austin County seat, the town was named for Thomas Bell, one of Stephen F. Austin's "Old Three Hundred," as his first colony has been labeled by history. The best time to visit is during the spring Country Livin' Festival, when nature lines the routes into the town with bluebonnets and Indian paintbrush. During that festival the chamber of commerce sets up roadside booths where you can get maps and directions to the best flower displays. They also sell packets of bluebonnet seeds in the hope that you will sow some of next year's color yourself. For information on Bellville—including antique shops, galleries, etc.—contact the chamber of commerce, 36 South Bell Street (P.O. Box 670), Bellville 77418, or call (409) 865–3407.

Restoration is bringing back the architectural integrity of the old town square. Numerous building fronts have been returned to their original design. More than a dozen housed antique stores at last count. There also are new boutiques and art galleries, a few of which open on Sunday afternoons in good weather.

One handsome Bellville home, circa 1906, has been restored by Anna and George Horton into the High Cotton Inn, a cozy Victorian retreat for bed and breakfast (409–865–9796). When the guests couldn't resist sneaking her luscious cookies, Anna took the hint and opened up the Cookie Factory in the inn's garage. Mason jars filled with Anna's cookies (and her rum cakes as well) are sold at the inn and at various outlets in Houston.

Although there are many historical markers in town, no vintage homes are currently open for scheduled tours. For a modest donation however, members of the Bellville Historical Foundation can open some of those doors for you on a guided tour. One of the special sites they access is Sam Houston's Texian Army encampment at Raccoon Bend on the west bank of the Brazos, currently undergoing an archeological dig.

WHAT TO DO

Bluebonnet Farms. 746 FM–529, 33 miles west of T–6 and 7 miles east of Bellville. This 100-acre farm breeds and trains American saddlebred horses and has several national champions in its paddocks. Visitors are welcome only if they have a sincere interest in the riding and training of horses; no sightseers or casual drop-ins, please. Appointments required. (409)865–5051.**Christmas Tree Farms.** You can choose your own and haul it home at Fortune's Farm, (409) 865–5826, and Teague's Trees, (409) 865–5390.

    The 1896 Jailhouse Museum. 36 South Bell Street. The sheriff's office has been restored to its turn-of-the-century look, and exhibits include artifacts from the Texian Army encampment at Raccoon Bend as well as assorted weapons, many of which were confiscated from prisoners during the jail's serious years. Open weekday mornings; call for appointments at other times. (409) 865–3754.

    Red Deer Farm. 205 Clens Road, 1.1 mile from Bellville via T–159. The first commercial deer farm in the United States when it was established in 1984, this handsome 200-acre facility is riding high on the newest wave of Texas agriculture, commercial deer farming. Some 200 head of farm-bred deer from Canada, New Zealand, Nova Scotia, and England are scattered among eleven paddocks, each animal a mini-gold mine in itself. Foals sired by a leading stag can sell for as much as $4,500; prices for outstanding mature hinds (females) hover around $10,000. Two of North America's most noted breeding stags, Romulus and Crown Prince, are here; the latter has double-crowned spikes on his antlers and is the first of that type to be imported into the United States. Note: This is not a wild animal park or petting zoo, and children under ten are not permitted on the premises under any circumstances. The farm and its tour are aimed at education, not entertainment and are of value only to persons interested in agriculture. Visitors with advance reservations can tour at feeding time on Friday afternoons (fee) and agricultural student groups are particularly welcome. The gates are unlocked only for those with advance appointments, and tour space is limited. Tip: The stags are in velvet in spring, a spectacular sight. (409) 865–8181, (409) 865–9601.

WHERE TO EAT

Bellville Provision Company. 239 FM–2429. This is a good place for those two Texas favorites, barbecue and chicken-fried steak. Open for lunch and dinner daily except Monday. $–$$. (409) 865–2510.

Bellville Restaurant. 103 East Main, across from the court-house. The building dates from 1885, the restaurant from the 1930s. Lunch here is a daily ritual for Bellville's businessmen. The steam table with its many choices of entrees and vegetables is popular, plus there are daily specials and a regular menu. Open twenty-four hours daily. $–$$; (CC). (409) 865–9710.

Newman's Bakery. 201 East Main. In addition to the usual Napoleons and éclairs, this fragrant place is also a local favorite for kolaches, ham and cheese croissants, and pigs-in-a-blanket. Nor is it just take-out. There's sit-down service for soups, salads, and sandwiches as well. Open daily from 6 a.m. $. (409) 865–9804.

Sillavan's Restaurant. 472 T–36, between Bellville and Brenham. Good old American standards like chicken-fried steak, hamburgers, and pot roast are served here, including a blue plate special at lunch. Open for lunch and dinner Tuesday–Saturday, Sunday until 2 p.m. $–$$. (409) 865–5066.

The Tea Rose, The Tap Room, and the Townsquare Inn. 17 South Bell, across from the courthouse. It's often standing-room-only in these connecting establishments, run by Bob and Deborah Nolan and family. The Tea Rose's daily lunches are light and tasty, and the Saturday evening dinners are table d'hôte, ranging from home-done beef Wellington to pot roast and chicken-'n'-dumplings. The Tap Room is open nightly with a dinner menu on weeknights. $–$$. (409) 865–9720. If you're too drowsy to head home, just hope there is room in the adjacent Townsquare Inn, another Nolan venture. In addition to claw-footed bathtubs, there's a honeymoon suite with a giant hand-carved canopied bed. (409) 865–9021.

WANDERING THE BACKROADS

To return to Houston from Bellville, you again have a choice. FM–529 east is a rural route that intersects T–6 north of the Bear Creek business area on the northwest side of Houston. If you live in south Houston, your best bet from Bellville is T–36 south 15 miles to Sealy (Trip 1, this sector), then east on I–10 toward home.

SOUTHWEST

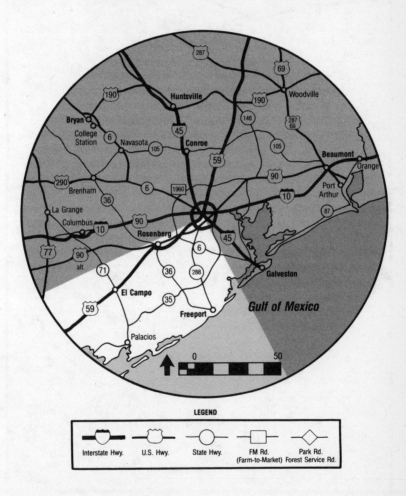

Gulf of Mexico

0   50

LEGEND

Interstate Hwy.   U.S. Hwy.   State Hwy.   FM Rd. (Farm-to-Market)   Park Rd. Forest Service Rd.

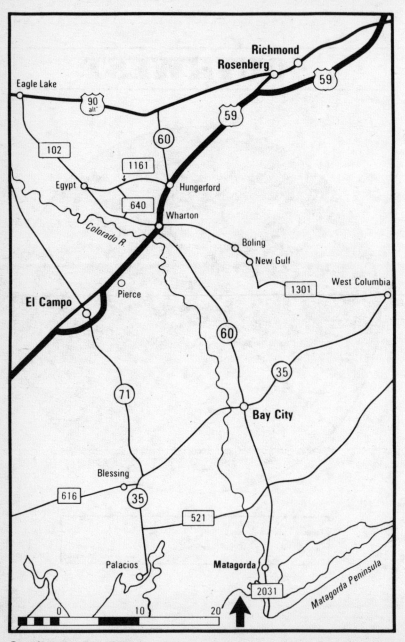

Southwest: Day Trip 1

Day Trip 1

WHARTON
EL CAMPO
PALACIOS and BLESSING
MATAGORDA

WHARTON

The trip through Wharton, El Campo, Palacios, and Matagorda covers a lot of territory, so you may want to make a weekend out of it with an overnight at the Luther Hotel in Palacios. Take your fishing and crabbing gear and have fun.

Start your trip via US–59 south to Wharton. While not a gee-whiz destination in itself, Wharton has several pleasures. This rich agricultural land drew Stephen F. Austin's early settlers, and the town of Wharton began about 1846.

Although no homes are open to the public on a regular basis, it's interesting to drive down Wharton's oak-shaded streets. Don't miss driving by the old Wharton home at 219 Burleson Street, a private residence that is often on the Christmas Homes Tour. For information on local events as well as a list of antique shops, contact the Wharton Chamber of Commerce, 225 Richmond Road, Wharton 77488. (409) 532–1862.

WHAT TO DO

Cotton Ginning. There are not many places left in Texas to watch a cotton gin do its thing. If you are interested and planning to visit Wharton during the August–September ginning season, you can visit the Moses Gin by advance arrangement with the Caney Valley Cotton Co., Box 470, Wharton 77488. (409) 532–5210 or 532–3522.

Egypt Plantation. On FM–102 north between Wharton and Eagle Lake. The tiny crossroads town of Egypt was settled by Austin's second colony. Park at the old frame general store and go in for a chat and a cool drink. Then walk to the "new" post office with its two vintage gas pumps before looking around the rest of this tiny town. FM–1161, the short, one-lane road in front of the post office, ends at Egypt Plantation, one of the few original homesteads in Texas still owned by members of its founding family. Built in 1849, this durable pink brick homeplace is normally open only to groups of twelve or more. During the mid-March through April wildflower season in nearby Eagle Lake, however, owner Anita Northington welcomes individuals and families as well. The house tour includes the Northington-Heard Museum, a remarkable collection of Texana housed in the old Egypt-Santa Fe Railroad depot behind the plantation house. Reservations required. Fee. Box 277, Egypt 77436. (409) 677–3562.

Gundermann's Orchard. Take the Eagle Lake exit from US–59 south and follow FM–102 north into Glen Flora. Watch for signs. If tornadoes, freezes, and droughts have left the crops intact, visitors are welcome to pick the apples, vegetables, and sometimes peaches starting in mid-May. Ever see a cider press doing its job? You may be able to here in June if the size of the apple crop allows (fee). A selection of country arts and crafts, and sometimes cider, is sold here. Call for crop information. (409) 677–3319.

James G. Martin Nuts. 117 South Sunset Street, Wharton. This local pecan broker has six mechanical pecan crackers that rarely stop during the harvest months of October through January. You are welcome to stop in and watch. He sells both wholesale and retail, so you can pack some home. Open Monday–Saturday. (409) 532–2345.

Pierce. Eight miles south of Wharton via US–59; turn left at the second road past the Precinct 4 barn. "Shanghai" Pierce was the Lone Star state's first real cattle baron. After serving in the Civil War, he amassed a 250,000-acre cattle empire on these flatlands. Historic markers as well as a restored church and store now mark the site.

The Real McCoy Hunting Club. Guided or unguided duck and geese hunting on 900 acres of prime rice-growing land at the edge of the Lissie-Egypt prairie. Contact Bill Sherrill, 425 Croom Drive, Wharton 77488. (713) 485–0081.

Riverfront Park at the Port of Wharton. This new civic project has a playground, picnic tables, and a deck overlooking the river. Stop here with your picnic, and then tour the nearby museum and Monterey Square in front of the 1888 courthouse. The square is one of the Main Street projects fostered by the National Trust for Historic Preservation.

Wharton County Museum. 231 South Fulton Street, near the river in Wharton. Some interesting bits and pieces of Wharton's past are gathered here in what was the old jail. Donations are appreciated; closed on Monday. (409) 532–2600.

WHERE TO EAT

City Cafe. Arthur and Main streets, Garwood. If tummy is empty and purse is tight, you can't do better than Mary Schoellmann's place. Hearty breakfasts are in the $2–$3 range, lunches of the fried chicken/Swiss steak/meat loaf genre top out at $3.95. Burgers and sandwiches are even less. Nothing fancy, just good food for local folks in what was an old pool hall. Open Monday–Saturday. $. (409) 758–3085.

Hinze's Bar-B-Que. 3940 Highway 59 Loop, Wharton. Local folks think this family-run place has the best barbecue in the region—not to mention their homemade chocolate, coconut, and pecan pies. Try them out on a take-out. Open daily. $–$$; (CC). (409) 532–2710.

Mama John's. 814 East Milam. The "Home-burgers" are flavorful and juicy here because John grinds his own chuck meat, and the buffet lunch on weekdays is an equally tasty buy. Everything is fresh (only frozen if out of season)—not even the buffet vegetables come from cans—and John makes 90 percent of his own seasonings. Test those out on the blackened fish of the day; all his seafood is bought off the boats in Matagorda or Palacios. Open daily except Sunday. $–$$. (409) 532–8761.

Pier 59. 211 West Elm. Aside from good prime rib, lobster, salad bar, etc., the big attraction here is the deck overlooking the Colorado River, a great spot to end a day of exploring. Open for lunch and dinner Monday–Saturday. $$; (CC). (409) 532–3030.

WANDERING THE BACKROADS

Much of Wharton County sits atop vast underground sulphur deposits. At the Texas Gulf Sulphur headquarters, 12 miles east of Wharton on FM–1301 between Boling and New Gulf, you can see mountains of the yellow mineral literally dwarfing nearby railroad cars.

Wharton is surrounded by vast cotton, corn, and rice fields, and the early spring months along any rural road in the area produce a vision of fresh green, punctuated by bright wildflowers. Local folks think there is no prettier drive in Texas than FM–102 between Wharton and Eagle Lake.

Another nice rural drive is along the Spanish Camp Road, FM–640. Watch for the Glen Flora Plantation home (private) on your left, a hint of the Old South.

EL CAMPO

This spreading town, 68 miles south of Houston on US–59, sits amid a vast coastal grass plain used for open cattle range since the early 1800s. By the 1850s, this area was the starting point for cattle drives across East Texas on the Opelousas and Atascosito trails, heading for the railroad terminals at New Orleans and Mobile.

The railroad eventually made it to this part of Texas, and by the early 1880s the area had an official railroad name, Prairie Switch. Mexican cowboys handling the large herds would camp nearby—thus the name El Campo, which was officially adopted in 1902 when the town was incorporated. Early settlers came from Germany, Sweden, Czechoslovakia, and Ireland, an ethnic mix celebrated on El Campo Grande Day every August.

For information on El Campo, contact the local Chamber of Commerce, Box 446, El Campo 77437, (409) 543–2713. The Jackson County Chamber of Commerce has area information: P.O. Box 788 (317 West Main Street), Edna 77957, (512) 782–2382.

WHAT TO DO

El Campo Museum of Art, Science, and History. 2350 North Mechanic, in the new Civic Center on T–71 north at FM–2765. The main local attraction is the big-game trophy exhibit at this elaborate and extensive museum, originally a private collection of a local family. Shell and rock displays have been added, along with a waterfowl exhibit and a collection of clowns (ceramic, needlepoint, painted, and so on). Temporary shows are mounted four times a year. Open Monday–Saturday. Free, but donations are appreciated. (409) 543–2714.

Heritage Center. 101 South Mechanic, across from the post office in downtown El Campo. These three refurbished buildings date from 1906 and may be the start of a larger vintage development along the lines of Old Town Spring. Stop in at Churchill Downs for antiques, followed by homemade soups and sandwiches in the back of the store. Open Tuesday–Saturday. $; (CC). (409) 543–5611.

Lake Texana. Twenty-one miles southwest of El Campo via US–59. This 11,000-acre lake is noted for its catfish and bass, plus there's good camping and picnicking under shady oaks. All water sports are here, either at Lake Texana State Park, (512) 782–5718 or (800) 792–1112, or at Lake Texana Marina and Brackenridge Plantation Campground, (512) 782–7145.

Interesting to know: The lake now covers the old town site of Texana, which was a well-established Indian village back in 1685 when La Salle's expedition was in the area. In 1832, it became the first town founded in Jackson County, and a few years later the Allen brothers thought it would be the ideal location for their dream city because of its location on the Navidad River, which provided deep-water access to the Gulf of Mexico. Feeling it could be a great port, they offered $100 in gold for the land. When the owner demanded $200, the Allen brothers moved northeast and ultimately bought a tract of land in Harris County upon which they founded their dream city—Houston.

Artifacts from Texana's early days were uncovered by archeologists before the site was inundated with water; they now are on display at the Lavaca-Navidad River Authority headquarters, north of Palmetto Bend Dam on FM–3131. Free and open weekdays.

WHERE TO EAT

Churchill Downs. 101 South Mechanic. (See **Heritage Center** in "What to Do" section above.)

Hillje's Smokehouse. On US–59, 4 miles west of El Campo. Using an old family recipe, Mike and Betty Jo Prasek turn out memorable smoked sausage and beef jerky. If you call ahead, they'll have sandwiches ready to go when you arrive. Open daily from 7 a.m. until early evening. $–$$; (CC). (409) 543–8312.

Mikeska's Bar-B-Q. 209 Merchant Street, El Campo. Centrally located, this is a favorite spot to pick up some picnic sandwiches or take a road break. $. Open daily. (409) 543–5471.

PALACIOS and BLESSING

When you want to get away from it all, take T–71 south from El Campo to the sleepy fishing community of Palacios. Whatever you want to escape, it isn't here. The big activity for visitors is walking from the Luther Hotel to Petersen's Restaurant, with a short stroll along the newly refurbished bayfront thrown in for excitement. The hotel also is a popular haven for boaters.

The area was named Tres Palacios several centuries ago by shipwrecked Spanish sailors who claimed they saw a vision of three palaces on this bay. Unfortunately, the tiny town that began here around the turn of the century doesn't quite live up to the vision. For day-trippers, however, Palacios is the perfect low-key escape.

There are two lighted fishing piers (bring your own bait and gear), numerous other wooden jetties on the bay, a new shell beach, and several public playgrounds and boat ramps. A 1.5-mile-long walkway curves along the seawall, and a new, rather grand public beach area is under construction just south of the Luther Hotel. The biggest event of the year is the July Fourth Firecracker 200 which attracts some of the most powerful hydro racers in the country.

The old town of Blessing, 13 miles north of Palacios via T–35, is a real piece of the past. When the tracks of the New York Central (Missouri Pacific) Railroad and the Southern Pacific Railroad finally crossed on the Texas prairie in 1902, legend says that developer J. E. "Shanghai" Pierce said, "Thank God," and set aside 640 acres for a town of that name. The post office demurred, and Blessing was chosen as a compromise. Pierce's burial site is here in Hawley Cemetery, along with his likeness atop a ten-foot column so that he could continue to oversee his lands even after death.

Care to cut your own Christmas tree while touring the area? Holiday Pines Plantation is near Blessing. (512) 588–7673.

WHERE TO EAT

Blessing Hotel Coffee Shop. Avenue B and Tenth Street, in Blessing, which is south of El Campo and north of Palacios via T–35 and FM–616. The hotel, circa 1906, is now owned by the Blessing Historical Foundation and is under slow restoration; its twenty rooms are simple and inexpensive. What was the hotel's ballroom is now a coffee shop with a well-earned reputation of its own. You pay your money and fill your plate from pots of delicious country-style food lined up on top of old stoves. The breakfasts are incredible, and the lunches are large enough to satisfy a hardworking field hand. No cutesy quiches here; the noon meal on Sunday is like Thanksgiving all year long. Open daily except Christmas. $. (512) 588–6623.

Petersen's Restaurant. 420 Main Street. Almost everything that swims in the gulf ends up on the table at Petersen's, and the toasted French bread is in a class by itself. Open daily for breakfast, lunch, and dinner. $$; (CC). (512) 972–2413.

WHERE TO STAY

The Luther Hotel. 408 South Bay Boulevard, on the bay between Fifth and Sixth streets in Palacios. Quality always lasts, and this rambling white-frame hostelry has survived many a storm since its construction in 1903. Sited with dignity on a large lawn, this is the kind of place where you contently watch twilight creep across Palacios Bay while lounging in a chaise on the front porch. Resort it isn't, relaxing it is. Members of the Luther family still run this historic hotel and suggest you make reservations, as they hang out the NO VACANCY sign with regularity. The rooms are comfortable, with air conditioning and/or ceiling fans and private baths. Several have kitchens, and there's a third-floor "penthouse" if you feel like splurging. Be aware that no food is served at the hotel. (512) 972–2313.

WANDERING THE BACKROADS

The main route into Palacios is T–71 south from El Campo. A short jog east on County Road 46 (11 miles south of El Campo) brings you to Danevang Lutheran Church and a memorial to the Danish pioneers who settled here in 1894.

T–60 is an alternate route to Palacios through neat and orderly Bay City. Take a break here at the Matagorda County Museum, 1824 Sixth Street, and examine its collection of early Texas maps, carpenter's tools, and other Matagorda-related archival material. Open Tuesday, Wednesday, and Sunday afternoons. (409) 245–7502.

If you travel between Palacios and Matagorda, take scenic FM–521. You can't miss Houston Light and Power Company's South Texas Nuclear Plant on the south side of the road. The free Visitor Center explains all, and tours of the project can be arranged. Open daily except Sunday. (409) 245–1477 or (512) 972–5023.

While driving FM–521 near the power plant, watch for tiny St. Francis Catholic Church and its cemetery on the north side of the road. This was originally a Polish village, but after the 1895 hurricane swept the settlement away only the church was rebuilt.

MATAGORDA

Founded in 1829 with Stephen F. Austin as one of its original proprietors, Matagorda thrived as a port and was the third largest town in Texas by 1834. One of the early freight routes that supplied central Texas with the basics of life ran between Matagorda and Austin; wagons left both cities on the first and the fifteenth of every month.

The railroad had steamed across Texas by 1853 but bypassed Matagorda in favor of Bay City. A hurricane in 1854 dealt another blow, and Matagorda never regained its early prominence.

Visitors today find two historic churches (1838 and 1839; both the first of their denominations in Texas), an 1830 cemetery, and a double-lock system operated by the U.S. Army Corps of Engineers on the Intracoastal canal. One medallion home is interesting to drive by: the Dale-Rugley-Sisk House (private), built in 1830 at the corner of Catalpa and Fisher streets.

If it's crabbing, seining, or beaching you want, turn south on FM–2031 (locally called River Road) in the center of town and follow it to the gulf. There are many fine crabbing and fishing holes along the way, and the road ends at a new county park and 20 miles of beach stretching as far as you can see. There are several charter fishing operations on River Road, among them Allen's Landing, (409) 863–7729; Blue Gem Charters, (409) 863–9909; and River Bend Marina, (409) 863–2310.

WHERE TO EAT

Seabreeze Restaurant. Corner of Market and Matagorda streets. It's a good thing this is a super place to eat, because it's the only game in town. They buy their fish straight from boats that dock practically in their backyard, which means the flounder, shrimp, and soft-shell crab couldn't be fresher. The shrimp salad holds its own against the best of the coast, and the seasonal oysters come from nearby shoals. Contrary to the general rule of "don't order beef in a seafood restaurant," the burgers and steaks win local raves. Open Wednesday–Sunday for lunch and dinner. Bring cash; they don't take credit cards. $–$$. (409) 863–7875.

Day Trip 2

ANGLETON
BRAZOSPORT
EAST AND WEST COLUMBIA
RICHMOND AND ROSENBERG

ANGLETON

Two routes, T–288 and T–35, come south from Houston and meet in Angleton before continuing on to the Brazosport area as T–288. You'll pass the old Brazoria County Courthouse in Angleton, built in 1896 and expanded in 1916 and again in 1927. It now houses the Brazoria County Museum.

If you enjoy canoeing, explore Bastrop Bayou, about 5 miles south of Angleton via either FM–523 or T–288. The best put-in for this 5-mile float is at the FM–2004 bridge, south of the intersection with FM–523. The best take-out is 2 miles (by road) further on at the old T–288 bridge (watch for a railroad track). Current is generally not a problem, so you have two options: either float downstream as far as you want from the FM–2004 bridge and then paddle back; or put in at the T–288 bridge, paddle upstream, and then float back to your car.

WHAT TO DO

Brazoria County Museum. 100 East Cedar Street, at intersection with T–288. A general store and doctor's office from Brazoria County's past is recreated here, along with a plantation bedroom, dioramas, and economics exhibits. Well worth a stop, if only to shop the museum's interesting store. Free. Open Tuesday–Saturday. (713) 331–6101, ext. 1208.

Chenango Orchards. Beginning in mid-May and continuing through June, you can pick peaches, nectarines, and produce at reasonable cost at this farm near Rosharon. Call for directions. (713) 431–2138.

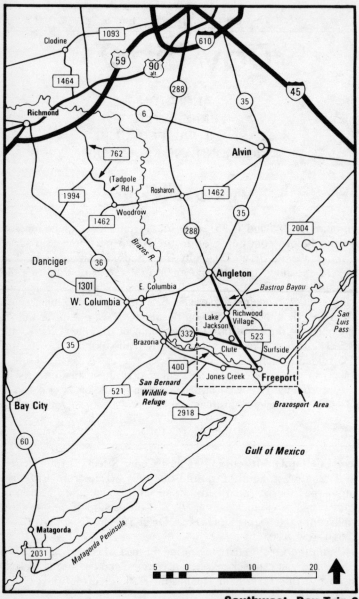

Southwest: Day Trip 2

BRAZOSPORT

It's hard to find the name Brazosport on current maps, but that's because it's really nine communities: Brazoria, Freeport, Lake Jackson, Quintana, Richwood, Surfside, Oyster Creek, Jones Creek, and Clute. Their common bond is the mighty (and usually muddy) Brazos River as it empties into the Gulf of Mexico.

The name has its origins on seventeenth-century nautical charts, marking where the Brazos meets the sea; and today Brazosport is the only mainland community actually on the gulf-front coast of Texas.

This is historic country—Stephen F. Austin and his colonies entered Texas here—but there is little physical evidence left to provide tourist interest. The area's biggest draws are the free and unrestricted beaches. Any sunny weekend finds thousands of cars lined up on the sand, boom boxes going full blast. Most of the beach-related businesses shut down after Labor Day, and Brazosport quickly reverts to the industrial and oil-refining community it basically is.

There's something going on in at least one of the nine towns almost every month of the year. For a schedule of special events as well as information on marinas, vacation rentals, deep-sea charter and party-boat fishing, etc., contact the Brazosport Visitors and Convention Council, P.O. Box 1361, Clute 77531, (409) 265–2508. For on-site assistance weekdays, you'll find them at 420 West T–332, in Clute.

WHAT TO DO

Antonelli's Root Beer Stand. In Freeport Municipal Park, off T–227. For years, Mr. Antonelli's root beer stand was the spot to be, but when he died, his root beer recipe died with him. When sentimental citizens began to dismantle his tiny shop for preservation in the park, they found the recipe taped under a drawer. So now, Thursday through Saturday afternoons during the warm weather months, Antonelli's root beer is once again available in Freeport, served up in a frosty glass mug at almost old-timey prices. (409) 233–4141.

The Beaches. The old mouth of the Brazos River becomes, through engineering, the Brazos Harbor Channel and is framed by two jetties ideal for free fishing and crabbing. This channel also divides the beaches. Northeast to San Luis Pass via FM–3005 and the Bluewater Highway (County Road 257) are Surfside and Follet's Island beaches (14 miles of sand); southwest of the channel are Quintana Beach and

Bryan Beach State Park. The latter's 878 acres are undeveloped but good for fishing, beachcombing, and bird-watching; use four-wheel drive and keep a wary eye on the tide or you may be stranded by rising water. Both Quintana and Bryan Beach are reached from T–288 south (Brazosport Boulevard) and County Road 1495.

Quintana Beach has an excellent county park, which includes a restored historic house with ecology lab, picnic pavilions, restrooms and showers, fishing pier, playground and sports courts, World War II gun mounts, and both primitive camping and RV sites. The latter requires reservations. (409) 233–1461 or (800) 872–7578.

With the exception of Quintana and a small section of Surfside, automobile traffic is allowed on all beaches. You can camp pretty much where you wish. There are no hook-ups, and public restroom facilities are extremely limited. Surfside has the most commercial development. If it's solitude you seek, Bryan Beach is your best bet.

Big Boggy National Wildlife Refuge. On the north shore of East Matagorda Bay. Difficult to access, this wild area is open for seasonal wildfowl hunting only. (409) 849–6062.

Brazoria National Wildlife Refuge. On the north shore of West Galveston Bay. From T–288 south in Lake Jackson, turn east on FM–2004 for 5 miles, then right on FM–523 for 8 miles and follow signs. This 42,200-acre reserve is open the first full weekend of every month for birding and nature photography. There's also seasonal access for wildfowl hunting. (409) 849–6062.

Brazosport Center for the Arts and Sciences. 400 College Drive, Lake Jackson, on the Brazosport College campus off T–288. This large cultural complex is of interest to day visitors primarily for the gem of a natural science museum it contains. Exhibits at the Brazosport Museum of Natural Science interpret this coastal region through shells, plants, animals, fossils, minerals, and Indian artifacts. The shell exhibit is particularly well done and will turn your beach trips into expeditions. The Brazosport Nature Center and Planetarium has star shows for the public on Tuesday evenings. A self-guided nature trail along Oyster Creek reveals more than 200 species of riverbottom vegetation. Closed Monday. (409) 265–7661.

Captain Elliott's Party Boats, Inc. 1010 West Second Street, Freeport. In addition to daily deep-sea fishing trips to the snapper banks 30 to 60 miles offshore, this firm offers two-hour sightseeing trips on the Old Brazos River by private charter. Fee; (CC). Reservations advised. (409) 233–1811.

Dido's Houseboat Rides on the San Bernard River. See "Where to Eat" listings.

Girouard's General Store. 626 West Second Street, Freeport. When *Texas Monthly* magazine labels something the "best" in the state, it's worth a good look. You'll find the wrenches over the bread, plumber's helpers near the piñatas, and nearly everything else tucked somewhere. This is an outstanding example of a nearly extinct type of store. If you forgot your crabbing or seining gear, just stop here. Open daily except Sunday. (409) 233–4211.

San Bernard Wildlife Refuge. Ten miles west of Freeport on FM–2918. This 24,455-acre prairie and marsh preserve is accessed by boat from the Intracoastal Waterway and via FM–2004 west from T–288 in Lake Jackson. Established as a quality habitat for wintering migratory waterfowl and other birds, the refuge has recorded more than 400 species of wildlife. There is limited land access for birding, wildlife photography, and general nature observation, but new and improved land facilities are in the planning stages. For on-site assistance, try the maintenance facilities on County Road 306, inside the refuge boundaries. Gates are always open; no fee. Information: P.O. Drawer 1088, Angleton 77516. (409) 849–7771.

Scuba diving. Licensed captain and divemaster Brian Elenbaas runs one-day diving trips on weekends year-round to either the *V. A. Fogg* shipwreck or coral formations around offshore oil platforms 30 to 35 miles south into the gulf. Both spots take about three hours to reach aboard his 30-foot sport fishing boat, the *Trigger III.* Departures are from Kirby Marina on Oyster Creek. (409) 233–8359 (home/evenings), 238–1710 (day).

Another option is *The Fling,* a 100-foot-long ship that's air-conditioned and outfitted with bunks and showers for overnight trips, makes two- and three-day trips to both Stetson Bank and the Flower Gardens; the latter, 110 miles offshore, is one of the northernmost coral reefs in the Western Hemisphere. For information, contact Gary Winn through Captain Elliott's Party Boats. (409) 233–1811.

For additional information on Brazosport area scuba trips, contact Dove Safari, (409) 265–8401.

WHERE TO EAT

Cafe Laredo. T–332 at West Way in Lake Jackson. The chef makes his own tortillas and hot sauce, two reasons why this Mexican place is a hands-down local favorite. Open Monday–Saturday for lunch and dinner. $; (CC). (409) 297–0696.

Dido's. From FM–521 in Brazoria, turn left on T–36, right on FM–311, and right on FM–519 to the river. Dido runs his own shrimp boats, which makes for good eating, either in the air-conditioned dining room or on the outside deck. Open for lunch and dinner daily except on summertime Wednesdays; in winter, open weekdays except Wednesday for dinner, weekends for lunch and dinner. $–$$; (CC). (409) 964–3167.

On The River. 920 West Second Street, Freeport. The fish, whether fried, boiled, blackened, or baked, is great here, particularly the catfish; plus there are plenty of steaks and chicken dishes as well. If weather permits, ask for a table on the screened porch upstairs, overlooking the water. Open for dinner nightly, for lunch on Friday. $–$$; (CC). (409) 233–0503.

WANDERING THE BACKROADS

From Brazosport and environs, this day trip continues north to East and West Columbia. Although T–36 is the swiftest route, you might prefer to mosey a while along the old river road that runs beside the Brazos from Jones Creek to Brazoria. To do that, start north on T–36 from Freeport, turn east (right) on County Road 400, and continue northwest along the river. At the intersection with FM–521, turn west (left) for about three-quarters of a mile to intersect T–36 and the original routing for this trip.

As you pass through Brazoria, take time to explore. Most of the original town has been flooded by the river, but there are several historical markers worth a read.

As an alternative to continuing on T–36 to the Columbias, you can follow FM–521 west and T–60 south to Matagorda (Trip 1, this sector).

THE COLUMBIAS—EAST AND WEST

As you drive into these two small towns on T–36 and T–35, it's hard to believe they were among the most thriving communities in the state in 1836. East Columbia originally was Bell's Landing, a small port on the Brazos River established in 1824 by Josiah H. Bell, one of Austin's first colonists. Today East Columbia is almost a ghost town with only a few fine old homes to hint at its earlier importance.

West Columbia was another enterprise of Josiah Bell. In 1826, he cut a road across the prairie on the west side of the Brazos and created a new town, which he called Columbia. Within three years it was one of the major trading areas in Texas, and by 1836 some 3,000 people lived here, the rich Brazos bottomlands nurturing a thriving plantation economy.

After Sam Houston's victory over Santa Anna at San Jacinto, West Columbia came into its own. The most powerful men in Texas came here, made it the first state capital, created a constitution, and elected Sam Houston the first president of the new republic.

Such glory was short-lived. The town wasn't big enough to house everyone who came to the governmental proceedings, and in 1837 the legislature moved to Houston. But West Columbia had snagged its place in history, and visitors today can visit several interesting sites and antique shops along Brazos Street. For maps and advance information, contact the West Columbia Chamber of Commerce, 247 East Brazos Street, West Columbia 77486. (409) 345–3921 (weekday mornings only).

WHAT TO DO

Ammon Underwood House. On the river side of Main Street in East Columbia. Built about 1835 and enlarged twice, this stately old home has been surprisingly mobile. It has been moved three times to save it from tumbling into the Brazos. It is the oldest house in the East Columbia community and is currently owned and under restoration by the First Capitol Historical Foundation of West Columbia. Many of the furnishings and some of the wallpaper are original, and one room has been left unfinished to show early construction techniques. A log cabin built prior to 1850 has been moved onto the land behind the Underwood House and is being restored and furnished as a kitchen. Open during the San Jacinto Festival and by appointment through the West Columbia Chamber of Commerce. (409) 345–3921.

Columbia Historical Museum. 247 East Brazos Street, West Columbia. Local antiques plus exhibits on area ranching, the oil boom days of the 1920s and present times. Call for hours. (409) 345–3921.

Danciger Observatory. On a three-acre rural plot near Danciger, far from Houston's bright lights and polluted skies. Public star parties are held one Saturday night a month for up to twenty people interested in astronomy, from beginner to expert. Highly experienced volunteers from the nonprofit Danciger Astronomy Group (several of whom teach astronomy professionally) built and now operate a 10-foot-tall, 32-inch telescope designed specifically to give a bright picture of meteors and the Milky Way. The basic observation plan begins at dark and runs until midnight, following the skies from west to east. Bring folding chairs and/or sleeping bags, dress warmly (the observatory has a roll-off roof that exposes the entire night sky), and wear shoes you can wash after walking through a cow pasture. No alcohol is allowed. Fee; advance reservations required. (713) 482–6781 or (713) 482–5190 (evenings).

Hanson's Riverside Park. On the San Bernard River, 2.5 miles west of West Columbia on T–35. This great picnic spot has grills, a playground, a fishing pier, and an old-fashioned swimming hole.

Replica of the First Capitol. On Fourteenth Street, behind the West Columbia post office. This successful Bicentennial project re-creates the small clapboard building that served as the first capitol of Texas. The original building was a store that subsequently had a variety of tenants before it was destroyed in the violent storm of 1900 that devastated much of the Texas coast. The shed room to the right as you enter is an attempt to reproduce Stephen F. Austin's office at the time when he served as the first secretary of state for the republic; the furnishings of the building, while not original, are antiques from that period. Open Monday–Friday.

The Varner-Hogg State Historic Park. One mile north of T–35 on FM–2852. This land was one of the original land grants from Mexico, part of approximately 4,500 acres given to Martin Varner in 1824. Varner built a small cabin, began running stock, and in 1826 built a rum distillery on his holdings. Stephen F. Austin referred to this last enterprise as the first "ardent spirits" made in the Texas colonies. Varner sold his holdings in 1834, and the following year the new owner built the two-story brick house which survives today. Varner's original cabin is believed to be incorporated into the house, and the bricks of the existing house were made by slaves from clay found in the nearby Brazos riverbed. By the late 1800s, this plantation was prospering with sugarcane, cotton, corn, and livestock. In 1901, the first native-born governor of Texas, James Hogg, bought the old plantation and regarded the house as the first permanent home his family had. In 1920, the four Hogg children began remodeling the old house. Donated to the state in 1958, it underwent further restoration in 1981. There is a shaded picnic area, and guided tours are given whenever a small group forms. Closed Monday–Tuesday. (409) 345–4656.

WHERE TO EAT

Columbia Lakes Country Club, Resort, and Conference Center.
188 Freeman Street, West Columbia. Although the sporting facilities
are for members only, the hotel and two dining rooms are open to all.
One is formal (no shorts or abbreviated sports clothes, please), and
the second is more casual and overlooks the golf course. The buffets
laid out at breakfast and again at weekday lunches are good bets.
Open daily for breakfast, lunch, and dinner. $–$$$; (CC). (409)
345–5151.

My Cousin's Sandwich Shop. 521 South Seventeenth, West
Columbia. Far more than a sandwich is available here. The weekday
buffet lunch is all-you-can-eat, and the menu ranges from chicken-
fried steak to Philly steak sandwiches. They also make all the
desserts in-house, so save room. Open daily, with varying hours. $;
(CC). (409) 345–6670.

A Taste of Texas. 817 South Seventeenth, West Columbia. Why
not start a weekend trip with the breakfast buffet at Scott and Sheri
Leopold's place? Scott's a junk man at heart, so expect nostalgic
decor. Breakfast aside, the house specialty is the barbecue cooked
slowly over live oak coals. The results must be good; they sell some
3,000 pounds of barbecue a week in what is essentially a very small
town. Breads also are homemade, so the sandwiches are super. Open
daily; call for hours. $; (CC). (409) 345–6162.

RICHMOND and ROSENBERG

Enjoy Richmond while you can. Within a decade it may be swal-
lowed by Houston's urban creep, a historic oasis amid acres of subdi-
visions. For now, just getting to Richmond and its sidekick city of
Rosenberg is a pleasure, whether you come north via T–36 from the
Columbias or west on US–90A from Houston. The countryside pri-
marily is farms and ranches shaded by mature pecan trees and pleas-
ant to ride through any time of the year.

Richmond literally flows into Rosenberg, the larger of the two towns.
An early shipping site on the Brazos, Rosenberg really boomed in 1883
when the railroad came to town. While it remains the commercial center,
the two towns have shared a common history for the past century. For
day-trippers, Richmond is the more historically interesting destination.

By Texas time, Richmond is very old, one of the first permanent
settlements of Stephen F. Austin's original 300 colonists. For centuries

the Brazos River had made a big bend here, each flood leaving more rich soil in its wake. Shortly after Christmas Day, 1821, five men staked their fortunes on this fertile land, building a two-room fort just below the bend—thus the name Fort Bend County. A marker now stands at this site, almost lost between the eastbound and westbound bridges of US–90A as they span the Brazos.

The settlement thrived with the addition of Thompson's ferry, northwest in the bend of the river, and in 1837 the town of Richmond was formally laid out on the site of the old fort. By 1843, a sugar mill was in operation at nearby Sugar Land—the forerunner of today's Imperial Sugar plant—and sugarcane plantations were thriving throughout the area by the 1860s.

Richmond had some now-famous residents, among them Mirabeau Lamar, Deaf Smith, and Jane Long. Carrie Nation ran a hotel on the corner of Fourth and Morton streets before she took up her crusade against demon rum.

Visitors today find several reminders of Richmond's colonial past, but the overriding feeling is that of small-town America, circa 1920. Somehow it is reassuring to discover a corner drugstore and a five-and-dime within the shadow of an old-fashioned courthouse. A walk along Richmond's main drag, Morton Street, is a visual antidote to Houston's skyscrapers.

A detailed map guides you along the oak-shaded streets to all the historic sites, courtesy of the Fort Bend County Museum. The maps are available at the museum (see "What to Do" section) or from the Richmond-Rosenberg Chamber of Commerce, 4120 Avenue H, Rosenberg 77471, (713) 342–5464. A strong Czech population leads to the annual Czech Fest on the first weekend of May at the Fort Bend County Fairgrounds. The Fort Bend County Fair again livens things up in early October.

WHAT TO DO

The A. P. George Ranch. 10215 FM–762, 8 miles southeast of Richmond on FM–762. What was life like in rural Texas between 1890 and 1930? This 470-acre living history project (part of a 23,000-acre working ranch) turns back the years and lets you participate as well. Costumed actors recreate Victorian life at the J. H. P. Davis home (1880s) and more modern times at the George ranch house (1930s); cowboys rope and ride; ranch hands demonstrate cattle-dipping, blacksmithing, woodworking, etc.; and horse-drawn carryalls haul you around the grounds. Nearly every weekend between

Memorial Day and Labor Day has a special theme, plus the George Ranch Summer Theater puts on plays in the Old Lodge Hall. Don't miss Texian Market Day the last weekend of October. Special events such as rodeos and trail rides can be arranged year-round for corporate meetings, conventions, and private groups. Open Wednesday–Sunday in summer, weekends in May, September, and October (fee). (713) 545–9212 or 343–0218.

Brazos Bend State Park. On FM–762 (Tadpole Road), 20 miles south of Richmond. One of the newest parks in the system, this is a wild beauty along Big Creek, a tributary of the Brazos. Overnight facilities include screened shelters, trailer sites with hookups, tent sites with water, and primitive sites with no water that require a hike in; almost all are shaded by massive oaks. In addition to two large fishing piers where you can angle for bass, catfish, or crappie, there are hiking and nature trails, several large playing fields, seven photography platforms for focusing on the park's exceptional wildlife, and an interpretive center. Caution: This is alligator country, and no one may enter any of the park waters for any reason. All visitors are given a guide to alligator etiquette when they arrive. Fee. Park information: (409) 553–3243 or (800) 792–1112.

The George Observatory, a satellite facility of the Houston Museum of Natural Science, is also in the park. General public viewing through the large telescope is limited to Saturday evenings, and passes are required. The planetarium opens at 3 p.m. Saturday, and the free viewing passes are given out on a first-come, first-served basis at 5 p.m. Be there by 3:30, however, when the "pass" line begins to form, or you will be doomed to disappointment. No pass? Console yourself with a look through the smaller telescopes set up on the planetarium's top deck. For information on the George Planetarium, call (713) 242–3005 or 639–4634.

Christmas Tree Farms. You can cut your own tannenbaum at Vacek Christmas Tree Farm near East Bernard, (409) 335–6386; and at Orchard Farms near Orchard, (409) 478–6204.

The Confederate Museum at Old South Plantation. On FM–359, approximately 5 miles north of Richmond. The South may rise again. This miniature Tara houses a collection of muskets, rifles, guns, uniforms, furniture, pictures, money, letters, and other memorabilia relating to the Civil War. Open Tuesday, Thursday, Saturday, and Sunday, or by special arrangement. Donation. (713) 342–8787.

Decker Park. North of the railroad tracks at Sixth and Preston streets. The three buildings moved here mark the very slow beginning of a living history museum: a 1902 railroad depot, a log-cabin replica of the 1822 fort, and the 1850s McNabb House, once owned by Carrie Nation's daughter. The Victorian brick relic across Preston Avenue was the county jail from 1896 to 1948.

The Fort Bend County Courthouse. Fourth and Jackson streets. This fifth courthouse was built with an air of majesty in 1908 and was so well refurbished in 1981 that it was cited by the Houston chapter of the American Institute of Architects. It is also the only public building in Fort Bend County listed in the National Register of Historic Places. Its more notable features are the three-story rotunda, the mosaic tile floors, and the rich woodwork on the stairs and in the main courtroom. Free. Open Monday–Friday.

Fort Bend Museum. Fifth and Houston streets. Just about every aspect of area history is covered here with displays including items or manuscripts of Mirabeau Lamar, Jane Long, and Austin's first colony. One diorama tells the harrowing tale of early railroad crossings on the Brazos, and special exhibits include the hatchet Carrie Nation used on a Houston saloon in 1905. A clapboard house that stood on property owned by Jane Long from 1837 to 1859 stands next to the museum and is open for special exhibits.

The museum staff also gives demonstrations of frontier skills and guides historical tours of Richmond by advance arrangement. Closed Monday. (713) 342–6478.

Imperial Sugar Co. 198 Kempner Street, Sugar Land. From US–90A, turn north on Kempner. On the site of the S. M. Williams plantation established in the 1840s, this modern plant gives visitors a look at cane sugar from the raw product to final packaging. The free tours are interesting; reservations are not necessary except for groups. Open Monday–Friday. (713) 491–9181.

John H. Moore House. Fifth and Liberty streets. Built in 1883 on what is now the present museum grounds, this gracious old home with its turn-of-the-century furnishings is a mini-museum in itself. Fee. Open only for guided tours on Sunday afternoon. (713) 342–6478.

McFarland House. On Jackson Street, in front of the courthouse. Beautifully restored, this 1880s Victorian cottage has some antique furnishings, an interesting past, and a ghost. Tours are handled by the volunteer McFarland House Committee. To visit, call Richmond's city secretary, (713) 342–5456, for name and telephone number of current tour manager.

Morton Cemetery. On Second Street, north of Jackson. Used during the 1838–41 period, this is the last resting place of Mirabeau Lamar and the "Mother of Texas," Jane Long.

WHERE TO EAT

Brazos Bottom Inn. 7010 FM–762. This country cafe is an ideal place to stop for tasty vittles en route to either the George Ranch or Brazos Bend State Park. House specialties include seafood and hand-cut steaks, but the luncheon salads and burgers are great also. Save room for the "really homemade" desserts, particularly the Brazos Bottom Pie. They count the calories in this chocolate mousse/cream cheese/whipped cream beauty so you won't have to. Open for lunch and dinner, Sunday–Friday, dinner only on Saturday. $–$$; (CC). (713) 341–5210.

Quail Hollow Inn. 214 Morton Street, Richmond. When Swiss chef Karl Camenzind takes on the likes of beef Wellington, wiener schnitzel, or sweetbreads in marsala wine cream sauce, it's worth the trip from Houston just to sample the results. Chocoholics line up for his Chocolate Sin torte. This former hotel chef is picky about the seafood he uses—it has to be very fresh—and all steaks are topped with a garlic herb butter that will spoil you for anything else. There's also a wild game menu; quail comes four ways here, even in a nest of chestnut puree. Now for the surprise: Prices are well under those charged for similar multicourse meals in metro Houston. The ambience isn't bad either, a 100-year-old building furnished with a smattering of antiques on Richmond's quiet main street. The big question is whether there are enough true "foodies" in Houston to keep this quality, out-of-the-way place going. Open for lunch and dinner Tuesday–Saturday; brunch on Sunday. $–$$$; (CC). (713) 341–6733.

WANDERING THE BACKROADS

An alternate route from Houston to Richmond forsakes US–59 and US–90A and instead rambles west on Westheimer (FM–1093) past its intersection with T–6. At Clodine, turn south (left) on FM–1464 for about 10 miles and then west (right) on US–90A into Richmond. For restaurants on this route, see Day Trip 1, West Sector.

Another country ramble takes the long way home. From Richmond, turn south on FM–762 (Eleventh Street/Thompson Road) and follow its zigzag southeasterly course through the countryside. Just beyond Crabb, FM–762 turns further south as the A. P. George Road (sign also will read FM–1994). Stay on FM–762 as it jogs onto Tadpole Road. At the intersection with FM–1462 at Woodrow, turn east (left) to intersect T–288 and then north (left) toward home and Houston.

NORTHEAST

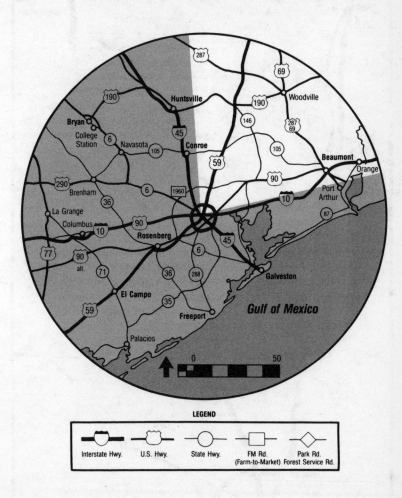

LEGEND

| Interstate Hwy. | U.S. Hwy. | State Hwy. | FM Rd. (Farm-to-Market) | Park Rd. Forest Service Rd. |

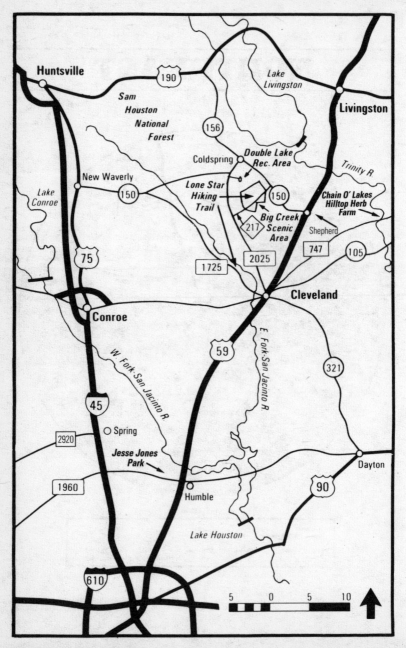

Northeast: Day Trip 1

Day Trip 1

HUMBLE
CLEVELAND
COLDSPRING

HUMBLE

Like the small town of Spring in north Harris County, there are two Humbles—old and new. The new is easy to find, a plastic forest of franchise signs and shopping centers around the US–59 north/FM–1960 interchange. Old Humble lies quietly behind, east of the railroad tracks and south of FM–1960.

Back in 1865, a fisherman named Pleasant Smith Humble established a small ferry across the San Jacinto River close to where US–59 crosses it today. Things remained quiet until the railroad came to town in 1878, and Humble became a flag stop on the narrow-gauge HE & WT line, running between Houston and Shepherd. Settlers came, and by 1886 it was officially a town.

Rich with timber, Humble fed a growing logging industry. Back in 1887, a local lumberman, Jim H. Slaughter, rafted logs down the San Jacinto for milling. Pulling into a small backwater to make an overnight camp, he noticed bubbles seeping along the river bank. When his match brought a flame, he rightly concluded the presence of natural gas and subsequently bought 60 acres of land in the area. Although he personally didn't profit greatly, this was the beginning of the oil fields in Humble and Harris County.

The first wells came into production in 1904, and by mid–1905 the field was producing more barrels per day than any other in the state. The Moonshine Hill area east of town soon had a population of 25,000, and Humble got busy earning its reputation as one of the toughest towns in Texas. The Texas Rangers often had to be called on to keep some semblance of law and order.

In 1909, the Humble Oil and Refining Company was formed in a small, tin-roofed building on Humble's Main Street, one of its organizers being the local feed store owner, Ross Sterling. The company was successful and ultimately became part of the Exxon we know today. Sterling didn't do too badly either. Previously the owner of a chain of feed stores, he soon bought the Humble State Bank and carved a niche in the state's history as a newpaper publisher, oil man, and governor of Texas from 1931 to 33.

As quickly as it had come, the oil boom disappeared—no new wells were coming in—and by 1915 Humble once again was a small, quiet community strongly dependent on lumber and agriculture for its financial base. Then a second oil strike at greater depth in 1929 brought new life, and Humble was chartered as a city in 1933. Visitors today can tour the still-working oil field (look for the Moonshine Hill Loop sign 2 miles east of town on FM–1960). This stretch of road between Humble and Moonshine Hill was the first concrete road in Harris County.

Humble's Main Street now is a stroll through small-town Americana. An antique store or two and other less glamorous small businesses thrive here because rents are relatively low. A renewed interest in preserving Humble's past keeps things moderately spiffed up. Stop for a moment at the corner of FM–1960 and North Houston Avenue to see the oldest artesian well in the area, drilled as a wildcat oil venture in 1912. For additional information on the area, contact the Humble Chamber of Commerce, P.O. Box 3337, Humble 77347. (713) 446–2128.

WHAT TO DO

Humble Historical Museum. 110 West Main Street, next to City Hall. A grassroots result of the Bicentennial, this small museum is bursting with a collection of old things donated by local residents. Open Tuesday–Saturday. Free; donations appreciated. (713) 446–9881.

Jesse H. Jones Park. 20634 Kenswick Drive. From US–59 north, go west 1.7 miles on FM–1960 and turn right on Kenswick Drive; the park is at the end of the road. This large wilderness preserve on Cypress Creek has ten hiking trails, a playground and picnic area, and a three-acre beach on the creek for fishing (no swimming); with a Texas fishing license you can angle for white bass, crappie, catfish, and alligator gar. Nature photography is popular here, as are birding and canoeing. About 85 percent of the trails are black-topped for use by the handicapped. Birders can pick up a list at the Nature Center Building which also has wildlife exhibits, including common poisonous snakes and a cutaway look at a working beehive. This park is the take-out for an 8-mile, five-hour canoe float from Mercer Arboretum, upstream. Free and open daily except major holidays. (713) 446–8588.

Lake Houston. The best play areas (picnicking, swimming, boating) are Dwight D. Eisenhower Park and Alexander Duessen Park, both near the dam. Take the Duessen Drive exit from the Sam Houston Tollway and follow signs.

Old McDonald's Farm. FM–1960 east bypass. Under development. Call (713) 446–2128.

SafariLand of Texas. 231 McClellan Road, Kingwood. Exotic animals from many parts of the world come almost within reach at this wildlife ranch. You tour by tram and feed many of the animals by hand. Open daily April–September; closed on Monday, October–March. Call for directions. Fee. (713) 359–1946.

World Kaleidoscope. In Deerbrook Mall; use the Casa Ole entrance. Want to impress on your children that we have to take care of our world? This unique educational museum brings conservation and recycling down to kid-play level. (713) 441–2628.

WHERE TO EAT

Chez Nous. 217 South Avenue G, South Humble. In addition to a menu that features many French classics, chef/owner Gerard Brach and his wife Sandra offer outstanding daily specials such as fresh Dover sole or swordfish in an avocado/lime butter or pineapple salsa. French-born and trained, Gerard also has taught a wine course at the Four Seasons in NYC, an expertise that is evident from the wine list. This jewel of a restaurant is in an unlikely setting, a 100-year-old church. You'll want to dress up for this dining experience. Like Quail Hollow Inn in Richmond, this restaurant is worth a trip to Humble in itself if you enjoy fine food prepared with skill and care. Open Monday–Saturday for dinner; reservations strongly advised. Ask for specific directions when you call; it's hard to find. $$–$$$; (CC). (713) 446–6717.

Mama Hattie's. 217 FM–1960 east bypass. When this Irish pub-style place opened, its quarter-pounders blew a few hamburger chains out of town. Hoorah for the little guy. Expect English and Irish beers and ales, and a dart board on the wall. Open for lunch and dinner Monday–Saturday. $. (713) 446–6785.

Menciu's Gourmet Hunan. 1379 Kingwood Drive, in Kingwood development north of Humble via US–59. Popular with local residents, this family-run place uses only fresh foods to prepare its tasty dishes. The lunch specials are excellent values. Open for lunch and dinner Monday–Saturday, dinner nightly. $–$$; (CC). (713) 359–8489.

The Outback. 9753 FM–1960 bypass. G'day, Mate, and welcome to this Australian-theme steakhouse. The steaks on this giant barbie are prime and choice grain-fed beef, the chickens have never seen a freezer, and everything else is made from scratch, on-site. Is an

Aussie beer really better than a long-neck? Are Australian wines different from their Texas cousins? Find out for yourself here. Open for dinner nightly. $$–$$$; (CC). (713) 446–4329.

Two Cooks. 502 Staitti Street, at corner of D Street in Humble. The catering ladies at this serve-yourself eatery fix one entree each day, complete with green salad, fruit, roll, and your choice of dessert and beverage. The porch of this eighty-year-old home is delightful in nice weather. Open Tuesday–Friday, lunch only. $. (713) 446–1005.

To continue this day trip, go north on US–59 to Cleveland.

CLEVELAND

Back in the 1880s this railroad town on US–59 north of Houston thrived with lumber shipping. Now it is better known as the main gateway to the forest and water wonderland that covers most of San Jacinto County. Entrances to the Lone Star Hiking Trail are marked on FM–1725 and FM–945 near Cleveland, and the local Chamber of Commerce has a brochure listing activities in the area: Box 1733, Cleveland 77327; (713) 592–8786. A Discover Cleveland Fest is held downtown the first Saturday night of every month. If you come in early summer, consider picking a year's supply of blueberries at Clear Water Berry Farm, (713) 592–4351.

WHAT TO DO

Big Creek Scenic Area. This 1,130-acre preserve has numerous hiking trails, wild and varied topography, spring-fed creeks, and abundant wildlife. Part of the 350,000-acre Big Thicket that spatters across vast portions of southeast Texas, Big Creek claims the state champion magnolia tree. The Lone Star Hiking Trail begins near Montague Church on FM–1725 and loops through the scenic area. From Cleveland, continue on US–59 north 12 miles to Shepherd, then west on T–150 for 6 miles to Forest Service Road 217. Information: San Jacinto District Office, Sam Houston National Forest, 407 North Belcher Street, Cleveland 77327; (713) 592–6462.

Big Thicket Downs. From US–59, turn right at the second traffic light in Cleveland, then left on FM–787 east and go 15.2 miles; this brush track will be on your right. What's a brush track? It's 80,000 yards of top soil hauled from Trinity River bottomlands and spread around a half-mile oval carved from the east Texas woods. A training track for young thoroughbreds and quarterhorses from a four-state area, Big Thicket Downs is organized racing at its most elementary level (no pari-mutuel). There's an electric starting gate and timer and between ten and twenty horseraces every Sunday (year-round if entry numbers permit). You can walk through the stables, the horses are close enough to touch during the post parade, and the jockey club is a picnic table under the trees. No matter when you come, you'll find stables full of horses and training sessions going on. Saturdays are good-time play days when local folks race their horses and parade them around for sale. If you are thinking of buying a horse, this is a good place to comparison-shop. At this writing, this is the only racetrack open to the public in the Houston area, and it's fun. But come prepared; if it has been raining, the track and parking lot will be muddy, and if it hasn't been raining, they'll be dusty. Folding chairs come in handy. The snack bar can wet your whistle, plus it serves some of the best hamburgers in the region. Fee. (713) 592–8087 or 692–5509 (evenings).

Chain-O-Lakes Resort and Conference Center. Eighteen miles east of Cleveland, between T–787 and T–146 on the Daniel Ranch Road. Adjacent to the Daniel Ranch (which was colonized in 1818 and was the first Anglo settlement in Texas), this long-time campground has grown into a quality family resort strongly oriented toward day visitors. There are 130 acres of lakes, all stocked and interconnected, and no fishing license is required. Come ready for some serious angling; eight-pound bass are caught every summer. You can either bring your own boat or rent one of theirs, and the bank fishing is good too, particularly if you angle with purple plastic worms. You are welcome to bring bicycles and ride the roads through the woods (they also rent golf carts), plus there's a two-and-a-half-acre artesian-fed swimming lake with diving platforms and a kiddie area. The Rampage, a 40-foot-long water coaster, splashes into another pool, and its additional all-day fee ($3) includes the use of a plastic raft. There are horse-drawn carriage rides, horseback trail rides, and hayrides. The outdoor ROPES course provides a team-building experience for corporate types on executive retreat. In addition to standard hook-up and wilderness campsites, owners Jim and Beverly Smith have built fourteen new and well-designed log cabins that are furnished with antiques and sleep from two to ten people. Open daily, year-round. Bonus: The Smith's Hilltop Herb Farm is adjacent (see "Where to Eat," below). (713) 592–2150 or 592–7705.

Christmas Tree Farms. Call for directions to the following: Fairchild's Home-grown Christmas Trees, (409) 298–2941, and Triple "J" Christmas Tree Farm, (713) 593–1578.

Clark's Limited Editions. On FM–1725, 11.2 miles north of T–105, east of Cleveland. If you call in advance, Mrs. Molly Clark will be pleased to show you her outstanding collection of miniature horses. Standing less than 34 inches in height, they take only one or two cups of food per feeding and are very gentle; but they cannot be ridden, of course. Visitors are allowed to mingle with the animals in their pens, so bring your camera. Two of the Clark's miniatures qualified for the 1987 National Championships. (713) 443–8645 (direct Houston line) or (713) 592–1648.

Double Lake Recreation Area. On FM–2025, 15 miles north of Cleveland. This twenty-five-acre lake is edged by picnic and camping areas and has a beach and a bathhouse with showers. No motorboats are allowed, but you can paddle your own canoe here, if you want. Information: See **Big Creek Scenic Area** listing, above.

Ronald Sweeten Studios. Local artist Ronald Sweeten has expanded from taxidermy to western and wildlife bronzes, cast by the lost-wax technique. His work is in numerous collections, and visitors are welcome at his gallery and foundry on US–59, 1 mile north of Cleveland. Open Monday–Saturday; call for directions. (CC). (713) 592–5661.

WHERE TO EAT

Boyett's Restaurant. 1002 South Washington Street (US–59). Homecooked Texas standards fill the platters here, and the cinnamon rolls have been named the best in the state by *Texas Monthly.* Open daily for breakfast, lunch, and dinner. $–$$; (CC). (713) 592–2601.

Hilltop Herb Farm. Eighteen miles east of Cleveland, between FM–787 and TX–146 on the Daniel Ranch Road at Chain-O-Lakes Resort and Campground. The best of what was the Hilltop Herb Farm eatery west of Cleveland has jumped to larger quarters east of town, and creator Madalene Hill's original format and unique recipes for a series of five-course table d'hôte meals based on the creative use of fresh herbs have survived the move in grand style. Now owned and operated by Jim and Beverly Smith of Chain-O-Lakes Resort and Conference Center, this famed restaurant is open to groups daily by prearrangement and to individuals by reservation only for Saturday night dinner (ask about menu when you call) and Sunday buffet (more than thirty selections). Dining here includes walks through the indoor and outdoor greenhouses, the herb garden, and store. Almost everyone ends up buying some mint-touched Tranquilitea mix for home. $$–$$$; (CC). (713) 592–5859.

Jo Anna's Italian Restaurant. 211 North College Street, Cleveland. Many locals think this is the best Italian restaurant in the region because everything—from the lasagna and Italian salad to the heavily loaded pizzas—is made on-site from fresh ingredients. Open for lunch and dinner, Monday–Saturday. $–$$; (CC). (713) 592–4587.

WANDERING THE BACKROADS

Continuing on to Coldspring is a day-tripper's delight. From Cleveland, take FM–2025 north for 17 miles, then go east on T–150 another 2 miles. This takes you through a major portion of the Sam Houston National Forest. An alternate route leaves US–59 north at Shepard and follows T–150 west 11 miles to Coldspring.

An 8-mile jaunt southeast of Cleveland on T–321 toward Dayton will bring you to Well's Store, formerly the gathering place for the Tarkington Prairie community and a stage stop on the old Lynchburg-Nacogdoches Road. The center portion of this old mercantile store was built in 1875, and the grounds are used for an antique fair in the spring.

COLDSPRING

This old community (pop. 569) was called Coonskin when it was founded in 1847. Now the San Jacinto County seat, it is showing signs of life as a budding tourist center. Most of the structures on Main Street were built between 1916 and 1923. There are numerous historical markers in Coldspring, including one on the United Methodist Church (1848), one of the oldest Methodist churches in Texas. A good time to come is the fourth Saturday of every month from March to November, the popular Trades Day for arts, crafts, and antiques, (409) 653–2184.

WHAT TO DO

Christmas Tree Farms. This is good Christmas tree cutting country in November and December; call the following for directions: Iron Creek Christmas Tree Farm, (409) 767–4541; D-Bar-D Christmas Tree Farm, (409) 628–3114.

Old Town Heritage Center. Coldspring's original Courthouse Square now is home to a small but interesting museum in the old 1880s jail and the transplanted Waverly Schoolhouse, circa 1926.

Other memorabilia are scattered around the grounds, including an old Ford fire engine and the replica of a blacksmith shop. Museum is open Thursday–Saturday or by appointment (409) 653–2009.

WHERE TO EAT

County Seat Restaurant. One block from Courthouse Square at the end of Slade Street. Famous for its fried catfish, fried pickles, and hot water corn bread, this rustic place is under new ownership that also emphasizes fresh *everything* prepared in a variety of ways. Expect thick steaks, homemade hamburgers, a variety of chicken dishes, and fresh-fruit cobblers better than Mom ever fixed. Drinks are served in mason jars, and if you are a Houston-area celebrity, they retire your jar—a "Doug Johnson and Ron Stone drank here" sort of display. The huge live oak justifiably known as the "old hanging tree" shades all; an outdoor patio is planned. Open for lunch and dinner, Tuesday–Saturday. $–$$; (CC). (409) 653–4001.

    Miracle Mile Inn. On the right, 8 miles north toward Lake Livingston on T–156. A favorite eating spot for Lake Livingston regulars, this simple place is known for outstanding fried catfish and chicken-fried steak. Expect the East Texas cafe basics: red-and-white checked oilcloth on the tables, plastic-covered menus, and a friendly staff. Lunch and dinner, Thursday–through Sunday. $. (409) 377–4966.

WANDERING THE BACKROADS

From Coldspring you can continue west on T–150 and connect with I–45 at New Waverly (Trip 2, Northwest Sector). From there, turn north (right) on I–45 to Huntsville and Madisonville. If it's time to go home, head south on I–45; from New Waverly, it's 55 miles to the Houston city limits.

    An alternate: If you want to visit the Lake Livingston area (Trip 2, this sector) from Coldspring, take T–156 north to its intersection with US–190 and turn east. From Livingston, take US–59 south to home.

Day Trip 2

LIVINGSTON
WOODVILLE

LIVINGSTON

A fire wiped out three downtown blocks around the turn of the century, so little is left of Livingston's beginnings back in 1846. The seat of Polk County, this timber town 76 miles north of the heart of Houston via US–59 is important to day-trippers in several ways.

Every fall, the forest around Livingston resembles the rolling hills of western Massachusetts when the frosts bring up the color in the maple, sassafras, oak, sweet gum, sumac, and hickory trees. One of the town's biggest attractions is Lake Livingston, 15 miles west of downtown. The 90,000-acre lake is essentially an impoundment of the Trinity River, and there are three short but beautiful river-float trips possible below the dam. Access for canoes is at the dam: from the US–59 crossing south of Livingston and from FM–105 near Romayor. The final take-out is at the FM–162 crossing east of Cleveland.

All of Polk County is crossed with old Indian traces, the remains of which are noted on highway signs. The trails no longer exist, but each is marked in several places. For information on Lake Livingston or the area in general, contact the Polk County Chamber of Commerce, 516 West Church Street, Livingston, 77351. (409) 327–4929.

WHAT TO DO

Alabama-Coushatta Indian Reservation. On US–190, 17 miles east of Livingston. Established by Sam Houston in 1854, this 4,600-acre reservation in the Big Thicket is struggling with the economy and both the state and federal governments. Some of their legal battles now are behind them, and the future looks promising. At present, however, visitors find a well-executed camping/recreation/tourist complex that doesn't quite achieve its potential.

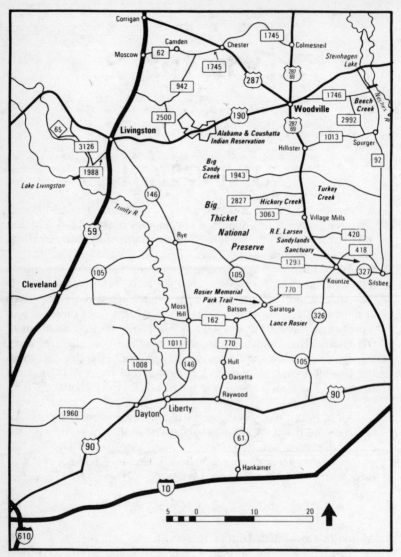

Northeast: Day Trips 2 and 3

Start at the museum for some historical background, and then tour the Big Thicket forest by either the Indian Chief train or open bus. Except for a trail, this is the only public access to the Big Sandy Creek unit of the Big Thicket National Preserve. More than 100 species of trees are native to this reservation, including eight varieties of oak, the state champion water hickory and laurel oak trees, and a huge 200-year-old magnolia. The tours go through virgin forest, and you may surprise an alligator or two in the swamp regions. (Fee).

There's also a historical museum, the Inn of the Twelve Clans restaurant, and an Indian village replica where tribal members do a good job of demonstrating early housing, crafts, and foods. Tribal dances representing war, courtship, harvest, and tribute are performed daily in summer, on weekends the rest of the year. (Fee).

One place the Alabama-Coushatta truly shine is in their beautiful baskets, woven from the rare long-leaf pine. Many have lids and are shaped like animals, and all are considered collector's items. A few are usually for sale in the village store, and some rare oldies are displayed in the Polk County Museum in Livingston.

Slightly removed from the central complex is twenty-six-acre Lake Tombigbee, nice for quiet camping, picnicking, and swimming. Canoeing and fishing for bass, perch, and catfish also are popular. The reservation is open daily in summer and Friday–Sunday in spring and fall; it is closed December–February. Information: Route 3, Box 640, Livingston 77351. (409) 563–4391 or (800) 444–3507.

Blueberry Farms. You can pick an annual supply at reasonable cost at either Smith Sandy Foot Farm, (409) 327–2744, or Hamilton's Berry Farm, (409) 563–4910.

Christmas Tree Farms. Call the following for directions: Cockrell's, (409) 632–2905, and Goosby's Christmas Tree Farm, (409) 646–3450.

Colquitt's Syrup Mill. From Livingston, continue north 9 miles on US–59, then go east (right) on FM–942 for approximately 15 miles. Turn right on a dirt road just before Beard's Cemetery and swing right again at the first fork to find one of the few old-fashioned sugar cane mills left in East Texas. Just stop at the first house on your left and knock on the door. Mr. and Mrs. Colquitt, the owners, will be glad to show you the small mill out back.

The crushers in this old mill are more than 100 years old and still going strong, driven by a belt from a tractor motor. The juice is sluiced off into long open pans and boiled down into syrup, a simple, time-honored process.

The crushing season starts about the second week in November and lasts as long as the cane does or until a hard freeze hits. The mill often runs full-tilt seven days a week until Christmas, so November and December are prime times to visit here. You can watch, sample a bit and buy some cans of the moderately priced light and tasty syrup. Some folks come just to buy the raw juice as basis for their own home brew.

The rest of the year the mill is abandoned to weeds and the elements, and there isn't much to see, although the Colquitts sell syrup until there isn't any left. If you want to check on the syrup supply or make sure the mill is in operation (a wise idea; sometimes there isn't much of a cane crop in these parts), give them a call at (409) 563–2340, or check with the Polk County Chamber of Commerce (weekdays only), (409) 327–4929.

Johnson's Rock Shop. Ten miles east of Livingston off US–190 in the Indian Springs Lakes Estates; call for directions. You'll see more than 1.5 million pounds of rock, and just about that many varieties, plus the equipment used to cut, polish, and finish it. Visitors are welcome, and there's no fee for a personal tour. Open daily. (409) 563–4438.

Lake Livingston. From Livingston, take US–59 south 2.5 miles and turn west on FM–1988, then north on FM–3126 to Park Road 65. There is good public access at Lake Livingston State Park. Facilities include a swimming pool, boat rental, activity center, hiking and biking trails, picnic areas, campsites, and screened shelters. Numerous private resorts, marinas, and campgrounds along this route offer fishing guides and rent boats. Information: Route 9, Box 1300, Livingston 77351. (409) 365–2201.

Polk County Museum. 601 West Church, in the Murphy Memorial Library. Exhibits focus on the early days of Polk County, plus there are some interesting Indian artifacts. Note the old Jonas Davis log cabin across the street. Donation. Open Monday–Friday. (409) 327–8192.

WHERE TO EAT

Catfish Bill's. On north side of US–190, 2 miles west of the US–59 bypass. This mom-and-pop place is locally loved for its catfish and loaded buffet. Open through dinner, Wednesday–Saturday; Sunday until 4. $; (CC). (409) 967–8134.

Shrimp Boat Manny's. 1324 West Church, Livington, one block east of the US–59 bypass. Formerly Rachal's ("Ra-shallz"), this unassuming place specializes in seafood prepared Cajun-style. Manny and Nancy Rachal are from Lafayette in "Luziana" and serve a mean étouffée, boiled and fried shrimp, raw and fried oysters, and seafood gumbo. Open Monday–Saturday, $–$$. (409) 327–0100.

Southland Park Restaurant. Four and a half miles west on FM–1988, at the base of the dam. In addition to a grand view of the lake and the dam, locals say this popular place serves the best catfish "you ever put your lips around." The rest of the menu is equally good, and includes choice steaks, chicken, and a variety of seafood. Open daily for lunch and dinner. $–$$; (CC). (409) 365–2063.

This day trip continues through the forest to Woodville, 33 miles northeast of Livingston via US–190.

WOODVILLE

Although history has been relatively quiet here, the town has some surprises in store for those who take the time to poke around. Not only are there twenty-one historical markers in the area—the entire town is a bird sanctuary and serves as the northern gateway to the Big Thicket.

Founded in 1846-47 as the seat of the newly created Tyler County, Woodville is aptly named because it is surrounded by miles of rolling forest. The best times to go are late March and early April when the Tyler County Dogwood Festival stirs things up a bit, or in the fall, after the first cold snap coats the woods with some of the prettiest colors in the state. Brochures, maps, and updates on the current status of spring and fall scenery are available from the Tyler County Chamber of Commerce, 201 North Magnolia Street, Woodville 75979, (409) 283–2632. The office is inside the Woodville Inn, and brochures about area attractions are available after hours. Weekday mornings are the best time to call.

The courthouse in the heart of town is no longer the distinctive architectural showplace it was when built in 1891 for the grand sum of $21,609. An ill-advised remodeling in the 1930s stole its baroque charm and reduced it to the mundane and functional. Visitors today find the antique shops and ice-cream parlor across the street far more interesting.

WHAT TO DO

Alan Shivers Library and Museum. 303 North Charlton, 2 blocks north of the courthouse. The late Governor Alan Shivers had his roots in Woodville, and this restored Victorian showplace houses his papers as well as memorabilia of the Shivers family and the town. Fee. Open Monday–Saturday, Sunday by appointment. (409) 283–3709.

Big Thicket Information. The north district office of the Big Thicket National Preserve is at 507 North Pine, in Woodville. Open Monday–Friday. (409) 283–5824.

Blueberry Farms. June and July are prime picking months at Ling's Farm, (409) 837–2263 or 283–2664; Mott's Blueberry Farm, (409) 429–3196; and Wilbank's Farm, (409) 969–2507.

Christmas Tree Farms. Call for directions to the following choose-and-cut operations: Tom and Ruth Drawhorn, (409) 429–3277; Twin Lake Estate, (409) 429–3406; Hudson's Christmas Tree Farm, (409) 429–3486; Wright Christmas Trees, (409) 429–5293; and Currie's Christmas Tree Farm, (409) 283–2422.

Dogwood Trail. This 1.5-mile trail along Theuvenin Creek is maintained by the International Paper Company. Watch for their sign 3 miles east of Woodville on US–190.

Heritage Village. Two miles west of Woodville on US–190. Never underestimate the power of women with a mission. In 1987, when it looked like Woodville's best-known tourist attraction might either close or move, the ladies of the Tyler County Heritage Society turned local pockets inside out to raise the money to buy the property and its restaurant. Now what was a weathering conglomeration of early Americana is an outstanding open-air museum devoted to Texas history in general, and specifically to Tyler County and the Big Thicket territory. Visitors walk among a number of homely historic structures filled with artifacts of early pioneer life (barbershop, blacksmith shop, syrup mill, whiskey still, pawnshop, apothecary, newspaper, etc.). Docents in historical dress provide commentary, a smithy works the forge, and artists demonstrate their skills among the refurbished buildings. Walkers note: Eleven and a half acres of neighboring woodlands are threaded with trails. The heritage society also owns and operates the Pickett House restaurant (see "Where to Eat"), and the gift shop specializes in East Texas handcrafts and art. Want a quilt or pine-needle basket? How about an inlaid domino set? This is the place. Open daily except December 24-25. Fee. (409) 283–2272.

James Edward Wheat House. At the corner of Charlton and Wheat streets. One portion of this house was built in 1848. It is a private residence, but you are welcome to enjoy the exterior.

Jones Country Music Park. On Route 255, north of Colmesneil (watch for signs). Country and western star George Jones was born in nearby Saratoga and returned to his native piney woods to develop this project. His home is on the property, and when he isn't singing in Nashville or on the road, this is where he lives. The project includes the Possom Holler Club (see "Where to Eat"), a ballroom that swings with live music on weekends, and a large outdoor stage, where some of the nation's top C&W names perform on Labor Day, Memorial Day, and the Fourth of July. Loretta Lynn, Mel Tillis, Merle Haggard, Willie Nelson—that's the caliber of those holiday shows. There's also a store, playground, RV park, and picnic tables on-site. Tickets are available at the gate (no credit cards). For camping, program, and advance ticket information, contact P.O. Box 730, Ducette 75942. (409) 837–5463 or 837–5544.

Lake Tejas. Eleven miles north of Woodville via US–69, then east 1 mile on FM–256. When summer's heat hits this neck of the woods, this super swimming hole is the place to be. Operated by the local school district, the lake is open on May weekends and daily from June to Labor Day. This sand-bottom lake boasts a two-level diving platform, sundecks over the water, lifeguards, bathhouse, and both picnicking and camping (year-round). Fee. (409) 837–5201 or 837–2225 weekdays.

Martin Dies, Jr., State Park. On Steinhagen Lake, 14 miles east of Woodville on US–190. The usual water activities, such as fishing, picnicking, and camping, are here. For information, contact Route 4, Box 274, Jasper 75951. (409) 384–5231.

The Peanut Factory. 307 West Bluff (US–190). The mesquite craze has hit even peanut butter. You can sample five flavors of this all-American favorite here, from unique mesquite to savory cinnamon and salt-free. This enterprising firm also roasts, seasons, and packages peanuts; plus you can watch the factory at work if you make arrangements in advance. Five flavors of peanuts can be bought in sizes ranging from a tiny bag to a two-and-a-half-pound tub. Open weekdays only. (CC). (409) 283–2495.

River Floating. Steinhagen Lake, east of Woodville on US–190, also is known as Dam B, an impounding of the Neches River. If you are interested in floating the Neches below the dam, call the U.S. Army Corps of Engineers at Steinhagen Lake (409–429–3491) to find out whether the river is floatable.

WHERE TO EAT

The Homestead Restaurant. In Hillister; take US–69/287 south 8 miles from Woodville, go east for 1 block on FM–1013, and then turn right just before the railroad tracks. Don't worry—there are signs, and this restaurant is worth searching for. Two refugees from Houston, Emily and Otho Sumner, offer country dining with a gourmet touch in a spacious old home they have restored. Built around 1912 in nearby

Hillister, the house was moved by the Sumners to its present shady thirteen-acre site and fixed up with charm—including rockers and a swing on the porch. In addition to some nice touches on the standard fish, steak, and chicken offerings, most of the veggies are grown out back, and they make their own salad dressings. Every entree is prepared to order, and because Emily Sumner is a pie freak, the cook goes crazy with an ever-changing selection such as tollhouse, coconut cream, buttermilk pecan, chocolate gold brick, pumpkin/ginger snap, or Japanese fruit pies. While reservations are not absolutely essential, they are strongly advised, particularly if you want to sit in a room cleverly adorned with vintage clothing. No liquor is served, but glasses and ice buckets are provided for those who wish to bring their own wine. Open for dinner Thursday–Saturday, lunch only on Sunday. $–$$. And if you feel like spending the night, the Sumners also have a fully equipped guest retreat on the banks of Theuvinen Creek, 6 miles from their restaurant. Available to nonsmoking adults only, this two-bedroom house has a fireplace, a screened porch, and a great fishing hole in bass territory. (409) 283–7324.

Pickett House. Two miles west on US–190, behind Heritage Village. This old schoolhouse has been converted into an all-you-can-stuff-in kind of place, with bright circus posters on the walls and chicken and dumplings in the pot. The menu also offers fried chicken, but no hamburgers, steaks, etc., are served. These boarding house-style meals also include your choice of fresh buttermilk or real made-from-scratch ice tea, three vegetables, tomato relish, watermelon rind preserves, corn bread, hot biscuits, and fruit cobbler. You fetch your own drinks and then take your dirty dishes to the kitchen, just like home. Open daily for lunch and dinner March–August; September–February it's lunch only on weekdays, lunch and dinner on Saturday and Sunday. $–$$. (409) 283–3946.

Possom Holler Club. On Route 255, north of Colmesneil. Part of the Jones Country Music Park, this large rustic place specializes in steaks, catfish, shrimp, and hamburgers. C&W fans will love the memorabilia scene. Open daily in summer; usually Thursday–Sunday in winter (call in advance to be sure). $–$$; (CC). (409) 837–2256.

WANDERING THE BACKROADS

From Woodville, you can drive northwest on US–287 to the small community of Chester and make a 1.6-mile detour north on FM–2097 east to see Peach Tree Village, John Henry Kirby's community meetinghouse and chapel. Built in 1912 as a community hall by lumber magnate Kirby, it is under restoration by the Tyler County Historical Society. If it isn't open and you want to see inside, ask at the caretaker's house. The site is an old Alabama Indian headquarters camp called Ta Ku la, and two pioneer trails crossed here.

Another scenic drive takes you from Woodville to Saratoga and Big Thicket National Preserve (Trip 3, this sector). Take US–69/287 south from Woodville to Kountze, swing southwest on T–326, and turn right on FM–770 to Saratoga, in the heart of the Big Thicket. To continue home to Houston, follow FM–770 south to US–90 and turn west.

Although the wild azalea canyons near Newton are beyond the geographic scope of this book, they are well worth viewing during their pink and white blooming season which usually falls between the last week of March and first week of April. Tip your hat to the Temple Eastex Lumber Industries for preserving these beauties, and walk carefully—bird's-foot violets, cinnamon fern, and jack-in-the-pulpit wildflowers may be underfoot. Newton is 48 miles east/northeast from Woodville via US-190. For information, contact the Newton Chamber of Commerce, Drawer 66, Newton 75966. (409) 379–5527.

If you need a swifter return home from Woodville, retrace your route back to Livingston via US–190 and turn south on US–59.

Day Trip 3

LIBERTY and DAYTON
BIG THICKET

LIBERTY and DAYTON

Although this area, east of Houston on US–90, is rich with history, much of what survives remains privately owned, and the towns have little with which to illustrate their heritages to the general public. Take away the historical markers, and the casual tourist might conclude that nothing much ever happened here—which is far from the truth.

Originally, this southern corner of East Texas was called the Atascosito District, a municipality first of Spain and then of Mexico. Now broken into ten counties, the early focus of the district was the outpost of Atascosito, shown as a freshwater spring on maps as early as 1757. To reach the original site of Atascosito today, take T–146 northeast from Liberty approximately 4 miles and turn left on FM–1011. A marker is just beyond the intersection, and the spring still flows nearby.

After 1821, this wilderness was controlled by Mexico, and Anglo settlers were welcome. For the most part, those early settlers were independent individuals who came here because they could not gain grants through Austin's colonization farther to the west. They formed settlements like Liberty and Dayton, as well as many other places whose names have faded from map and memory.

The Atascosito Road crossed the district, running from Goliad and Refugio to Opelousas, Louisiana. Today, its route is roughly paralleled by US–90, and the town of Dayton straddles the historic path.

In 1831 the Villa de la Santissima Trinidad de la Libertad was established slightly south of the spring and officially laid out with six public squares. Now called Liberty, it is considered, by tradition, to be the third oldest town in Texas.

Two maps available from the chamber of commerce will direct you to most of the sites of interest, including St. Stephen's Episcopal Church (1898), 2041 Trinity Street; the Cleveland-Partlow Home (1860), 2131 Grand Street (private); and the T. J. Chambers Home (1861), 624 Milam Street (private). Graveyard historians love Liberty—there are at least four historic cemeteries in the area. For information, contact the Liberty-Dayton Chamber of Commerce, Box 1270, Liberty 77575. (409) 336–5736.

Six miles west on US–90 and across the Trinity River is Dayton. Originally, it was called West Liberty and then Day's Town in honor of an early settler, I. C. Day. At first it was a lumber and farming community; later, Dayton got a financial boost with the coming of the railroad in the 1870s, and again with the development of oil in the early 1920s. When you pass through, take time to read the historical marker concerning the Runaway Scrape (Trip 3, West Sector). This marker is on the eastern outskirts of Dayton on US–90 east.

WHAT TO DO

Blueberry Farms. Liberty and Hardin counties are prime blueberry territory. You can pick your own at the following: Tanner Blueberry Farm, (409) 298–2382; Lynch Blueberry Patch, (409) 385–1200 or 385–7221; Paradise Patch, (409) 385–0804; Blueberry Basket, (409) 246–4754 or 755–6006; Lee's Berry Haven, (409) 385–5179; and Gates Berry Farm, (409) 246–2387.

Christmas Tree Farm. If you are en route to Dayton or Liberty in the late fall, you can pick out your Christmas tree at Londa's Christmas Tree Farm in Crosby, (713) 328–1156.

Cleveland-Partlow House. 2131 Grand Street, Liberty. Now open to visitors on Tuesday from 10 a.m. to 2 p.m., or by appointment. Fee. (409) 336–5488.

Geraldine Humphreys Cultural Center. 1710 Sam Houston Street, Liberty. Displays of local and pioneer history as well as special art exhibits are mounted here, plus the Valley Players theater company stages plays and musicals at the center. For their current playbill, call (409) 336–5887. A contemporary bell tower houses an exact replica of the famous Liberty Bell, cast in 1960 by a London foundry from the original pattern and mold. The bell rings twice a year—on New Year's Day and again on the Fourth of July during an old-fashioned Independence Day celebration on the center grounds. Free. Open Monday–Saturday. (409) 336–8901 (Liberty Library).

Old French Cemetery. Approximately 3 miles east of Dayton on FM–1008. Established in 1830, this is the burial place of some of the early settlers of the Atascosito District. One grave notes an 1821 death; others are enclosed inside antique iron fences.

Sam Houston Regional Library and Research Center. Four miles north of Liberty via T–146 and a turn northwest (left) on FM–1011. Appropriately sited very near the original settlement of

Atascosito on a high knoll shaded by mature pecan trees, this massive repository is owned by the state and operated by the Texas State Library. Within its fireproof vaults are valuable historic records, documents, portraits, and other artifacts of the original Atascosito District. It also is one of the state's least known and most interesting museums. There are three public display rooms full of goodies like the pirate Jean Lafitte's personal diary and other remnants of the days when Liberty was a major steamboat port on the Trinity River. Genealogists, take note: This library has reprints of the *Atascosito Census of 1826,* significant because it lists the maiden names of wives.

The historic Gillard-Duncan home is on the museum grounds, restored and furnished to its period. Built about 1848 in Ames, an early Creole community south of Liberty, the house is shown by appointment. Free. Open Monday–Saturday. (409) 336–8821.

Timber Ridge Tours. This company specializes in comprehensive guided trips on the lands and waters of East Texas, from Woodville to the Bolivar Peninsula and including the Big Thicket. Call for a list of their adventures. (409) 246–3107 or 429–5796.

WHERE TO EAT

Frank's Restaurant. 603 East US–90 (south side of US–90 east in Dayton). Nothing on the outside of this roadside restaurant would indicate that people drive from Houston and Beaumont just to eat seafood, chicken, or steak here. Breakfast, lunch, and dinner served Wednesday–Sunday. $–$$; (CC). (409) 258–2598.

Layl's Sandwich Shop. 2118 Commerce, 1 block north of US–90 in Liberty. This has been the "meeting and eating" place in Liberty since 1929, so if you want to know what local folks are up to, come here. The breakfasts, in particular, are outstanding, and they sell their homemade mayhaw jelly and picante sauce by the jar. Open for breakfast, lunch, and dinner daily. $. (409) 336–3531.

WANDERING THE BACKROADS

After viewing the local sights, continue this day trip to the Big Thicket via Moss Hill, Batson, and Saratoga. From Liberty, take T–146 north 15 miles to Moss Hill, turn east (right) on FM–162 to Batson, and then northeast (left) on FM–770 to Saratoga.

Moss Hill is a farming and ranch area named for the Spanish moss draped in the surrounding woods. Batson was a small village called Otto prior to the discovery of the Batson Oil Field in 1903. It also was the scene of the 1904 Batson Roundup when all the unmarried women were gathered together and auctioned off to prospective husbands. It's a bit of a racy story, so ask locally or check out the faded pictures from the event at Heritage Village in Woodville (Trip 2, this sector).

Saratoga was named for the famous New York State spa because it had several medicinal hot springs. A hotel catering to the health seekers burned decades ago, but some of the old foundation still can be found. No word on the fate of the hot springs. Saratoga today is the gateway to the Big Thicket.

BIG THICKET

The Big Thicket National Preserve is often described as the biological crossroads of North America. It is a unique place: eight major ecosystems where the flora and fauna mix from all points of the compass. Ferns, orchids, giant palmettos, mushrooms, virgin pine—the abundance and variety is almost unequaled anywhere else on the globe.

Unfortunately, many folks visit what they think is the Big Thicket and come home wondering what all the shouting is about. The problem is that there are twelve Big Thickets in all, and you have to know where to look to find them. The preserve is composed of eight land sections and four river/stream corridors and spreads out over 84,550 acres and seven counties. The beautiful, biologically unique portions lie well away from the highways. Just driving through won't do.

The above statistics refer to acreage either within or earmarked for the national preserve. In general terms, the Big Thicket covers 3.5 million acres of East Texas, including portions of Harris County.

All Texans love a tall tale, and the Big Thicket has its share. One concerns the Kaiser Burnout at Honey Island, near Kountze. Local residents called "jayhawkers," who had no sympathy for the Confederate side in the Civil War, hid out in the woods to escape conscription. Charged with capturing them, Confederate Captain James Kaiser set a fire and flushed them out. Two were killed, a few captured, and the rest vanished once more. Some claim the descendants of those Jayhawkers still live in the depths of the Big Thicket. As more people explore this wilderness, there may be an update on the story.

Then there's the mysterious light that spooks travelers on the Bragg Road, a pencil-straight graded lane that follows the old railroad right-of-way between Saratoga and Bragg. Sometimes called a ghost or the "Saratoga light," it appears as a pulsating phenomenon and has been seen by enough people to warrant serious investigation. Some say it is the ghost lantern of a railway worker killed on the old line; other less imaginative minds claim it's just swamp gas or the reflected lights of cars on a nearby highway. Whatever, it adds to the Big Thicket mystique.

In addition to the backroads route to Saratoga listed in the previous day trip, Houstonians have several ways of getting to the area. The most direct route follows US–90 east to a left turn on FM–770 north at Raywood, continuing on to Saratoga. An alternative is to take I–10 east to Hankamer, then north on T–61 to US–90. Go west 4 miles to FM–770 north to Raywood.

Depending on what unit of the Big Thicket you visit, there also is good access from Woodville, Kountze, Cleveland, and Beaumont. A state map is indispensable.

WHERE TO GO

The Turkey Creek, Beech Creek, Hickory Creek Savannah, and Big Sandy units of the national preserve are open to visitors. The Nature Conservancy operates the Roy E. Larsen Sandyland Sanctuary near Kountze. Big Thicket Association operates Rosier Memorial Park in Saratoga.

Turkey Creek is noted for its changing habitats and carnivorous plants. There is a visitor information center on FM–420, 2.5 miles east of US–69 between Warren and Kountze. **The Kirby Nature Trail** is here, a 1.7- or 2.4-mile loop walk down to Village Creek and back. The information center is open daily, March–December; Thursday–Monday during January and February. It often closes early on Friday. (409) 246–2337.

For a longer hike, the 9.2-mile **Turkey Creek Trail** begins on FM–1943, about 3 miles east of US–90, and ends on County Line Road, slightly east of the intersection of FM–3063 and US–69.

Beech Creek, off FM–2992 southeast of Woodville, is a 4,856-acre beech/magnolia/loblolly pine plant community. However, a 1975 beetle epidemic killed almost all of the loblolly pines, so the forest is not as pretty as it was. A 1.5-mile loop trail passes through a mature stand of hardwoods.

The Hickory Creek Savannah unit, one-half mile west of US–69 and FM–2827 on a dirt road, combines the longleaf pine forest and wetlands with the dry, sandy soil found in the uplands. The

Sundew Trail (one mile) is open to the public, and there is a new a one-half-mile trail for the handicapped and elderly.

The Big Sandy Creek unit includes a rich diversity of plant and animal life. The 5.4-mile **Woodland Trail,** at the northwestern edge of the unit (near the Alabama-Coushatta Indian Reservation), covers a floodplain, dense mature mixed forest, and upland pine stands. The trail entrance, 3.3 miles south of US–190 on FM–1276, is not well marked. The trail also offers two shorter loops.

The Roy E. Larsen Sandylands Sanctuary is on T–327, 3 miles east of Kountze. Although it is considered an excellent example of the arid sandylands, it has 9 miles of frontage along Village Creek. The canoe float from FM–418 to FM–327 has some good swimming holes and white sandbars; about three hours paddle time in length, it is one of the most popular outings in the park (see **Boating** section under "What to Do" for canoe livery services). If you prefer to walk, a 6-mile trail is open daily, and guides can be arranged by writing to P.O. Box 909, Silsbee 77656, or calling (409) 385–4135.

The Rosier Memorial Park Trail is a one-half-mile loop through a palmetto-hardwoods plant community on the western outskirts of Saratoga, near the intersection of FM–770 and FM–787. Open daily, and guides can be arranged through the Big Thicket Museum (see below).

WHERE TO START

The Big Thicket Museum. On FM–770 in the tiny town of Saratoga. The museum offers exhibits, slide shows, maps, and free advice. Open Tuesday–Sunday. Information: Box 198, Saratoga 77585; (409) 274–5000.

All-day canoe trips (fee) and in-depth hikes are offered on weekends and are listed in brochures available free from the museum. There also are five interpreter-guides, each one specializing in some particular aspect of the Big Thicket. If you prefer to explore on your own, stop at the museum for orientation and a map and then head for one of the six units listed previously. Do remember that this is a young park, expanding slowly on very limited funds, and that many of the areas are recovering still from man's earlier abuse.

Membership in the Big Thicket Association is inexpensive and strongly advised (same address as museum). Members receive the *Big Thicket Bulletin* and schedules of special events, plus the satisfaction of aiding the growth and conservation of this unique preserve.

WHAT TO DO

Birding. Excellent, particularly from late March through early May, when hundreds of species pass north on their way up the Mississippi flyway.

Photography. There is a great range of nature subjects, many requiring macro and telephoto lenses. Most of the beautiful things are found in deep shade, so bring high speed film and a tripod. Several outstanding photographic books on the Big Thicket are available at Houston libraries and bookstores to start those creative juices flowing. Some of the Big Thicket Museum tours are designed for and led by photographers. Check with the museum for information. (409) 274–5000.

Camping. Primitive backpacking is allowed by free permit from the National Park Service (409–839–2689) in the Jackgore Baygall, Beech Creek, Big Sandy, and Lance Rosier units. The Big Thicket Museum allows campers on its grounds by reservation only. (409) 274–5000. Kitchen and shelter available to camping groups.

Fishing. Allowed in all waters. A license is required.

Hunting and Trapping. Allowed in specific areas. Permit required. For information and season details, contact the National Park Service, P.O. Box 7408, Beaumont 77706. (409) 839–2689.

Boating. Fishing and sightseeing trips on the Neches River can be arranged through Timber Ridge Tours, (409) 246–3107 or 429–5796.

Small watercraft can be launched at several places on the Trinity River, Neches River, Pine Island Bayou, and Village and Turkey creeks. The water level fluctuates; check before you make firm plans. The national preserve organizes free trips several times a month with a naturalist guide. However, you must bring your own canoe, life jacket, paddles, etc. The preserve does provide shuttle service at the end of the trip back to the starting point. (409) 839–2689.

The Big Thicket Museum also sponsors Saturday and Sunday guided all-day canoe trips in the spring, summer, and fall. These usually focus on the more remote areas, and many do not finish until sunset. All gear is provided—just bring a big lunch and water bottle. Another museum specialty is close-up canoe trips with specialists in ornithology, botany, herpetology, etc. For information and reservations, call (409) 274–5892 between 6 and 9 p.m., or write P.O. Box 198, Saratoga 77585.

Exploring the Big Thicket waterways on your own can be difficult. There are few take-outs, and much of the land bordering on the creeks is privately owned, which makes canoe folks subject to trespass charges. Seek advice and equipment from one of the following canoe livery services: (409) 274–5892 in Saratoga; (409) 246–4481 in Kountze; (409) 892–3600 in Beaumont; (713) 522–2848 in Houston; and (409) 962–1241 in Groves.

Hiking. Wear sturdy, water-repellent boots. This is rain country at certain times of the year, and the shady trails often have standing water. Mosquito-repellent is an absolute necessity. Pets and vehicles are not permitted on any of the trails, and you must register your hike at the trailhead. Absolutely do not wander off-trail on your own. The Big Thicket has earned its name, and it is easy to get lost.

Guided Trips. Timber Ridge Tours operates a variety of customized guided trips within the Big Thicket National Preserve. For information, contact them at P.O. Box 115, Kountze 77625. (409) 246–3107 or 429–5796.

WHERE TO EAT

Jack and Sue's Catfish Kitchen. 205 West Avenue N. (FM–327), Silsbee. This simple brick place serves good-sized breakfasts and has a daily luncheon buffet full of good home cooking. In addition to catfish, they serve a great seafood buffet Thursday–Saturday. Open daily for breakfast, lunch, and dinner; Sundays until 3 p.m. $–$$; (CC). (409) 385–3685.

The Lumber Company. 305 Kirby Ave. (US–92 north), Silsbee. Built on the site of the old Kirby Lumber Company, this popular restaurant specializes in homestyle favorites at lunch and an extensive fresh seafood buffet at dinner. Open for lunch and dinner Tuesday–Friday, dinner only on Saturday, and lunch only on Sunday. $–$$; (CC). (409) 385–9388.

In addition to the Homestead Restaurant in Hillister (Trip 2, this sector), you may be able to catch some good homecooking at the Big Thicket Museum. They cater to groups of fifteen or more by reservation only, but may fit individual families or travelers into an already scheduled group if space and food quantity permit. Call for costs and reservations: (409) 274–5000.

EAST

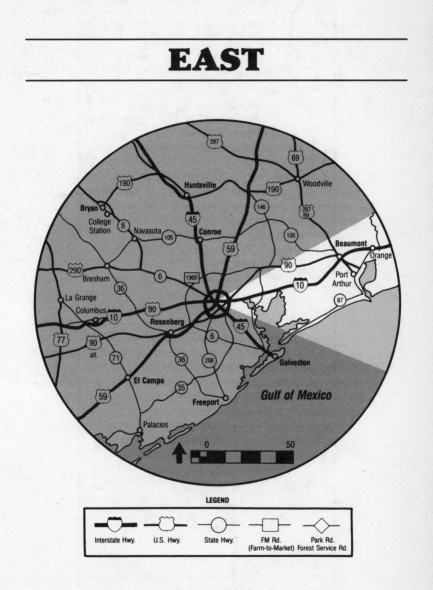

287

69

190   Huntsville   190   Woodville

Bryan   146   287
College   45   69
Station   6   Navasota   105   Conroe   105
290   Brenham   59   Beaumont   Orange
La Grange   6   1960   90   Port
Columbus   36   90   10   Arthur
77   10   Rosenberg   45   87
90   6
alt.   71   36   288   Galveston
El Campo   35
59   Freeport   **Gulf of Mexico**
Palacios

0   50

LEGEND

Interstate Hwy.   U.S. Hwy.   State Hwy.   FM Rd.   Park Rd.
(Farm-to-Market)   Forest Service Rd.

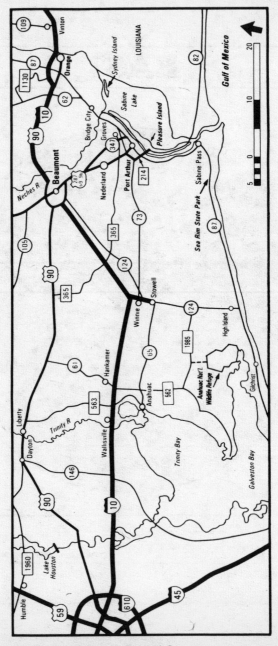

East: Day Trips 1, 2, and 3

Day Trip 1

BEAUMONT

The prospect of a day trip to Beaumont may evoke all the wild enthusiasm usually reserved for kissing your sister. But a little exploration in and around this river city may change your mind. There are a surprising number of things to do, not only in Beaumont proper but in the Golden Triangle area (Beaumont/Orange/Port Arthur) that surrounds it. From Houston, there's only one way to get there—due east on I–10.

Although history hasn't painted the town with the color found in Austin's cradle country west of Houston, Beaumont is equally as old. The first land grant by Mexico to an Anglo in Texas was issued to Noah Tevis around 1820 and covered 2,214 acres of richly forested area along the Neches River. Today, that land is downtown Beaumont. By 1825, there was an active trading post here, and Jefferson County, of which Beaumont is the county seat, is one of the original counties formed by the Texas Republic in 1836. Since that time Beaumont has made its own brand of history in several ways.

Most vivid and important to modern America was the Lucas gusher in 1901. Not only was it a precursor of the giant Spindletop oil field, it produced between 90,000 and 100,000 barrels of oil daily in its first ten days, the largest strike up to that time. The quality of that oil and the drilling methods subsequently developed at Spindletop ushered in the petroleum industry technology of today and enabled the United States to convert from coal to fuel oil for basic energy.

Almost overnight, Beaumont grew from 8,500 souls to 30,000 folks with advanced cases of oil fever, and a wooden shanty town called Gladys City was hammered into instant life on Spindletop Hill. By the end of that decade the oil was gone, and Gladys City was a ghost town of wooden shacks. Those glory days live again in the recreation of Gladys City, one-half mile north of its actual site, at Beaumont's successful Bicentennial project.

Economically linked with the volatile oil and petrochemical industry, Beaumont has had its ups and downs in recent years. By the late 1960s, shifting financial winds had created another ghost town of sorts in the downtown area. But that scene slowly is changing, thanks to major commitments from both the public and private sectors. During the past decade more than $120 million worth of capital improvements have been made downtown, including new municipal and county government complexes. The $10 million Steadman Building project at Park and Crockett streets (similar to the West End Market in Dallas) is drawing crowds with its restaurants, night clubs, and shops; work also is underway on major office projects; and the new $5 million Art Museum of Southeast Texas opened in 1987 to raves. Other commercial projects involve the restoration of classic buildings listed on the National Register of Historic Places.

For free maps, brochures, and advice, stop at the Visitor Information Center in the Babe Didrikson Zaharias Memorial (take the Gulf Street exit from I–10). Open Monday–Saturday year-round, and on Sunday from March through September; (409) 763–2469. The Beaumont Convention and Visitors Bureau is another good source, P.O. Box 3827, Beaumont 77704, (800) 392–4401.

A prerecorded monthly calendar of events called "What's Happening in Beaumont" can be dialed at (409) 838–3634.

WHAT TO DO

Art Museum of Southeast Texas. 550 Main Street. This handsome, $5 million museum showcases a wide variety of art. Exhibits change every six weeks. Open Tuesday–Sunday. Free. (409) 832–3432.

Babe Didrikson Zaharias Memorial. Gulf Street exit from I–10. In her time, this outstanding woman athlete put Beaumont on the map, and the town repaid her with a love and admiration that live on beyond her death from cancer in 1956. This memorial museum chronicles a life and career that saw her named the Woman Athlete of the Year six times by the Associated Press. Free. Open daily. (409) 833–4622.

Blueberry Farms. Call the following for directions to pick-your-own berry patches: Lazy D. Berry Farm, (409) 296–2882; A Patch of Blues in Lumberton, (409) 755–1879; Texas Blueberry Plantation, (409) 753–2890; and Dishman Brothers Berry Farm, (409) 752–2161.

Christmas Tree Farms. There are any number of places to cut your own tree in Chambers, Jasper, and Jefferson counties: Dennis Dugat Farms, (409) 296–4716; Ferguson's Christmas Tree Farm, (409) 374–2365; Double S Christmas Tree Farm, (713) 479–1898 or (409) 994–3395; Huckleberry Hollow Farm, (409) 994–2134; Rudolph's Pasture, (409) 423–5961; Five "O" Evergreens, (409) 994–3686; B's Tree Plantation, (409) 794–1593; Hubert's Christmas Tree Farm, (713)

470–0365 or (409) 796–1516; Beavers Christmas Tree Farm, (409) 253–2372; and F & W Enterprises, (409) 983–1271 or 837–5642.

Eastex Canoes. 5865 Cole Street. Why not take a paddle on the Neches or Sabine rivers? This rental and livery service provides everything including maps and basic instruction. Open daily. (409) 892–3600.

The Edison Plaza Museum. 350 Pine Street. What was the old Travis Street substation of Gulf State Facilities now houses various adventures in electricity, including inventions of Thomas A. Edison. Open weekdays. (409) 839–3089.

The Fire Museum of Texas. 400 Walnut Street. This 1927 fire hall now contains a good collection of old fire equipment and memorabilia, including seven major fire fighting units used from 1779 to the present. Open weekdays. (409) 880–3917.

The French Trading Post. 2985 French Road. (Delaware exit from US–69/96/287 north; turn west and watch for signs). This substantial museum was John J. French's trading post and home back in 1845, now restored and operated by the Beaumont Heritage Society in a beautiful woods setting north of town. Fee. (409) 898–3267.

Gladys City Boomtown. At the intersection of University Drive and US–287. Although it lacks the grime of the original, this reconstruction is a good look at 1910 America as well as life in an oil-field boomtown. A rickety boardwalk connects most of the structures, just as it did eight decades ago.

The furnished replicas include a surveying and engineering office, the pharmacy and doctor's office, a photographic studio, a general store, and more. Vintage oil-field equipment is scattered around, and the Lucas Gusher Monument is out back on its own site.

From I–10 take the US–287 turnoff to Port Arthur and then the Highland Avenue/Sulphur Drive exit. Signs take you from there. Fee. Closed Monday. (409) 835–0823.

Historical Tours. The Beaumont Heritage Society offers a variety of area tours on an hourly fee basis. (409) 898–0348.

McFaddin-Ward House. 1906 McFaddin Street. Don't leave Beaumont without touring this impressive home; it is one of the few restored Beaux Arts/Colonial houses in the United States. Built in 1906 on land granted by the Mexican government to earlier generations of the McFaddin family, it was occupied by that oil-wealthy and socially prominent family until 1982. Tours begin every thirty minutes with an excellent slide show and continue through numerous rooms, a kaleidoscope of family life and American decor styles from the 1907 period on. Most of the furniture is American, most of the accessories are European, and the Pink Parlor (1908) is particularly grand. Open Tuesday–Saturday and on Sunday afternoon; no children are allowed. The last tours begin at 3 p.m. Fee. (409) 832–2134.

Old Town. East of Calder and Eleventh streets. When the first Gladys City was in its heyday, this portion of Beaumont was a highly desirable tree-lined residential neighborhood. Today it still is. Some of the homes remain impressive, and many now house galleries, restaurants, and specialty shops.

A free map helps you find out what's what in this thirty-block area. Pick one up at the Tourist Information Center or order it in advance from the Beaumont Convention and Visitors Bureau, Box 3827, Beaumont 77704, (409) 838–1424 or (800) 392–4401.

Port of Beaumont. 1255 Main Street. You'll have a bird's view of the busy port from an observation deck on top of the Harbor Island Transit Warehouse; ask the security guard at the Main Street entrance for directions. Guided tours can be arranged by calling the telephone number below. This modern port handles more than 30 million tons of cargo annually and is one of the four largest ports in the country in terms of tonnage. However, the far banks of the Neches River remain richly forested and undeveloped, just as they were when clipper ships stopped here a century ago. (409) 832–1546.

Riverfront Park. On the Neches River behind City Hall at Main and College streets. "Sunday in the Park" is the big summer event here from April through November. Civic groups host fun and games every Sunday from 2 to 4 p.m., and the activities are different every week. Great for kids, so bring a picnic and spend the afternoon. Free.

Texas Energy Museum. 600 Main Street at Forsyth, across from the civic center complex. Exhibits about Beaumont before and after Spindletop are featured in this new $5 million showcase, along with the entire collection of oil-patch artifacts of the Western Company Museum of Fort Worth. Exhibits animated with Cine-robots show how oil is created, found, pumped, and refined. Open Tuesday–Sunday. Fee. (409) 833–5100.

Tyrrell Historical Library. 695 Pearl Street. People come from all parts of the world to research their roots at this genealogical library, built in 1906 as a Baptist church. Open Tuesday–Saturday. (409) 833–2759.

WHERE TO EAT

Bando's. 4310 Calder Street. Owner/chef Debbie Bando has created one of Beaumont's favorite bistros, similar in many ways to the Cafe Express in Houston. The smell of freshly baked bread brings your taste buds to attention first. Then you have to decide between dining inside or on the patio. Next comes the hard stuff: which of the four major entrees, twenty salads, twenty kinds of coffee, fifteen to twenty wines (available by the glass), or uncountable sandwiches to order at the counter? Nor do you have to stand around clutching a number; your order is brought to your table. There are super desserts and a wide variety of cheeses, pâtés, and other gourmet goodies, because this is also a retail food and gift shop. Unless you pull up at the drive-in and order snacks or a picnic to go, real china and linen nappery are the rule. Bando's is one of the few places in Beaumont serving authentic espresso and cappuccino. Open from 9:30 a.m. to 5 p.m., Monday–Saturday, but you can buy an early-morning snack and drink from the drive-in before they open if you are desperate. $. (409) 898–8638.

The Boondocks. Jap Road at Taylor Bayou, in the Fannett area. How about some raccoons and alligators with your catfish? This casual place delivers all three, particularly in summer. The catfish is on the menu; the raccoons and alligators are outside, eagerly awaiting your leftovers. Open for dinner Tuesday–Friday, lunch and dinner on Saturday and Sunday. $–$$; (CC). (409) 796–1482.

Carlo's. 2570 Calder Street. If you want Italian and the spouse wants Greek, this is the place. They specialize in both. Open for lunch and dinner Monday–Friday, dinner only on Saturday. $$; (CC). (409) 833–0108.

David's Upstairs. 745 North Eleventh Street. Can't make it to New Orleans? This classy continental restaurant brings the French Quarter to Beaumont, right down to the live jazz and rhythm and blues music nightly. Chef Jim Morrison adds his own flair to classics like beef Wellington and steak Diane, and his oysters stuffed with crabmeat and Bailey's Irish Cream cake are originals. Popular with Beaumont's young professional crowd, this dining club has an à la carte menu and an adults-only policy after 8 p.m. Open for lunch and dinner Monday–Friday, dinner only on Saturday. $$–$$$; (CC). (409) 898–0214.

The Green Beanery Cafe. 2121 McFaddin Avenue at Sixth in Old Town. This chef-owned restaurant offers tasty, unusual twists on classic American and continental dishes, and all the veggies are fresh and crisp. Several small shops share this old home complex. Open Monday–Saturday for lunch and dinner, and reservations are required. $$; (CC). (409) 833–5913.

Patrizi's Other Place. 2050 I–10 southbound, between Washington and College streets. Newly refurbished, this family–owned restaurant features more than thirty entrees, homemade soups, and freshly baked breads, all from the owner's own recipes. Open for lunch and dinner Sunday–Friday; dinner only on Saturday. $–$$; (CC). (409) 842–5151.

Day Trip 2

ORANGE

Anyone who thinks chili is the definitive Texas dish hasn't been in Orange for the International Gumbo Cook-off on the first Saturday in May. More than 20,000 folks mob this annual event, proving that the Cajun heritage thrives in this part of the state.

Others pass by Orange on their way to play the ponies at Delta Downs Racetrack, just over the bridge in Vinton, Louisiana. Whatever your reasons for day-tripping this way, stop to enjoy this neat little city. Some 32 miles east of Beaumont, and the last gasp of Texas on I–10 before you find yourself in Louisiana, Orange has some interesting places to visit.

Founded officially in 1836, the city's traceable history really starts about 1600 when the Attacapas Indians settled here. French fur traders came a century later, followed by the Spanish, and the city's name comes from this latter period—early French and Spanish boatmen looked for the wild oranges that grew along the banks of the Sabine River. Anglo settlers ventured west across the Sabine in the early 1800s, but little is left to mark those times. Most of Orange's tourist attractions date from the prosperous lumber and ranching days of 1880 to 1920.

Local information, including a list of antique stores, can be had from the Orange Chamber of Commerce, 1012 Green Avenue, Orange 77620; (409) 883–3536. Do cross the Sabine when you make this day trip; the Louisiana State Information Center combined with the Sabine National Wildlife Refuge is on the right just beyond the bridge. There's an outstanding picnic area and boardwalk through the marshes where you may see numerous water birds, nutria, etc., so bring your camera, preferably one with a telephoto lens.

WHAT TO DO

Blueberry Farms. Pick to your heart's content at the following: Clegg Blueberry Farm, (409) 994–2549 or 994–3425; Buna Blueberry Ranch, (409) 994–5427; or J and J Blueberry Farm, (409) 745–2225 or 746–2600.

Christmas Tree Farms. Orange County may be the Virginia pine capital of Texas. Call any of the following for directions: Armstrong's Christmas Tree Farm, (409) 883–2441; K & K Evergreen Christmas Tree Farm, (409) 746–2412 or 746–3268; Nichols Christmas Trees, (409) 746–2276; Ramac, (409) 886–2595 or 883–2923; Rees Farm, (409) 962–4676; Spell's Golden Triangle Trees, (409) 746–2337 or 746–2250; Holiday Christmas Tree Ranch, (409) 745–1608; Reaves Christmas Tree Farm, (409) 746–2522; "The Original" Christmas Tree Farm, (409) 745–1826; and Carpenter's Christmas Tree Farm, (409) 886–5127.

Delta Downs. Twenty miles east via I–10, then north on L–109. Slightly beyond the two-hour, 110–mile limit of this book, this track still is a good reason to visit the Beaumont/Orange/Port Arthur area. September–March is for thoroughbreds only, and April–Labor Day is strictly for quarter horses. For information, contact P.O. Box 175, Vinton, LA 70668. (800) 737–3358 (reservations) or (318) 589–7441.

Farmer's Mercantile. Corner of Sixth and Division streets, just where it's been since 1928. Saddles rest next to bins of nuts and bolts, onion sets are offered just below packets of bluebonnet seeds, and horse collars line the high walls. Whatever you might need, it's here—somewhere. People have been known to dawdle here for hours, remarking on the old wood stoves, bottle cappers, and such. You can't miss the place—just look for hay bales on the sidewalk. Open Monday–Saturday. (409) 883–2941.

First Presbyterian Church. 902 Green Avenue. One wonders what there would be to see or do in Orange without the Lutcher and Stark families (see entries on Stark House and Stark Museum that follow). This impressive domed building is another Lutcher-Stark contribution to the city, finished in 1908 and noted for its handsome interior and stained-glass windows. Fun to know: The air-conditioning system in this church and that of New York City's Chrysler Building were completed within days of each other in 1908, and records are unclear as to which was officially America's "first" commercial building with AC. At that time the City of Orange could not provide enough electricity to the church to operate both the lights and the AC at the same time, so a powerhouse with a coal-fired generator were part of the church's original construction. Operated by a full-time engineer, the system used ammonia and dry ice to "condition" the air, a real marvel to Texans of that time. Tours are available for six or more by advance reservation. If you can't meet those tour requirements, come for Sunday services. (409) 883–2097.

Heritage House. 905 West Division Street. While not as elegant as the Stark House (see below), this turn-of-the-century home is worth a stop. Not only is it furnished as an upper-middle-class home would have been in those times, but there are several "see-and-touch" exhibits for children as well as historical items of interest. Fee. Closed Saturday and Monday. (409) 886–5385.

Linden of Pinehurst (Brown Center of Lamar University). US–90 (business route), just off I–10 on the western outskirts of Orange. When Mrs. Gladys Brown saw a famous Natchez antebellum home called Linden, she ordered its duplicate built in 1956 at Pinehurst, the Browns' ranch in Orange. Along with its furnishings and forty-eight acres of parklike grounds, it was donated in 1976 to Lamar University by the Brown estate and is open to the public unless a special conference is being held on the premises. Note: The gate sign says PINEHURST RANCH, and a nearby gate says LINDENWOOD which leads to a subdivision. Go past Lindenwood and a cemetery; the home will be on your right. Tours may be arranged through Brown Center of Lamar University, 4205 Park Avenue, Orange 77630. (409) 883–2939.

Lutcher Theater. Orange Civic Plaza. If you are coming over for the weekend anytime during the September–May season, call to see what's playing. Recent offerings have ranged from Harry Belafonte and Arlo Guthrie to the Gatlin Brothers. (409) 886–5535.

Piney Woods Country Wines. 3408 Willow Drive. This small vineyard produces some tasty fruit wines. Drop in for a sample of Texas-grown sunset muscadine or peach. The tasting room is open afternoons Tuesday–Saturday in spring and fall, all day Tuesday–Saturday in summer; closed in January and February. (409) 883–5408.

Stark Museum of Western Art. 700 Green Avenue, across from the Stark House. William H. Stark was a prominent financial and industrial leader in Orange who married Miriam Lutcher in 1881. She began collecting European art in the 1890s, and her son, Lutcher, and daughter-in-law, Nedda, continued the family tradition with further emphasis on art of the American West and the Taos School of New Mexico. The Audubon print and Steuben glass collections also are particularly worth seeing. This contemporary museum was completed by the Starks in 1976 and houses the varied and impressive collection. Free. Open Wednesday–Saturday and on Sunday afternoon. (409) 883–6661.

Super Gator Tours. 106 East Lutcher Drive, on the westbound side of I–10 (exit 878). Few thrills compare to skimming over water aboard an air boat. This firm welcomes families for hour-long explorations of the bayous and cypress swamplands that make up the Sabine River. Reservations suggested. Open daily year-round, weather permitting. Fee. (409) 883–7725.

W. H. Stark House. In the Stark Civic Center complex at Green and Sixth. Built in 1894, this massive, fifteen-room Victorian home with its gables and turrets is a visual delight, inside and out. A ten-year restoration project, it can be toured only by advance reservation. No children are allowed. Tours start in the carriage house where an excellent glass collection is on display. Open Tuesday–Saturday. Fee. (409) 883–0871.

WHERE TO EAT

Cody's. 3130 North Sixteenth Street, at I–10. Stop here for charcoal-broiled hamburgers, steaks, seafood, and salads. Their burgers have been rated best in Southeast Texas by *Texas Monthly*. Open for lunch and dinner Monday–Friday, dinner only on Saturday and Sunday. $–$$; (CC). (409) 883–2267.

Crawfish Capitol. At the intersection of T–12 and T–62 in Mauriceville, 8 miles north of Orange. Live or boiled, this is the place to get crawfish. Bill Harris purges the little devils (i.e., cleans their intestines) in fresh well water for twenty-four hours and then sells them live or cooks them up into tasty Cajun-style étouffée, gumbo, etc. Save time for a tour of the vats of crawfish outside. This is the only place in America that has live crawfish for sale year-round. Open daily for sales; restaurant is open from February 1 through midsummer. $–$$. (409) 745–3022.

Guadalajara. The Mexican food here is so authentic no one speaks much English. Closed on Sunday. $; (CC). Two locations: 106 Green, (409) 886–9063, and 137 MacArthur, (409) 883–4214.

Old Orange Cafe. 914 West Division Street. Bring your willpower when you have lunch here; the praline cheesecake will test your dietary resolve. Open weekdays only. $–$$; (CC). (409) 883–2233.

Ramada Inn. 2600 I–10 west. If you are eastbound, exit at Sixteenth Street; westbound, exit at Adams Bayou. Folks come from as far away as Beaumont for the Friday and Saturday night seafood buffets—mountains of fresh shrimp or crawfish, depending on the season. $$; (CC). Open daily for standard meals also. (409) 886–0570.

Day Trip 3

NEDERLAND
PORT ARTHUR

NEDERLAND

When you want to fish or hunt in Southeast Texas, you well could be headed for Port Arthur. From Houston, the most direct route is I–10 east to Beaumont, followed by a swing southeast on US–69/96/287. For the day-tripper, there are several activity options in the area, but first, let's take a look at one of the smaller towns you will pass on the way—Nederland.

You'll think you are in Cajun country when you first drive up the main street of this small community—the local market is usually advertising fresh boudain (sausage). Confusion sets in when you see some Dutch names on stores and a windmill at the end of the street. Established as a railroad town in 1897, Nederland was first settled by Dutch immigrants who soon were followed by French settlers from the Acadiana area of southwestern Louisiana, and both ethnic groups make Nederland what it is today.

WHAT TO DO

Maison Beausoleil. 701 Rue Beausoleil, off Grigsby Avenue in Port Neches Park, Port Neches. This 1810 Acadian home was barged in from Vermillion Parish, Louisiana. Fully furnished to its time, it can be toured by appointment. (409) 722–3446.

Windmill Museum and La Maison des Acadian Museum. 1528 Boston Avenue, in Tex Ritter Park, Nederland. These adjacent museums keep the dual heritage of Nederland alive. The first floor of the authentic Dutch windmill is devoted to mementos of Tex Ritter, a local boy who made the big time in country and western music, and the remaining two floors have a sparse but interesting collection of assorted cultural treasures. Best is the old pirogue, hollowed out of a cypress log prior to 1845 and in use until bought and donated to the museum in 1969.

La Maison des Acadian Museum honors the French Cajun culture. A Bicentennial project constructed by local volunteers, this authentic replica of a French Acadian cottage has furniture to match. Both museums are open Tuesday–Sunday, March through Labor Day, and Thursday–Sunday thereafter through February. Information: Nederland Chamber of Commerce, 1515 Boston Avenue, Nederland 77626. (409) 722–0279.

WHERE TO EAT

The Schooner. US–69/96/287 at FM–365. Famous for stuffed flounder and stuffed red snapper steak, this restaurant goes all the way with a few stuffed fish and game trophies for decor as well. Open daily for lunch and dinner. $$; (CC). (409) 722–2323.

PORT ARTHUR

From Nederland, continue southeast on US–69/96/287 to Port Arthur. The Sabine and Neches rivers merge to form Sabine Lake, which then empties into the Gulf of Mexico 8 miles south of Port Arthur. The town sits on the northwest bank of the lake.

Settled as Aurora about 1840, it was renamed Port Arthur in 1897 when it became the terminus of the Kansas City-Pittsburgh and Gulf Railroad. The ensuing oil strike in nearby Beaumont ushered in Port Arthur's golden age of growth. Today the city is primarily a large industrial and refining center with a growing number of things of interest to visitors; you can survey the scene on weekdays from an observation balcony on the fifth floor of City Hall, 444 Fourth Street, (409) 983–3321. Guided tours to the port of Port Arthur can be arranged by calling (409) 983–2029. The Port Arthur Convention and Visitors Bureau is a good source of specific information: 3401 Cultural Center Drive, Port Arthur 77642. (409) 985–7822 or (800) 235–7822.

WHAT TO DO

Airboat Rides. This activity comes and goes in Port Arthur. At this writing, you can explore the more than 15,000 acres of marsh in Sea Rim State Park aboard an airboat, a wonderful trip for anyone interested in wildlife, birding, or just being outdoors with the wind in your hair. Sea Rim Airboat Tours operates daily from March through October; year-round by appointment. Fee. (409) 727–4501 or 727–4487.

Fishing. You can fish in Sabine Lake, the freshwater bayous that feed it, or the Gulf of Mexico via Sabine Pass. Top game fish are speckled trout, red snapper, mackerel, billfish, and tarpon. A license is required except for party-boat excursions. For information on party boats, marinas, guides, etc., contact the Con-Vis bureau listed above.

Hunting. To see vast flocks of birds on the wing in sunrise light is unforgettable. Even seasoned hunters have been known to put down their guns in awe, although you will rarely find one who will admit it. You too can have that experience in the Port Arthur area. This is prime territory for duck and geese hunting, with four areas open to the public at various times during the November–January season. For overall information, contact Sea Rim State Park, P.O. Box 1066, Sabine Pass 77655. (409) 971–2559. Other areas open for public hunting include the Texas Point and McFaddin Beach national wildlife refuges, (409) 971–2909, and the J. D. Murphree Wildlife Management Area, (409) 736–2559.

Museum of the Gulf Coast. In Gates Memorial Library, on the Port Arthur campus of Lamar University, 317 Stilwell at Lakeshore Drive. Before the construction of the Intracoastal Canal there were beautiful sand beaches on Sabine Lake. Several sprouted luxury hotels that live on only in photographs on display with other area memorabilia in this interesting museum. The Port Arthur area has spawned a number of noted musical artists, among them Janis Joplin, Harry James, Aubrey "Moon" Mullican, Johnny Preston, and Ivory Joe Hunter. Their legacies, complete with gold records, are celebrated in the museum's outstanding Southeast Musical Heritage exhibit. Open weekdays. (409) 983–4921.

Oriental Village. 801 Ninth Avenue. More than 8,000 Vietnamese settled in the Port Arthur area in the early 1970s, 95 percent of them Roman Catholics and the other 5 percent Buddhists. Their culture and expressions of religion have changed the face of this town. Hoa-Binh (Area of Peace) shrine has a triple-life-size statue of the Virgin Mary, surrounded by ornamental gardens. A block of Vietnamese shops is adjacent. The Buddhists bought an old Baptist Church at 2701 Proctor Street and turned it into Buu Mon Buddhist Temple, complete with a lighted, four-tiered pagoda tower. Their dragon dances for Buddha's birthday and the Tet (New Year) celebration every year.

Pleasure Island. In Sabine Lake, across the Sabine-Neches ship channel and south from metro Port Arthur. Follow signs to the Martin Luther King Bridge and Pleasure Island. This multimillion-dollar development is stirring things up, and there's more to come. For now, there are miles of free levees for fishing and crabbing, a marina, a restaurant and golf course, a hotel and resort, spots for picnicking and camping, boat ramps, and a ten-acre concert park that hosts musicals and festivals from late spring through fall. Part of the lake around the island is reserved exclusively for sailboards.

Pompeiian Villa. 1953 Lakeshore Drive. Believe it or not, this is a billion-dollar house. Built in 1900 by Isaac Ellwood, the "barbed wire king," it later was sold to the president of Diamond Match Co. He, in turn, traded it for $10,000 worth of Texaco stock worth $1 billion on today's market—or so the story goes in Port Arthur. Is that figure before the Pennzoil judgment or after? Whichever, this pink stucco villa is listed in the National Register of Historic Places and is now owned by the Port Arthur Historical Society. Open Monday–Friday. Fee. (409) 983–5977.

Sea Rim State Park. About 23 miles south of metropolitan Port Arthur on T–87. Thanks to enlightened management, the sea rim marshlands between Port Arthur and Galveston are treated as the fragile natural resources they are. Important to the seafood industry as nursery grounds for shrimp and fish, they also provide a unique experience for the visitor.

Sea Rim State Park is far more than the usual seaside camping and sunning spot. With more than 15,000 acres, this is the third-largest state park in Texas, and it is divided into two distinct areas. The beach unit has camping with and without hook-ups; a main headquarters with restrooms; hot showers; concessions; an outstanding interpretive center; and the Gambusia Trail, a 3,640-foot-long boardwalk through the wetlands behind the dunes.

The second unit is a pristine marsh, explorable only by airboat, small powerboat, or canoe. You may surprise a flock of herons or egrets, or see an alligator or two—unless they see you first. There are four camping platforms and observation blinds within the marsh. If you want to explore these wetlands, you must bring your own craft; at this writing, there are no rentals or rides in or near the park, except for the airboat rides previously mentioned. You also must file a float plan with the rangers and have marsh maps to guide you through this water wilderness. Fee. Information: P.O. Box 1066, Sabine Pass 77655. (409) 971–2559.

Sidney Island. At the north end of Sabine Lake between the junction of the Sabine and Neches rivers, this wild place is protected and accessible only by authorized boat. Created from spoil left from the dredging of the Sabine-Neches Waterway in 1915, this small island has evolved into a protected natural habitat for thousands of birds, including, for a time, the roseate spoonbill. Unfortunately that rare bird has not been sighted on Sidney Island since 1988, although a few have been seen along the marshes and roads nearby. Owned by the State of Texas and leased to the Audubon Society, mile-long Sidney Island is best viewed through binoculars from Rob Bailey's Fish Camp. From T–87 in Bridge City, turn south on Lake Street and go to the end of the road, an interesting drive through a marsh. October visitors get a bonus. Migrating monarch butterflies come in on the Texas "Blue Norther" storms and rest here overnight en route to Mexico. Sue Bailey, the game warden for Sidney Island, welcomes questions, although actual visits to the island are nearly impossible to arrange. (409) 735–4298.

Snooper's Paradise. 5509 East Parkway, at the northwest corner of Thirty-ninth Street and T–73 in Groves. For thirty-two years, these folks have been importing antiques from Europe, and their 50,000-plus square-foot facility bulges with beautiful things, mostly from the period 1860 to 1900. Delivery to Houston is all in a day's work. Open Monday–Saturday. (CC). (409) 962–8427.

Vuilsteke Dutch Home. 1831 Lakeshore. This home was built in 1905 for the first Dutch consul to Port Arthur and contains its original furniture. Tours by appointment. Fee. (409) 984–4921.

Whitehaven. 2545 Lakeshore. Now owned by the DAR, this 1915 Greek Revival mansion is open for tours on Monday, Wednesday, and Friday or by appointment. Fee. (409) 982–3068.

WHERE TO EAT

Carpel's. Under the Rainbow Bridge on the Port Arthur side; look for signs on the west side of the road. Watching the boat traffic just outside the restaurant's windows is nearly as popular as the seafood. Open for dinner Tuesday–Sunday, lunch daily except Saturday. $–$$; (CC). (409) 962–5470.

Channel Inn. 5157 South Gulfway (T–87), Sabine Pass. How does an all-you-can-eat serving of barbecue crab sound? Or how about the seafood platter? Come here, and bring a bib. This is a real down-home place, right down to the rolls of paper towels on the tables. Don't come alone, though. The seafood platters are served only to two or more. Better yet, bring five friends, because reservations are accepted only for six or more; that will get you past the usual thirty-minute wait. Open for lunch and dinner daily. $–$$; (CC). (409) 971–2400.

Farm Royal Seafood Restaurant. 27001 Memorial Highway (US–69/96/287). Putting this restaurant in a guide book could be a mistake. It may become so popular we won't be able to get in. This place serves some of the best Cajun food in the Golden Triangle area.

Best bet probably is the crawfish dinner if you are here between January and June. Lunch and dinner Monday–Friday; dinner only on Saturday. $–$$; (CC). (409) 982–6483.

Spoonbill's. At the marina on Pleasure Island. The deck of this laid-back pub-snackery is the place to be when the roseate spoonbills fly over around 6 p.m. on a summer evening. Families love this kickback place, particularly when the end-of-the-day singing and dancing music starts. Expect a jazz trio on Wednesday evenings, a pianist on Saturday night, and a combo on Sunday. The audience often provides additional entertainment. Open Wednesday–Sunday from 7 a.m. $; (CC). (409) 983–3822.

WANDERING THE BACKROADS

The most logical and the swiftest access from Houston to the entire Golden Triangle area is via I–10 east. But if time is no problem and you prefer quiet country roads, detour south from the interstate just past the Trinity River Bridge and explore Wallisville and Anahuac.

One of the oldest towns in Chambers County, Wallisville was torn down in 1966 by the U.S. Army Corps of Engineers in preparation for a large dam that has not as yet materialized and remains mired in controversy. In 1979, the nonprofit Wallisville Heritage Park Foundation was created to restore the old town and preserve the adjacent El Orcoquisac Archaeological District. So far, only the old post office and school are back in business, but the town site is lovely, and the project gains a modicum more momentum every year.

From Wallisville, take Old Wallisville Road to its intersection with FM–563 and continue south to Anahuac. The road itself is a delight—no center stripe or traffic—and it's easy to imagine how things were in the old days when this was a horse-and-buggy route.

Anahuac has some bits of history and a large wildlife refuge, the latter of great interest to bird lovers. Some thirty species of ducks and geese winter here along with many shore birds and marsh mammals. This is nesting ground for the rare yellow and black rail. In all, the Anahuac refuge has 20 miles of all-season road (12 additional miles in dry weather) and hosts 253 species of birds, thirty to fifty species of mammals, and an extensive number of reptiles. There is a very short boardwalk along Shoveler Pond, and several ramps for launching small boats into eastern Galveston Bay. Hunting is allowed on two tracts in season; request information on times, restrictions, and required permits. Maps and leaflets are available at the visitor contact station. For information and a birding list, contact

Anahuac National Wildlife Refuge, P.O. Box 278, Anahuac 77514. (409) 267–3337.

Settled in 1821, Anahuac still has traces of Fort Anahuac, built about 1831 by the Mexican government. Look for remains in the small, somewhat rundown park at the end of Main Street on Trinity Bay. Two old homes of interest are on the courthouse square. The first is Chambersea, built in 1845 and notable for the Texas star window in its western gable. The second is an early doctor's office, floated in from its original site in Cedar Bayou and now used as a museum. For weekday access to either place, ask at the county clerk's office.

To continue to the Golden Triangle area from Anahuac, either take T–61 north to I–10 east, or FM–562 south and FM–1985 east to T–124 south. This connects with T–87 at High Island. Turn left and continue northeast along the coast to Sea Rim State Park, Sabine Pass, and Port Arthur. This section of T–87 is the only road along the water on the entire Texas coast, and portions of it usually have storm damage. You may find it one lane in several places.

From Anahuac, it's also possible to return to Houston via Galveston. Follow FM–562 south and FM–1985 east to T–124 at High Island and turn right on T–87. This takes you to Bolivar and the free ferry (long wait on good-weather weekends) to Galveston.

SOUTHEAST

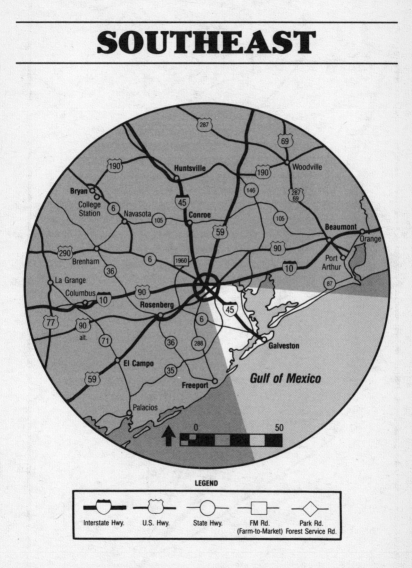

LEGEND

Interstate Hwy.	U.S. Hwy.	State Hwy.	FM Rd. (Farm-to-Market)	Park Rd. Forest Service Rd.

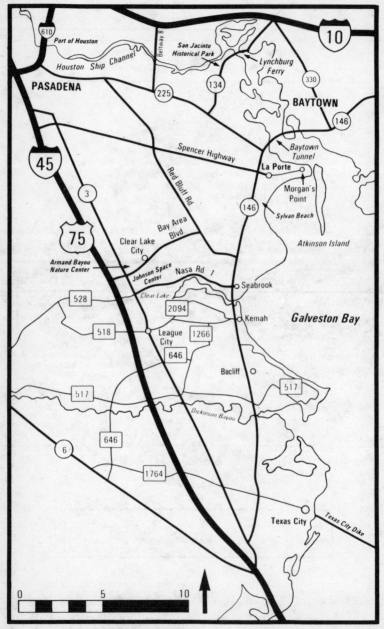

Southeast: Day Trips 1 and 2

Day Trip 1

PASADENA
LA PORTE
BAYTOWN
MORGAN'S POINT

PASADENA

As you drive southeast from Houston on I-45 and look east to the vast industrial-chemical complex that is Pasadena today, it's hard to believe that this once was projected to be Houston's garden. Such a bucolic future was altered permanently by two events: the completion of the Houston Ship Channel as a deep-water port in 1915, and the discovery of oil in nearby Baytown the following year.

Slightly off the usual Sunday drive itinerary, this upper bay region offers several things to see and do. Start with a tour of the Port of Houston and the ship channel, and then head east on T–225 to digest some history at San Jacinto Battleground State Historical Park in La Porte. From there, ride the free Lynchburg Ferry to Baytown and return to the Morgan's Point-La Porte area via the Baytown Tunnel. En route you'll find crabbing, swimming, and bird watching—all at a laid-back pace.

THINGS TO DO

The Beltway 8 Bridge. Accessible either from I–10 on the north or T–225 on the south. No reservations needed here, just some toll change for a fantastic bird's-eye-view of the port from atop the bridge.

The Pasadena Historical Museum and the Strawberry House. 201 Vince Street, in Memorial Park. The museum's fine displays include an authentic doctor's office and an early kitchen, complete with water pump. The adjacent Strawberry House originally stood on a nearby Mexican land grant and is furnished to illustrate three periods: the early 1880s when it was new; the 1920s; and the 1940s. Open Wednesday–Sunday. (713) 477–7237.

Port of Houston. 7300 Clinton Drive (Clinton exit from Loop 610 east). The observation deck on the northwest side of the turning basin is open daily, but a boat tour is better. The free ninety-minute trip aboard the *M-V Sam Houston* takes you close to huge ships from around the world, grain elevators, refineries, docks—the active heart of the third-largest port in America. This is an official inspection vessel, and reservations are required. Make them six to eight weeks in advance by writing to Port of Houston, P.O. Box 2562, Houston 77252. Closed on Monday, as well as for two weeks in April and for an additional month sometime during the year. (713) 225–4044.

Styled like a paddlewheeler, the *Bayou Bell* runs sightseeing and dinner cruises through the Ship Channel, departing Thursday–Sunday from Allen's Landing (Main and Commerce streets) in downtown Houston. Reservations required. $$–$$$; (CC). (713) 868–5323.

LA PORTE

Founded by French settlers in 1889, this modest community's boundaries now stretch north to include one of the state's most significant historical sites. See this portion of La Porte now, on your way to the Lynchburg Ferry, and the Sylvan Beach area on the final leg of this trip.

WHAT TO DO

San Jacinto Battleground State Historical Park. From Pasadena, continue east on T–225 to T–134, and turn north to Park Road 1836. Here, in just eighteen minutes, Sam Houston and his ragged Texian Army defeated the Mexican Army in 1836. Not only did this change the future of Texas, but that of the western half of the continental United States as well. The dramatic story is chiseled in granite and unfolds as you walk around the base of the 570–foot-tall San Jacinto Monument. There is no better capsule lesson in Texas history. Inside, the interesting **San Jacinto Museum of History** has artifacts from the Spanish-Mexican period (1519–1835) and the Anglo-American settlement years (1835–81). A documentary film, *Texas Forever! The Battle of San Jacinto,* brings history to life in the museum's Jesse H. Jones Theater for Texas Studies. The museum is free, but there are charges to see the film and to ride the elevator to the top of the monument. Open daily. (713) 479–2421.

The battlefield flanks the monument, and a free map available at the museum will guide you to markers and various positions of the Texas and Mexican armies. This oak-studded park land also has numerous picnic sites along one arm of the bay and on the ship channel, so bring your lunch and crabbing gear. (713) 479–2431.

The Battleship *Texas* is nearby. Moored here since 1948 and fresh from a major restoration, this is claimed to be the only surviving heavily armed dreadnought-class battleship, a relic of both world wars. Closed Monday and Tuesday. Fee. (713) 479–4414.

Lynchburg Ferry. From the cemetery and picnic area of the battleground park, continue northeast on T–134 to this free ferry, a survivor from pre-freeway days. You are welcome to park your car and take the fifteen-minute round-trip as a passenger, or you can drive aboard and then continue on to Baytown. The ferry operates twenty-four hours a day, year-round. (713) 424–3521.

Little Cedar Bayou Park. From T–146, turn left onto Fairmont Parkway, right on Eighth Street, and left on M Street. This pleasant city park has play and picnic areas, a mile-long nature trail that ends at Galveston Bay, and a WaterWorld-type wave pool that operates during the summer. Film and Float Night comes once a month during the summer—you lay on your inner tube and watch a major movie. (713) 471–5020.

Sylvan Beach. On T–146 in the bay-front portion of La Porte. This somewhat ramshackle county park has a playground, picnic areas, and free boat launch, but no swimming. There also is good crabbing, but the entire park could use some TLC. The old train depot at the park's entrance now serves as a historical museum for La Porte and is open by appointment. (713) 471–1123.

WHERE TO EAT

Monument Inn Restaurant. 2710 Battleground Road, La Porte. This is a long-standing favorite place known for its shrimp, steaks, and fish dinners. The huge aquarium is fascinating to adults as well as children. Open for lunch and dinner daily. $$–$$$; (CC). (713) 479–1521.

Vicker's Inn. 122 South First Street, La Porte. Featured on "The Eyes of Texas," this wonderful old Victorian home has come to life again as a top-notch restaurant. Owner/chef Tom Barrett specializes in nonfried foods, and there's nary a microwave on the premises. Expect everything from quiche to premium beef and fresh seafood; his shrimp salad won first place in the Houston Proud competition that preceded 1990's Economic Summit. Built in 1875, the Queen Anne-style house was moved to this site in 1905. Barrett has added a picket fence, dining patios front and back, and beautiful gardens—there's even a waterfall splashing into the goldfish pond.

Don't come to this dressy but casual place in a hurry; dinner here should be two hours of pleasure. Open daily for lunch and dinner, plus brunch on Sunday. $–$$; (CC). (713) 471–6505.

From the San Jacinto Monument area and La Porte, the Lynchburg Ferry takes you across the ship channel to Baytown, where you continue on T–134 to Decker Drive (T–330). Turn southeast (right) and drive through Baytown. At the intersection with R–146, make a right and continue to La Porte via the Baytown Tunnel.

BAYTOWN

Both Lynchburg and Baytown were early Anglo settlements, the former an important trading post, the latter originally a sawmill and a store. Baytown boomed after the Civil War and now is an industrial and residental community.

WHAT TO DO

Baytown Historical Museum. 220 West Defee Street. This interesting look at the area's past is housed in a 1936 post office. Note the fresco on the lobby wall, painted by noted artist Barse Miller as part of a WPA project during the Depression. Other major exhibits include replicas of an Indian hut and midden; the poetry of the "sage of Cedar Bayou," John P. Sjolander; and Humble-Exxon memorabilia from the early days in the oil patch. The Texas Room has artifacts relevant to David Burnet, Sam Houston, and Lorenzo de Zavalla, all of whom lived in the area. Open Tuesday–Saturday. Donations. (713) 427–8768.

Houston Raceway Park. 2525 FM–565 south. Take exit 798 from I–10 east of downtown, go south to T–146, then right to FM–565. Watch for signs. Billed as the world's fastest drag-racing track, this quarter-mile strip hosts the NHRA Fram Supernationals annually in late February/early March. Want to test your wheels in pro territory? Come on Wednesday night and bring $10. Some type of racing or special event is held on every Wednesday and weekend, year-round. Fee. (713) 383–2666.

WHERE TO EAT

Murray's Restaurant. 1001 Memorial Drive, Baytown. This large log cabin is a source of good, rib-stickin' country food, such as chicken-fried steak, chicken-'n'-dumplin's, pork chops, catfish, and barbecue. The salad bar is extensive and the soups, pies, and cobblers are made on-site. Open for lunch and dinner weekdays, dinner on Saturday, and lunch on Sunday. $–$$; (CC). (409) 422–5386.

MORGAN'S POINT

Back in those good old days, Morgan's Point combined with La Porte to provide a beach and bay playground for Houstonians. Big name bands brought crowds to the dance pavilion at Sylvan Beach, and folks drove around Morgan's Point just to see the handsome homes on the "Gold Coast."

A drive along Bayridge Road today still takes you past some of those places, among them a grand replica of the White House, built by Texas Governor Ross Sterling. It has been a landmark on the Houston Ship Channel for nearly three generations. At the end of Morgan's Point is an undeveloped beach area well known to birders. With binoculars, you can watch roseate spoonbills and other species on Atkinson Island, a sanctuary in this upper portion of Galveston Bay.

WANDERING THE BACKROADS

From the San Jacinto Monument, you can easily bypass tours of Baytown, La Porte, and Morgan's Point in favor of a jaunt to Clear Lake and Kemah (Trip 2, this sector). Just retrace your route back to T–225 and turn east (left) to its intersection with T–146. Turn south (right); it's approximately 10 miles to Clear Lake and Kemah.

Day Trip 2

CLEAR LAKE
SEABROOK and KEMAH
TEXAS CITY

CLEAR LAKE

A drive south from Houston on I–45 brings you to NASA Road One. Turn east to explore Clear Lake and the easygoing towns of Seabrook and Kemah.

The launching of *Sputnik* also kicked off America's space program and ultimately created the Lyndon B. Johnson Space Center, now the second largest tourist attraction in Texas. After following man's exploration of space, you can challenge some new frontiers on your own. A few miles away is nature at her most primitive, a wilderness bayou seemingly untouched by man. Nearby, a local air field offers lessons in sky diving, and you can arrange a ride in the jump plane to test it out. The less adventurous can sail on Clear Lake or stop at the docks in Seabrook and Kemah for fresh shrimp.

WHAT TO DO

NASA-Lyndon B. Johnson Space Center. From I–45 south, take NASA Road One exit and go east 3 miles. This focal point for America's manned space flight program is both interesting and exhausting. A full tour requires about three hours of standing and walking, so come well fed and in comfortable shoes. You also will want your camera and a flash unit to record the extensive displays of lunar material, space-shuttle trainers, Apollo 17 spacecraft, the Mercury capsule, skylab trainers, and other space exotica.

Most visitors start at Rocket Park, impossible to miss alongside the parking lot. From here, you walk to the Visitor Center and begin a self-guided tour that includes the main museum, two astronaut training areas and the cafeteria-gift shop. Briefings are conducted in the Mission Control Center on a first come, first served basis throughout the day; sign up at the information desk in Building Two as soon as you arrive. Free. Open daily (except Christmas Day). (713) 483–4321.

Armand Bayou Nature Center. 8600 Bay Area Boulevard. One of the last natural bayous around, this haven for wildlife is protected from development by the Johnson Space Center on the south and Bay Area Park on the west.

Start first at the Nature Center and learn the territory through exhibits. Then follow the 1.5-mile hiking trail through the woods and along the bayou, either on your own or on one of the free guided hikes offered twice daily on weekends. Also on the grounds is a three-acre working farm from the 1890s, complete with a restored and furnished farmhouse, barn, outbuildings, vegetable garden, and livestock. You can walk around the farm during the week or tour with a guide on the weekend (fee). Consider buying a family membership ($35) while you are at the nature center. Among the benefits are rental canoes ($20 a day) for exploring the bayou on your own. At this writing, pontoon boat rides through the bayou were being considered. Open daily, except major holidays. Fee except on Monday. (713) 474–2551.

Canoeing the Bayou. You can float through this wilderness on your own and not get lost, thanks to a free waterways map available from the Armand Bayou Nature Center. There is canoe access at Bay Area Park and at the NASA Road One bridge at Clear Lake Park, 5001 NASA Road One. In addition to those available to members of the nature center, canoes can be rented by the hour at Sneak In/Sneak Out Canoe Rentals, 2908 Red Bluff Road, (713) 474–7660, and at the Water Sports Center of Clear Lake, 5001 NASA Road One, in Harris County Park, (713) 326–2724, (deposit required). Inquire about car-top carriers or racks to transport canoes; you may need to bring your own.

Excursions on the Lake. A 100-foot paddlewheeler called the *Clear Lake Queen* carries up to 149 passengers around Clear Lake on ninety-minute cruises on Saturdays, Sundays, and holidays year-round. Heated, air-conditioned, and with three outdoor observation areas, she is the only working paddlewheeler in Texas that is certified by the U.S. Coast Guard. Fee. ($; no credit cards). The ship also sails on dinner cruises that feature live jazz on Saturday nights and is available for charter. Reservations are necessary, and beer, wine, and champagne are included in the dinner cruise price. $$$; (CC). (713) 333–3334.

Boating on the Lake and Bay. A 56-foot classic wooden bug-eye schooner, the *Morning Star,* departs from the Nassau Bay Hilton on two-hour sunset cruises nightly year-round, weather permitting. Fee. (CC). The ship also is available for half- and full-day charters for groups up to twenty-five. (713) 333–2339.

Another firm, Sailaway, offers a full-moon champagne cruise once a month year-round. Departures are from either the Nassau Bay Hilton or the Watergate Yachting Center in Kemah. They also charter yachts, with or without a captain, for four-hour sails on the bay (CC). (713) 334–5644.

Sackett's Sailing Center offers four-hour sails on Galveston Bay from Watergate Yachting Center on the Wednesday and Friday nights closest to the monthly full moon. This firm also rents and charters yachts and offers a twenty-four-hour course in basic sailing. (CC). (713) 334–4179.

At The Helm, a sailing school based at Watergate Marina in Kemah, has several ways of getting folks before the mast. One- to four-day courses range from basic sailing technique to advanced navigation. Their short cruise course prepares you for bare boat chartering, plus there's an executive team-building experience designed for the corporate world. Have you always wanted to sail on a regular basis but didn't want the expense and painful joys of owning your own yacht? At The Helm's sailing club may be the answer. Its $350–$450 annual membership fee allows you to sail 25- to 42-foot boats on any weekend throughout the year at no extra charge. Guests of members are charged an additional $37.50 each, however. (CC). (713) 334–4101.

Gulf Coast Sailing Center, 1206 FM–2094 on the south side of Clear Lake, offers full-day and half-day sailboat rentals. If you've always had a hankering to sail but don't know how, these folks claim their two- or six-hour practical course will have you skimming along on your own in a day. (713) 334–1722.

Another possibility if you want to learn to sail is Blue Marlin Sailing School. (713) 471–4801.

The Water Sports Center of Clear Lake in Harris County Park, 5001 NASA Road One, offers sailing lessons and rents sailboats, catamarans, wave runners, and canoes by the hour. (CC). (713) 326–2724. Other choices, if you just want to buzz around the lake for an hour or so, are the wave runners, jet skis, etc., available at the Hilton's Floating Dock Marina, (713) 333–2816. Ski boats and power cruisers can be rented by the hour or day from Club Nautico at South Shore Harbor Resort. (CC). (713) 334–2199.

Interlude Yacht Charters offers crewed yacht and sail charters on Galveston Bay by the hour, day, week, or month. The star of the fleet is the motor yacht *Interlude,* a wood hulled, 57-foot Constellation furnished with English, French, and Italian antiques, (713) 952–8984.

Odyssey Marina Management at the Nassau Bay Hilton rents houseboats and charters large power cruisers and sailboats by the day or week, (713) 333–1534. Boat charters also are available from the following: Classic Yacht Services, (713) 474–5443; Fat Barry's Charter Service, (713) 486–9734; and Houston Sailing Association, (713) 334–1856.

Sculling. Rowing as moveable art is the newest way to skim across Clear Lake, and you can learn the fundamentals with group or private lessons from the Oarlocker Rowing Club. (713) 334–3101.

Sailboarding. Lessons and rental equipment are available from Gulf Coast Sailing Center, (713) 334–5505, and from the Water Sports Center of Clear Lake in Harris County Park, (713) 326–2724.

Additional Information. Check with the Clear Lake Area Convention and Visitors Bureau, 1201 NASA Road One, Houston 77058, (713) 488–7676, in regard to sailboarding operations in Mud Lake (across from Harris County Park) and for a list of all boat ramps, bait and fuel spots, marinas, and charter party boats operating in the area.

Additional Canoeing Territory. Dickinson Bayou roughly parallels FM–517, both west and east from I–45. You'll find parking and a good put-in at the T–3 bridge in Dickinson, and then you have your choice of take-outs: either a carry at the FM–646 crossing (3.5 miles) or at Cemetery Road. This last section is the most beautiful and undisturbed.

Skydiving. At Skydive Spaceland, at the Houston Gulf Airport, east of League City. Take exit 20 from I–45, go east on FM–646 for 3.5 miles; turn north on FM–1266 for one-half mile. Observers are welcome, and usually there are plenty of people around to explain what is going on. If you want to ride along in one of the jump planes, it's best to arrange it in advance (fee). The six- to eight-hour Saturday classes include a skydive on your own, weather permitting. Reservations are required for classes. In a hurry? A thirty-minute training session will allow you to ride a parachute-built-for-two with a specially trained tandem master. Open Wednesday–Sunday. (CC). (713) 337–1713.

Bayou Wildlife Ranch. Take the Dickinson/FM–517 exit from I–45, then west on FM–517 for 6 miles; the entrance will be on your left. From antelopes to a zony (cross between a zebra and a pony), more than 260 animals (representing 42 species) roam this 86-acre preserve. Visitors tour with a guide via an open-air tram, and buckets of feed are part of the deal. This outstanding facility gives you a good look at major zoo-type animals roaming free in a natural environment. If you've never been nuzzled by a camel or scratched a giraffe's neck, this is the place. Also here: a feeding barn for young animals who need extra TLC, and a modest collection of antique cars and hearses. Open daily in summer, Tuesday–Sunday in winter. Fee. 713–337–6376.

From Clear Lake, continue this day trip by taking NASA Road One east and turning south (right) at the T–146 intersection in Seabrook. The north side of the bridge is Seabrook; the south side is Kemah.

SEABROOK AND KEMAH

Both of these fishing villages are heaven for shrimp lovers and boat watchers. The channel under the bridge is the only passage from Clear Lake into Galveston Bay, and the best view of the constant marine traffic is from the crest of the bridge itself.

If you want shrimp that are fresh and relatively cheap, go early in the morning and buy directly from the boats that dock on either side of the bridge. Shop around for the best price; sometimes you can do just as well at one of the dockside fish markets. The shrimp usually come "heads on," and you'll need an ice chest to cart them home.

Those who want to linger should call ahead to Bed and Breakfast on the Bay, the last house at the end of Eleventh Street in Seabrook, (713) 861–1333 or 781–7455. Guests have the use of two swimming pools, and the boat parade through the channel is right outside the door. There's also excellent crabbing and fishing under the bridge.

The quaint buildings of "old" Seabrook are blossoming anew with antique stores, boutiques, and specialty shops. NASA Road One becomes Second Street east of the T–146 stop light, so just mosey along until you see something of interest.

Much of what was the funky little fishing village of Kemah has been swept away by storms and bulldozers. The swanky new Lafayette Landing Marina complex is literally rebuilding the area at the south end of the bridge, but until it is fully occupied with shops, Kemah's big draws remain the shrimp boats and markets and the three excellent restaurants at the water's edge.

WHAT TO DO

Party Boat Fishing on Galveston Bay. Save yourself the run to Galveston. The 65-foot *Judy Beth,* operated since 1980 by Robert and Judy Connors, offers the most convenient party boat fishing for Houstonians. Departing from the Kemah docks March through mid-December with up to eighty passengers, it finds great fishing off Red-fish Island, the Houston Yacht Club, the entrance to the Houston Ship Channel, or around assorted oil-rig platforms in the gulf. Tackle and bait are available, and your catch can range from flounder and sand trout to croaker, whiting, or black drum, depending on the season. Reserve at least three days in advance for the Saturday morning trips. The boat goes out several times a day in good weather; call for current schedule. (CC). (713) 334–3760.

WHERE TO EAT

The Brass Parrot. 100 Bradford, Kemah; next to the Flying Dutchman. This casual place specializes in spicey Caribbean seafood and chicken—the popcorn shrimp and charbroiled tuna are good testers—and the drinks wear disguises like Typhoon Treat, Bahia Blast, Island Girl, etc. The deck outside is a great spot to catch some rays and watch the boating scene. Open daily for lunch and dinner. $–$$; (CC). (713) 334–1099.

The Crazy Cajun. 2825 NASA Road One, Seabrook. No way can you stay in a bad mood in this relaxed and zany place. The waiters will charm you right out of the blues, a cup of gumbo will rev up your taste buds, and the Cajun Shrimp Combo will hold off hunger pangs for hours. Open daily for lunch and dinner. $$–$$$; (CC). (713) 326–6055.

The Flying Dutchman Restaurant and Oyster Bar. 505 Second Street, Kemah. Ask the local residents where they go for good seafood and this place wins in a landslide. It's dressy duds upstairs, cut-offs and casual boatwear below. Open daily for lunch and dinner. $$; (CC). (713) 334–7575.

Joe Lee's Seafood Restaurant. Second and Kipp streets, Kemah. Casual indoor and outdoor dining on good gulf seafood and steaks. The oyster bar is a local favorite, as is the outdoor deck overlooking the boat parade from the lake to the bay. Open daily for lunch and dinner. $–$$; (CC). (713) 334–3711.

Landry's at Jimmy Walker's. 201 Kipp, Kemah. Seafood with a continental flair is the rule here, with fine dining on the second floor, a more casual atmosphere and outdoor tables on the first. If there's a see-and-be-seen place in the area, it's this pricey spot. Open daily for lunch and dinner. $$–$$$; (CC). (713) 334–2513.

Seabrook Classic Cafe. 2511A NASA Road One, Seabrook. This is a great place for weekend breakfasts, particularly if you have a fondness for those nifty little New Orleans donuts known as beignets. Everything is fresh here and made from scratch. Open for lunch and dinner daily; breakfast on weekends. $–$$; (CC). (713) 326–1512.

The Shrimp Hut. 1818 NASA Road One, at T–146, Seabrook. Success and renovation have changed a good small place into a good giant place, but the menu remains the same. The house specials remain crawfish in the spring, shrimp in the summer and fall, and oysters on the half-shell in the winter. The seafood po-boys are good, the fried or broiled seafood dinners are worth a drive from Conroe, and the patio dinners Friday–Sunday nights (March–November) will let you sample nearly everything. You also can buy steamed crab and shrimp here to pack home. Open for breakfast, lunch, and dinner Tuesday–Sunday. $–$$; (CC). (713) 474–5701.

T-Bone Tom's Smokehouse. 707 Highway 146, Kemah. Why anyone would want a great steak or barbecue in the midst of fresh fish territory is beyond understanding, but if that's your pleasure, this is the place. Open Monday–Saturday for lunch and dinner. $; (CC). (713) 334–2133.

Tookie's. 1202 T–146 (Bayport Boulevard), Seabrook. This spot is hard to miss: a green and gold barn on the east side of the road. When you are hankering for a real hamburger (they grind their own meat), real onion rings (thick and sweet), and real ice tea (huge and made with freshly brewed hot tea), come here. Open daily for lunch and dinner. $; (CC), (713) 474–3444.

Continuing south on T–146 from Kemah, you pass through the outskirts of heavily industrialized Texas City before connecting with I–45 just north of the causeway to Galveston Island. At that point you can continue on with Trip 3 of this sector, or swing north on the freeway toward home.

TEXAS CITY

Originally an 1880s settlement called Shoal Point, Texas City is of interest to day-trippers primarily for its 5-mile dike jutting out into Galveston Bay. The winds are fairly dependable here, so the beach areas along the dike are crowded with sailboards, small sailboats, and catamarans whenever the wind is up to filling sails.

Fishing and crabbing are wherever you find a spot, and there also are boat-launching facilities, bait and tackle shanties, some cafes, and a lighted fishing pier. However, the dike is often unpleasant with debris, and there are few amenities such as restrooms, designated parking areas, or drinking water.

The dike is easy to find—just drive east through town on FM–1764 (Palmer Highway), turn right at the end of the road, then left onto the dike road.

WHERE TO EAT

Clifton By The Sea. From T–146 south of Kemah, turn east (left) on FM–517 to the bay. The best reason for detouring to Bacliff is to eat fresh seafood and fine steaks at this former saloon, now spiffed up into a Nantucket-style family restaurant. Watch for signs along T–146 between Kemah and Texas City. Open for dinner Wednesday–Monday, lunch on weekends only. $–$$; (CC). (713) 339–2933.

Grand Prize Barbecue. 2223 Palmer Highway, Texas City. In addition to great barbecue in all its Texas forms, the big draw here is the authentic Texas decor. No decorator-imitation stuff or formula restaurant this. The staff haunts flea markets and antique shops for the trophy heads, vintage signs, and license plates that line the walls. Don't miss the stuffed rattlesnake or the rare 1946 Rockola jukebox that plays old 78-RPM records. On the barbecue side of things, you'll have a difficult choice between ribs, brisket, links, and ham, or one of the daily specials such as mesquite-grilled catfish, fajitas, T-bones, or chicken. Open daily for lunch and dinner. $–$$; (CC). (409) 948–6501.

Going home from Texas City means a trip north on I–45. Shoppers will have a hard time getting past exit 13 (Delany Road), the turnoff for the Lone Star State Factory Stores, which are open every day.

Day Trip 3

GALVESTON

GALVESTON

Cabeza de Vaca found it first. Later, in 1817, the pirate Jean Lafitte made this sliver of island his base of shady operations. Legend says his treasure still lies buried in the shifting sands, and hunting for it with metal detectors is a favorite Galveston pastime.

To Houstonians, this small city, one hour's drive south via I–45, has traditionally been a relief valve, a chance to escape from big-city life for a lazy day or weekend at the beach. But Galveston is far more than surf and sand. As the city's advertising says, ". . . the rest is history."

Long before Houston was much more than a landing on Buffalo Bayou, Galveston was a major port and the threshold to Texas for thousands of immigrants. By the 1870s, it was the wealthy and thriving "Queen City of the Southwest," and during the golden era of 1875–1900 some of the most remarkable architecture in America lined its streets.

A devastating hurricane in 1900 killed more than 6,000 people and swept much of the city out to sea. Vulnerable to every passing storm, Galveston seemed doomed to follow the earlier Texas coast ports of Indianola and Lavaca into oblivion. To save the city and ensure its future security, two massive engineering projects were undertaken, each remarkable for its time. The first was the building of a massive seawall, 17 feet tall and 10 miles long. The second was the raising of all the land behind that seawall from 4 to 17 feet.

These projects took seven years and were followed by yet another economic blow in 1915 when the successful completion of the Houston Ship Channel began to draw off the cream of the port trade. Galveston never recovered its pre-1900 commercial importance, ultimately degenerating into one of the wildest gambling towns in the state. The Texas Rangers finally brought down the law in the 1950s, and after that, Galveston slumbered along as a rather seedy seaside city.

But all is changing for the better. The renovation and restoration of many historic buildings, in addition to a growth in the hotel and convention sector, has sparked fresh capital investment, and Galveston is

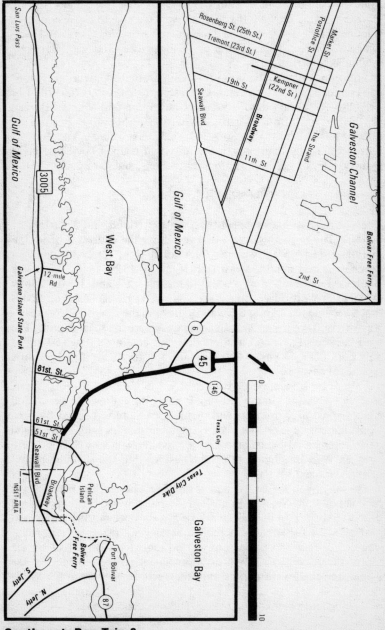

Southeast: Day Trip 3

now thriving once again. Don't miss a ride on the new $10 million rail trolley system that connects, in 1890s-1920s style, the Strand Historic District with the seawall. If you don't want to drive to Galveston, consider taking the Texas Limited excursion train that runs between Houston and Galveston Thursday through Sunday (see "Today's Galveston" section, below).

Information on Galveston is available from the Galveston Historical Foundation, (2016 Strand, Galveston 77550; 409–765–7834 or 713–280–3907) and the Galveston Convention and Visitors Bureau (2106 Seawall Boulevard, Galveston 77550; 409–763–4311, 800–351–4236 in Texas, 800–351–4237 elsewhere). The con-vis bureau offers, by mail only, a free discount coupon book that gives reduced rates on accommodations, attractions, and restaurants.

EXPLORING THE BEACHES

There are 32 miles of beachfront on the island and a variety of options. The decisions start after you cross the causeway from the mainland on I–45 and see the directional signs for East and West beaches. If you continue east (left lanes), I–45 becomes Broadway Boulevard and runs in an easterly direction up-island. If you follow the signs to West Beach from I–45, you will cross the island on Sixty-first Street, which ends at Seawall Boulevard, the island's second east-west artery. Turn right; West Beach starts where the seawall ends. The road becomes FM–3005 at this point and continues down-island to San Luis Pass. Do note that cars are not allowed on Galveston's beaches at any time.

There are several beach pocket-park facilities on FM–3005, operated by Galveston County. Each has changing rooms, showers, food concessions, playgrounds, and picnic areas and is backed by protected natural dunes. Horseback riding, parasailing, sailboarding, and other commercial beach activities are available nearby during warm weather. West Beach also offers the best jogging and shelling, particularly near San Luis Pass.

In town, you'll find numerous small beaches tucked between the rock jetties along Seawall Boulevard. Stop and watch the dolphins roll in the offshore swells, and then take a walk out onto the jetties and chat with the fishermen. There also are several places to rent roller skates, bicycles, and pedal surreys, and the wide sidewalk along the top of the seawall is a favorite promenade. At the east end of the island, the boulevard curves and intersects Broadway at Stewart's Beach. This city-run stretch of sand is popular with families because of its lifeguards, bathhouse, lockers, parking, concessions, etc.

A short drive farther east brings you to R. A. Apffel Park, a $2 million, 1980s development at the extreme end of East Beach. A favorite with fisherfolk and families, as well as teenagers looking for like kind, it has excellent boating and fishing facilities and a large recreation center that includes a bathhouse and concessions.

Galveston Island State Park. West of downtown Galveston on FM–3005, at the intersection with 13 Mile Road. Another beach facility with picnicking and camping, this 2,000-acre state park also offers birding from observation platforms and nature trails along its north boundary, which faces the protected waters of West Galveston Bay. The park's Mary Moody Northern Amphitheatre features major musical productions during the summer months.

Palm Beach. West of town in Moody Gardens: 1812 Hope Boulevard, off Eighty-first Street. This three-acre beach complex is on the bay and has white sand imported from Florida, whirlpools, lockers, a boardwalk, concessions, life guards, and freshwater swimming. This claims to be the only beach in Texas with palm trees. Fee. (409) 744–7256.

EXPLORING HISTORIC GALVESTON

Start at The Strand, once called the "Wall Street of the Southwest" and now the heart of one of the island's three historic districts. In itself, The Strand is considered one of the largest and best collections of nineteenth-century iron-front commercial buildings remaining in America. To get there from Broadway, go north on Rosenberg Avenue (Twenty-fifth Street) for 8 blocks. Most of the buildings along The Strand now house shops, galleries, businesses, and restaurants—the renaissance is in full swing. The Dickens-on-the-Strand Festival, which is held the first weekend in December, draws crowds in excess of 160,000 and is covered by the national press.

Stop first at The Strand Visitors Center, 2016 Strand, operated daily, year-round, by the Galveston Historical Foundation in the restored Hendley Row (1856-60). Brochures outlining walking and biking tours are available here, along with audio-guide equipment (fee) and information on Galveston's many points of interest. The following are among the main stops.

The Tremont House. 2300 Ship's Mechanic Row. This superb 1879 building now houses one of the most elegant small hotels in Texas. (409) 763–0300, (713) 480–8201, (800) 874–2300 (reservations only).

The 1871 League Building. Strand at Tremont. One of the nicest restorations in the city, and home to several interesting shops and the Wentletrap Restaurant (see "Where to Eat" listings).

Galveston Arts Center. 2127 Strand. If you like mixing art with history, drop by at this eclectic gallery. This is the old First National Bank Building, restored to its 1866 grandeur. Closed Tuesday. (409) 763–2403.

The Marx and Kempner Building. 2100 block of The Strand. Can you spot the clever *trompe l'oeil* mural? The original window detailing of this building was removed decades ago, and what looks like several vintage facades actually is hand-painted artwork.

The 1882 H. M. Trueheart-Adriance Building. 210 Kempner. This Nicholas Clayton-designed building is one of the most ornate and distinctive structures in the area. Its restoration in 1970 sparked The Strand's renaissance.

The *Elissa*. Pier 21, a block north of The Strand. One of the oldest ships in Lloyd's Register of Shipping, this 1877 square-rigged barque still sails several times a year and represents Texas in assorted tall-ship parades. The acquisition of the ship and its restoration are stories in themselves; be sure and see the *Elissa* film at the Strand Visitor's Center. Visitors can roam the restored after-cabins, the hold (self-guided), and the decks. The new Texas Seaport Museum is dockside. Open daily, unless *Elissa* is at sea. Fee. (409) 763–1877.

The Center for Transportation and Commerce. Strand at Twenty-fifth Street. Visitors step into a replica of the old Galveston train depot and then move through a series of brief sound-and-light shows depicting Galveston from the sixteenth century through the present day. Next comes the depot's original waiting room where life-size sculptures of travelers are frozen in a moment of 1932; unusual "hear"-phones allow visitors to eavesdrop on their conversations. Out back are restored steam locomotives, assorted railroad cars, a snack bar and picnic gazebo, and exhibits of steam-powered machines. Open daily. Fee. (409) 765–5700.

Galveston County Historical Museum. 2219 Market Street. The handsome City National Bank Building (circa 1919) houses more of Galveston's glorious past. Open daily. (409) 766–2340.

The East End Historical District. This special area includes forty blocks of Victoriana in the general area bounded by Broadway, Market, Nineteenth, and Eleventh streets. It can be driven or walked, but the best way to see the most is by bicycle or on the historical foundation's Homes Tour in early May.

The Bishop's Palace. 1402 Broadway. The only home in the East End Historical District that is open to the public, this massive place was built between 1887 and 1892 for the Walter Gresham family. Designed by noted Galveston architect Nicholas Clayton, it is considered by the American Institute of Architects to be one of the 100 most outstanding residential structures in America. Even more interesting than its turreted rococo exterior are the details and furnishings inside. Fee. Guided tours are given year-round (closed on Tuesday, September–June). (409) 762–2475.

The Silk Stocking Historical District. This nine-block area is loosely bound by Rosenberg, J, and N avenues and Tremont Street. Brochures on the most interesting homes open to the public are available at The Strand Visitors Center, the Galveston Island Convention and Visitors Bureau, and at Ashton Villa.

Ashton Villa. 2328 Broadway. This Italianate beauty was built in 1859 of bricks made on the island and survived both a disastrous island-wide fire in 1885 and the 1900 storm. It now is restored as the showplace of the Galveston Historical Foundation. The tours begin in the carriage house with an excellent film on the city and the storm of 1900. An interesting archaeological dig exposes a small portion of the home's original first floor, which became the basement when the level of the island was raised after the great hurricane. Open daily. Fee. (409) 762–3933.

The Moody Mansion and Museum. 2628 Broadway. This marvelous old home is the Smithsonian of Galveston. The city's grande dame, the late Mary Moody Northern, never threw anything away—archivists even found Christmas presents still in their original wrappings with full notation as to year and giver—and her lifelong home has been restored to the way it looked at her debut in 1911. Call for days and hours of operation. Fee. (409) 765–9770.

The 1839 Samuel May Williams Home. 3601 Bernardo de Galvez (Avenue P). One of the two oldest structures in Galveston, this charming restoration now looks as it did in 1854. Tapes tell about the Williams family as you move from room to room. Open daily. Fee. (409) 765–1839.

John Sydnor's 1847 Powhatan House. 3427 Avenue O. Home to the Galveston Garden Club, this handsome mansion and its oak-studded gardens are open only to groups. No high heels, please; they damage the beautiful pine floors. Fee. (409) 763–0077.

The 1894 Opera House. 2020 Post Office Street. The interior of this interesting building has been restored to its turn-of-the-century grandeur, and the stage once again hosts a variety of performing arts throughout the year. For box office information, call (409) 765–1894 or (713) 480–1894.

Historical Medical Sites. Numerous "firsts" are credited to Galveston's medical community. A brochure noting ten important sites is available from Galveston Historical Foundation (address previously given).

TODAY'S GALVESTON

If you've had it with history or are burned out with beaches, there is still plenty to do.

All About Town. Departing from Twenty-first and Seawall on the hour, this firm's Galveston Flyer Yellow Trolley Tour is a one-hour narrated look at the best of Galveston. One ticket is good for all day, so you can get on and off as you wish. Operates daily except Wednesday, year-round. Fee. (409) 744–6371.

Carriage Rides. Authentic horse-drawn surreys leave daily from the vicinity of Twenty-first and Strand for thirty- and sixty-minute tours of the various historic districts. Fee.

Galveston Sightseeing Train. Hop aboard at Moody Center, Twenty-first and Seawall. You'll get a ninety-minute, 17-mile guided tour of Galveston old and new. Fee. Several tours daily, weather permitting.(409) 765–9564.

David Taylor Classic Car Museum. 1918 Ship's Mechanic Row. This extensive collection of vintage wheels includes a 1955 Thunderbird convertible, a 1929 Chevy roadster, a classy 1931 Caddy roadster with rumble seat, and a 1934 Ford roadster convertible. Open Tuesday–Sunday afternoons. Fee. (409) 765–6590.

Fishing. In addition to the rock jetties along the seawall, there are commercial fishing piers at Twenty-fifth, Sixty-first, and Ninetieth streets and at Seawolf Park on Pelican Island. Surf fishing is allowed along most of the open beaches; common catches are speckled trout, flounder, catfish, and redfish,

Party boats for fishing in either the bay or gulf leave early in the morning, either from piers 18 or 19 or from the yacht basin. A Texas fishing license is required for everyone between the ages of seventeen and sixty-five unless you are fishing at least 10.5 miles offshore. Check to see if a license is required when you make your reservations. Common gulf catches include red snapper, sailfish, pompano, warsaw, marlin, ling, king mackerel, bonito, and dolphin. Medication for seasickness is advised—the gulf can get rough. For further information, call any of the following: Galveston Party Boats, (409) 763–5423 or (713) 222–7025; Williams Party Boats, (409) 762–8808 or (713) 223–4853; Aqua Safari Charters, (409) 935–4646; Yacht Brokers, (409) 763–3474; Galveston Charter Service, Inc., (713) 944–FISH; Southbound Charters, (409) 762–1601.

If you prefer to rent a boat and fish on your own, try Club Nautico at Payco Marina, accessed by the first exit at the Galveston end of the I–45 causeway. They rent power craft, the largest of which can take you 40 miles offshore. (713) 474–3802 or (409) 740–3024.

Harbor and Gulf Boat Tours. Pier 22. The *Colonel,* styled like an old-fashioned sternwheeler, churns its way around Galveston harbor on two-hour narrated cruises daily during the summer, and Friday–Sunday in winter. They also offer dinner, dance, and jazz cruises. Call for times. Fee. (409) 763–4666 or (713) 280–3980.

The 36-foot catamaran *Isla* takes passengers on daily sails in Galveston Bay at reasonable cost from March through November. Want to fish, play water volleyball, or anchor off an island and swim? Just tell the skipper, and he'll tailor the trip to your interest. Fee. (409) 740–0497.

The 67-foot *Rachel B. Jackson* docks next to the *Elissa* at Pier 21. This gaff-rigged tops'l schooner is available for two charter cruises daily, Thursday–Sunday. Fee. (409) 763–1877.

Horseback Riding. Weather permitting, you can rent a steed from either Sandy Hoof Stables (11118 West Beach between 7 Mile and 8 Mile roads; 409–740–3481) or Gulf Stream Stables (8 Mile Road; 409–744–1004).

Lone Star Flight Museum. 2002 Terminal Drive, at Scholes Field (Galveston Airport). Sited on what was a military air field during World War II, this growing collection of 1940s aircraft includes fighters, bombers, a rare F-7-F Tigercat, and one of only two P-47-G Thunderbolts remaining in the world—all of them close enough to touch. The gift shop is stocked with WW II memorabilia; aircraft engines are displayed, some with cutaway views; and the research library is a find for historians. Don't miss the remarkable essay on what World War II was all about, particularly if you have teens in tow. Open daily, except for major holidays. Fee. (409) 740–7722.

Mary Moody Northern Amphitheatre. Galveston Island State Park, west on FM–3005 at the intersection with 13 Mile Road. Historical musicals and Broadway favorites light up this stage Monday–Saturday from Memorial Day through Labor Day. Tickets are available at Houston ticket centers and at the gate. A barbecue dinner is available before the performance. Fee. (409) 737–3440, (713) 530–3600, or (800) 992–8000.

Moody Gardens. 1812 Hope Boulevard, near the Galveston Municipal Airport. This $18 million, twenty-year botanical project is well underway on the banks of Offats Bayou. (409) 744–7388.

The *Pride.* Sailing from Pier 21, Galveston. Billed as providing "the excitement of Las Vegas, the romance of a cruise," this full-size liner has eight day or evening gambling cruises every week into the international waters of the Gulf of Mexico. Price includes a buffet meal and Las Vegas-style entertainment. There's a pool for swimming, cabins for renting, and music for dancing. The only problem is getting through their maddening electronic telephone information system if you want to ask a question before booking. Tip: They often discount the cruise price by 50 percent if you book a week in advance. Call and ask about bargains as well as extra charges. (CC). (800) 72–PRIDE.

Seawolf Park on Pelican Island. Accessible from Broadway via a turn north on Fifty-first Street. Adults enjoy watching Galveston's busy harbor from this unusual vantage point, and children love scrambling over a series of naval exhibits that include an airplane, a destroyer escort, and a submarine. Also here: The *Selma*, one of the ill-fated cement ships built as an experiment during World War I. It ran aground here years ago. Fee.

There is no swimming at Seawolf Park, but there are good facilities for fishing and picnics. Open daily. Parking fee.

Strand Street Theater. 2317 Ship's Mechanic Row. This local repertory company has something on the boards almost every weekend, year-round, plus children's theater as well. Call for schedule. (409) 763–4591.

Sailing, Surfing, and Waterskiing. T-Marina at Washington Park, Sixty-first Street at Offatts Bayou, has instruction and rentals for many water sports. (409) 744–9031. The sailing charter scene is ever changing. For a list of operators, contact the Galveston Convention and Visitors Bureau.

Tennis and Golf. Information on specific locations is available from the Galveston Con-Vis Bureau. If you are a hotel guest, ask about temporary membership privileges at private facilities on the island.

Texas Limited. Seven handsomely restored passenger cars from America's golden age of rail make the 50-mile trip between Houston and Galveston every Thursday through Sunday, with double trips on Saturday. Whether you ride in the Chimayo car (1938) of Santa Fe Railway's famous Super Chief, the California Zephyr's Silver Stirrup (1948) with its vista dome, or the opulent Silver Queen club car (1957), taking the *Flyer* turns a trip to Galveston into a travel experience. Houston departures are from the downtown Amtrak station; Galveston arrivals are at the Center for Transportation and Commerce, at Twenty-fifth and Strand. (713) 522–9090 (taped information), (713) 526–1709 or (800) 284–5780 (tickets through Ticketron).

WHERE TO EAT

Clary's. 8509 Teichman Road, across from the *Galveston Daily News.* Don't judge this place by its low-key exterior. Locals think it serves some of the best seafood on the island, often with a Creole touch. An off-menu item, spiced shrimp, is a house specialty. Slightly dressy crowd here, so no beach clothes, please. Open Monday–Friday for lunch and dinner, Saturday for dinner only. $$; (CC). (409) 740–0771.

Cody's. Strand at Twenty-third. You can't miss this place. Just find the giant white cement trumpet at the side of Old Galveston Square and look up. An offshoot of Houston's popular jazz club/restaurant of the same name, this establishment serves up tasty food and even better music. Best of all, you can sit on the balcony and watch The Strand's ever-present human comedy passing below. Call for days and hours of operation. $–$$; (CC). (409) 762–2639.

Gaido's. 3800 Seawall. Whether it's fried, broiled, or boiled, the fresh seafood here is excellent, partly because the dressings and sauces are made from scratch. The menu changes daily to reflect the best from the sea. Open daily for lunch and dinner. $$–$$$; (CC). (409) 762–9625. (Tip: If Gaido's is crowded, try Casey's next door; they share the same kitchen.)

Hill's Pier 19. Twentieth and Wharf. Almost always crowded, this is the place for fresh fish, salads, gumbo, and more, all served cafeteria-style. You can eat inside or up on the top deck overlooking the boat basin. Open daily for lunch and dinner. $–$$; (CC). (409) 763–7087.

The Phoenix Bakery and Coffee House. Ship's Mechanic Row and Twenty-third, 1 block south of The Strand. Although the great sandwiches and salads will tempt, go straight for the New Orleans-style beignets and café au lait, and then head for one of the umbrella tables in the patio. It's not quite like N.O.'s French Market, but close. Open daily for all three meals. $–$$; (CC). (409) 763–4611.

Shrimp and Stuff. Thirty-ninth Street and Avenue O. Beach-weary folks love this simple place for its tasty shrimp po-boys, home-made gumbo, and ample fish dinners. Open for lunch and dinner daily. $–$$; (CC). (409) 763–2805.

The Wentletrap. 2301 Strand. Many Texans consider this one of the finest restaurants in the state. Housed in the historic League Building, erected in 1871, the Wentletrap boasts an inventive menu and upscale, dressy decor. Open Monday–Saturday for lunch and dinner; Sunday for brunch. $$–$$$; (CC). (409) 765–5545 or (713) 225–6033.

Yaga's Cafe. 2314 Strand. "Tropical" is the operative adjective at this casual place, from decor to food to music. Try the spicey shrimp only if you have some very cool liquid to quench mouth fire. This is also a good spot for burgers and sandwiches, plus it jumps with reggae at night. Call for hours. $–$$; (CC). (409) 762–6676.

WANDERING THE BACKROADS

Driving southwest the length of the island on FM–3005 brings you to great fishing at San Luis Pass. Go over the causeway, and it's another 38 miles to Surfside Beach and Freeport. For activities there, see Trip 1, Southwest Sector.

Heading east from Galveston along the coast to Sea Rim State Park (Trip 3, East Sector) is possible. Just take the free Bolivar ferry and continue on T–87. In Galveston, the Bolivar ferry slip is at the end of Second Street (turn north from Broadway), but don't plan to go to Bolivar on a prime-time weekend unless you love waiting in long lines.

Once on Bolivar, you won't find much, which is its biggest attraction—just some fishing camps, a long and primitive beach, and an abandoned lighthouse built in 1872. The lighthouse and the small homes around it were used some years ago as sets for the filming of the Patty Duke movie, *My Sweet Charlie.*

Watch for signs to Fort Travis Seashore Park, on the right as you exit the ferry from Galveston. Long known as the place where Jane Long, the "Mother of Texas," gave birth to the first Anglo child on Texas soil, it also has the remains of a fort built before the turn of the century. There is stair-access to a 2,800-foot beach, excellent fishing off the rocks, picnic and camping areas, and very rustic cabanas for overnight stays. To arrange for the latter, contact the permit coordinator of the Galveston County Parks Department, (409) 766–2411.

CELEBRATIONS AND FESTIVALS

NOTE: Many of the telephone numbers listed below are for weekdays only. For specific dates, consult the current issue of *Texas Highways* magazine.

JANUARY

Baytown's "Goose Creek Texas Chili When It's Chilly" Cook-off. There's even a margarita mix-off competition to liven up the early January scene. (713) 422–8359.

Festival Hill. Concerts followed by dinner and a classic film lure you to Round Top once a month from August through April—always enjoyable, but most welcome during the quiet days of winter. The dinner includes wine, and overnight accommodations are available in attractive studio residences as well as in historic Menke House. (409) 249–3129.

Janis Joplin Birthday Bash. Port Arthur celebrates a native daughter with concerts and special displays. (409) 983–4921.

FEBRUARY

The Clear Lake Gem and Mineral Show. This event is one of the best of its kind in the country. (713) 488–7676.

Galveston Mardi Gras. This reincarnation of a long-gone tradition keeps the island swinging with parades and balls during the ten days prior to Lent. (409) 764–4311, (800) 351–4236 in Texas, (800) 351–4237 elsewhere.

Texas Independence Day. Washington-on-the-Brazos relives its brief moment in the Lone Star limelight every year on the weekend closest to March 2. (409) 878–2461 or 836–3696.

MARCH

The Dogwood Festival and Western Weekend. Woodville celebrates the beauty of spring in the East Texas woods with this annual event the last weekend in March and the first weekend in April. Fun ranges from a parade and historical pageant to a beard contest, rodeo, and trail ride. (409) 283–2632.

Historical Tour and Antique Show. Some of Brenham's surviving antebellum homes can be toured during this event. (409) 836–3695.

Nederland Heritage Festival. Complete with a tulip pageant, parade, tennis tournament, flea market, and minimarathon. On Boston Avenue, between Fourteenth and Seventeenth streets in front of the city hall. (409) 722–0279.

Pioneer Day at Jesse Jones Park and Nature Center. All the homely arts that ultimately tamed the Texas frontier are demonstrated, plus the park's reconstructed homestead is open to the public. (713) 446–8588.

APRIL

Blessing of the Fleet(s). Take your pick. Galveston and Freeport both host these festivals annually. Freeport. (409) 265–2508. Galveston. (409) 763–4311 or (800) 351–4236.

Bluebonnet Festival. Chappell Hill shows off its old things in this best of Texas seasons. (409) 836–3695.

Burton Cotton Gin Festival. The town's wonderful old gin is open for tours, and all manner of other events liven things up on a weekend late in the month. (409) 289–2863.

Country Livin' Festival. Formerly Bellville's Bluebonnet Festival, this annual event falls on an early April weekend when the wildflowers in the fields around town are at their peak. The chamber of commerce has booths around town where you can pick up packets of bluebonnet seeds and maps of driving tours to see the year's best color. At the park it's everything from Civil War battles to mock Indian dances, Cajun music and food, folk artists, and buggy rides. (409) 865–3407.

Eeyore's Birthday Party. Costumes are a tradition for this annual event, which also includes music, games, maypoles, a lollipop tree, and birthday cake for everyone. This is an ideal outing for families with small children. There's even Shakespeare in the evening in the old barn. (409) 278–3530.

The Good Oil Days Festival. Humble's streets fill with crafts and entertainment on a mid-April weekend. (713) 446–2128.

Montgomery Trek. Many of Montgomery's old homes open their doors to the public on a mid-April weekend. (409) 597–4155.

Neches River Festival. Beaumont celebrates for a week with historical pageants, shows, exhibitions, etc., all over town. (409) 838–1424 or (800) 392–4401.

Pilgrimage Homes Tour. Calvert opens the doors of its marvelous old homes. If you love Victoriana and antiques, don't miss it. (409) 364–2559.

Round Top Antique Fair. Annually on the first weekend in April, Round Top's old Rifle Association Hall is filled wall to wall with antique dealers showing their best. (713) 520–8057.

San Jacinto Day Festival. East and West Columbia celebrate the early days of the republic with guided bus tours of old homes and plantations, the replica of the first state capitol, and a shrimp boil. (409) 345–3921.

Sylvan Beach Festival. La Porte revives its heyday with a parade, a chili cook-off, and entertainment. (713) 471–1123.

Texas Crafts Exhibition. Combine a trip to the antique fair in Round Top with a stop at Winedale, just down the road, where you will find quality exhibitions of the state's best handcrafts, plus folklife demonstrations, picnicking, etc. (409) 278–3530.

Texas Trek. Anderson comes to life each spring to celebrate its history with a home tour, parade, and plenty of Main Street fun. (409) 873–2662.

Triathalon. This biking, running, and swimming competition in Bryan-College Station is open to all who preregister. (409) 260–9898.

Winedale Spring Festival and Texas Crafts Exhibition. Combine this with a trip to the antique festival at Round Top. Winedale is just down the road, and the fun includes pioneer demonstrations of old-time skills and crafts, a craft show with working artists, live musical entertainment, a barbecue-chicken picnic, and a barn dance. (409) 278–3530.

MAY

Czech Fest. Rosenberg celebrates its ethnic heritage every spring at the Fort Bend County Fairgrounds. (713) 342–5464.

Homes Tour. Galveston's annual peek behind historic doors. One of the best in the state. (713) 280–3907 or (409) 765–7834.

International Gumbo Cook-Off. On the first weekend in May, Orange and its Cajun folks relegate chili to the back burner in favor of every sort of gumbo brewed in the South. (409) 883–3536.

Kaleidoscope. Beaumont spreads out the best in creative arts and crafts on the art museum grounds. (409) 838–6581.

Magnolia Homes Tour. Columbus rolls back time the third weekend in May with a melodrama, parade, historic homes tour, and antique and craft shows. (409) 732–5881.

Maifest. Brenham hosts the oldest spring festival in the state in the heart of the wildflower season. (409) 836–3695.

Navasota Nostalgia Days. Family fun, plus tours of several historic private homes. (409) 825–6600.

Old Town Spring. Country Fair time on the first weekend in May. (713) 353–9310.

JUNE

Agricultural Society Barbecue. Cat Spring turns out for June Feast on the first Sunday of the month. (409) 865–2627.

Big Thicket Day. The tiny town of Saratoga swings annually with a bluegrass and country music party, plus country cooking, crafts, etc. (409) 274–5000.

Fiddler's Festival. Some old-time toe-tapping music in Crockett the second week in June. (409) 544–2359.

Firemen's Picnic. Frelsburg draws folks into town with this celebration on the second weekend of the month. (409) 732–3716.

Grimes County Fair. Head for the fairgrounds in Navasota for this one. (409) 825–6600.

Juneteenth Celebrations. Emancipation is cheered with special events in Huntsville, (800) 289–0389; Brenham, (409) 836–3695; and Beaumont, (409) 838–3613 or 736–2469.

Lobster Fiesta and Golf Tournament. Huntsville hosts golf at Elkins Lake and a feed at the Walker County Fairgrounds. (800) 289–0389.

Oleander Festival. Any excuse for a bloomin' party in fun-loving Galveston. (409) 763–4011 or (800) 351–4236 in Texas.

Pow Wow. Livingston and the Alabama-Coushatta Indian Reservation are your destinations for this ethnic celebration the first weekend of the month. (409) 327–4929, (409) 563–4391, or (800) 392–4794.

Sandcastle Building Contests. Freeport invites the public to try their hands at this timeless childhood art at Surfside Beach the second weekend of the month. (409) 265–2508. Galveston's contest is usually a week earlier. (409) 763–4311, (800) 351–4236 in Texas.

Thicket Country Picnic and Blueberry Eatin' Meetin'. This week-long celebration in Kountze in early August includes Redneck Recognition Day, blueberry farm tours, pageantry, and two hunts, one for treasure, the other for wild hogs. (409) 246–2470.

Tri-County Rodeo. The Montgomery County Fairgrounds in Conroe is the scene of lots of rough and tumble action. (409) 756–8331 or 756–6644.

Y'all Come Celebration. Brenham hosts some outdoor summer fun for families at the Washington County Fairgrounds. (409) 836–4112.

JULY

Annual Rodeo. Call Crockett's Chamber of Commerce for list of events. (409) 544–2359.

Ashton Villa's Old-Fashioned Family Outing; Armadillo Longneck Festival; and Jean Laffite Days. Take your pick. All three enliven Galveston around the Fourth of July. (409) 763–4311 or (800) 351–4236.

Fourth of July Celebrations. The following all have their own versions of the old-fashioned Independence Day. Beaumont, (409) 838–3435; Brenham, (409) 836–3695; Chappell Hill, (409) 836–6382; Clear Lake, (713) 488–7676; Columbus, (409) 732–5881; Crockett, (409) 544–2359; Huntsville, (800) 289–0389; Lake Jackson, (409) 265–2505; Navasota, (409) 825–6600; Port Arthur, (800) 235–7822; Round Top, (409) 249–3308; Seabrook, (713) 488–7676; Sealy, (409) 885–3222; and Woodville, (409) 283–2632.

Lunar Rendezvous. The Clear Lake area celebrates with two weeks' worth of art shows, festivals, tournaments, and a decorated boat parade. (713) 488–7676.

AUGUST

Antique Celebration. Calvert puts on a show and sale of quality antiques and collectibles on historic Main Street; includes horse-drawn tours of historic district. (409) 364–2933.

Good Times Arts and Crafts Festival. Port Arthur hosts this salute to summer. You can combine it with an excursion to Sea Rim State Park. (800) 235–7822.

Schulenburg Festival. Four days of fun in Wolters Park, including a stock show and parade. (409) 743–3023.

Shakespeare at Winedale. The historic old barn at this open-air historical museum rings with the undying words of the Bard every Thursday–Sunday evening. You can even come for dinner before the show. (409) 278–3530.

Shrimporee and Fishfest in Palacios. There's a parade of floats and a blessing of the fleet, plus anglers compete for cash fishing prizes. (512) 972–2615 or 972–3362.

SEPTEMBER

Antique Show. Cat Spring gathers the best of treasures in a country setting. (409) 865–3407.

County Fairs. This is the month, so plan a trip to La Grange, (409) 968–5756; Columbus, (409) 732–5881, Brenham, (409) 836–3695; Woodville, (409) 283–2632; Hempstead, (409) 826–6312; or Beaumont, (409) 838–6581.

Pasadena Stock Show and Rodeo. This week-long event is held at the rodeo grounds, 7600 Red Bluff Road. (713) 487–7871.

Spindletop Boom Days. Beaumont's oil days live on at this annual shindig in the reconstructed Gladys City. (409) 838–6581.

OCTOBER

Antique Show. Bellville traditionally has one of the most extensive shows in the state on either the third or fourth weekend in October in the city park pavilion. Also on the grounds are a farmer's market, pumpkin-decorating contest, folk art, quilting bee, rug weaving, pony rides, and country cooking. (409) 865–3407.

CavOilcade Celebration. Port Arthur's annual biggie, complete with street parade, old-timers' breakfast, boat races, golf and tennis tournaments, Hungry Artists' show, antique automobiles, and a thieves' market. (409) 985–7822.

County and Regional Fairs. Try the Fort Bend County Fair at Rosenberg, (713) 342–5464, or the South Texas State Fair in Beaumont, (409) 838–6581 or (800) 392–4401. Other possibilities are the Brazoria County Fair, (409) 265–2505, and the Austin County Fair with its PCRA-sanctioned rodeo in Bellville, (409) 865–3407.

Epicurean Evening. How about sampling special dishes from the best restaurants in Galveston? This annual event is held in Moody Center on Seawall Boulevard. (409) 763–4311 or (800) 351–4236.

Fall Fest. Canoe floats, field trips, and camping are part of the program on the grounds of the Big Thicket Museum in Saratoga. (409) 274–5000.

Heritage Holiday. The Old West lives again in Old Town Spring, site of this annual ethnic celebration for northwest Harris County. (713) 353–2317.

Lickskillet Celebration. Fayetteville relives its heritage. (409) 968–5756.

Octoberfest. Washington-on-the-Brazos increases its population by several thousand during this two-day event. Includes a parade, street dance, entertainers, and loads of German food. (409) 836–3695.

Oktoberfest. Round Top and Winedale combine efforts for this special celebration. Expect demonstrations of horseshoeing, muleskinning, fireplace cooking, soap making, etc.—all following a German heritage theme. (713) 520–8057 or (409) 278–3530.

Parada del Rodeo. League City (south of Clear Lake) puts on a two-night rodeo followed by a dance in the pavilion at the Galveston County Park on T–3. There's also a trail ride and chili cook-off. (713) 488–7676.

Polk County Pinecone Festival. Livingston spreads fun around the courthouse square in downtown. There are street dances, trail rides, hot-air balloon races, timber exhibits, food, crafts, etc. (409) 327–4929.

Renaissance Festival. England's sixteenth century is recreated every weekend this month in the woods between Magnolia and Plantersville. Amid parades, jousting, races, and games of skill, you'll chat with Robin Hood, assorted wenches, minstrels, comics, jugglers, knights and their elegant ladies, and other anachronistic characters. Dress to the theme and join in the fun. (713) 356–2178 or (409) 894–2516.

Scarecrow Festival. Chappell Hill's biggest event of the year includes a stew cook-off. (409) 836–3695.

Square Fair. Wharton's town square is the focus of an antique auto show, a parade, a dance, running races, etc. (409) 532–1862.

Strand Street Music Festival. Details change on this Galveston offering, so call (409) 765–7834 or (713) 280–3907.

Texas Rice Festival. The small town of Winnie (west of Beaumont on I–10) celebrates its prime crop with carnival, parades, art shows, rice-cooking contests, street and square dances, and professional entertainment. (409) 296–2231.

Texian Market Days. Reliving the early days of ranching, this late October weekend event has pioneer-life demonstrations, crafts and art booths, horse-drawn wagon rides, entertainment, and tours of two old homes on the A. P. George Ranch. There's also a re-creation of an 1860s Confederate military camp and the 1820s settlement of Stephen F. Austin's first colonists. (713) 342–6478.

Trinity Valley Exposition and Rodeo. Liberty gears up the third week of October with a variety of family activities, including a baby parade, held annually since 1909. (409) 336–5736.

NOVEMBER

Why not an outing on Thanksgiving weekend to cut your own Christmas tree? There are more than five dozen commercial Christmas tree farms within the area covered by this book. For a complete list, request the free Christmas Tree Farm brochure from the Texas Department of Agriculture, Box 12847, Austin 78711. (512) 463–7624.

Christmas Previews. You will find "Welcome to the holidays" celebrations at various times and in a variety of styles at the following. Brenham, (409) 836–1690; Bay City, (409) 244–7692; Bellville, (409) 865–3407; Groves, (409) 962–3631; Lake Jackson, (409) 265–2508; Tomball, (713) 351–7222; Port Neches, (409) 722–9154; Columbus, (409) 732–5881 or 732–5135; El Campo, (409) 543–2713; and Beaumont, (409) 835–7100.

Fall Rose Festival. Independence's Antique Rose Emporium hosts seminars, exhibits, demonstrations, shopping, and food early in the month. (409) 836–5548.

Antique Show. Beaumont's Heritage Society puts together a whopper of a show in the Civic Center the first weekend of this month. (409) 898–0348 or 898–3267.

Polderfaire Arts and Crafts Show. Great stocking-stuffers are to be found here, plus an antique car show in Nederland at the Jefferson County Airport. (409) 722–0279.

Galveston Island Jazz Festival. Top musicians perform in Galveston's Grand 1894 Opera House, The Strand swings with entertainment, and there are jazz cruises on *The Colonel* paddlewheeler. (409) 765–1894 or 763–7080.

Messina Hof Tours. Two November weekend events bring visitors to this Bryan-College Station winery. The first is an Italian Garden Party which introduces new vintages, and the second is a Thanksgiving tour and tasting. Reservations are required. (409) 778–9463.

Wild Goose Festival. Eagle Lake gets noisy with duck- and goose-calling contests, hunting-dog field trial demonstrations, runs and bike races, a chili cook-off, etc. (409) 234–2780.

DECEMBER

Bellville's Small Town Christmas and Holiday Home Tour. This also includes seasonal dramas in the Little Country Theater. (409) 865–3407.

Bryan-College Station's Christmas in the Park. This month-long lighting festival in Central Park brings viewers from miles around. (409) 764–3773.

Candlelight Tour of the John Jay French Museum, Beaumont. You can help costumed French characters decorate an old-time tree. (409) 898–3267.

Christmas Bird Count in Brazosport. Birders from all over the country gather here between Christmas and New Year's for this annual event. Some 226 species have been sighted in years past. Binoculars are essential. (409) 265–2505.

Christmas Boat Lane Parade. Seabrook and Kemah join forces for an evening to celebrate the season in their own unique way. (713) 488–7676.

Christmas Homes Tour in Wharton. Grand homes of the past open their doors to the public. (409) 532–1862.

Christmas Market and Festival of Lights in Sealy. The entire town turns out for this early December weekend event which includes a parade. (409) 885–3222.

Christmas Open House at Winedale. All the old German Christmas traditions seem right at home here for this one-night event. (409) 278–3530.

Dicken's Evening on the Strand. Galveston's famous Strand becomes a four-block-long stage for Victorian Christmases past. Dress up in your best period duds and join the fun. There will be a mix of characters from Dickens, as well as town criers, British bobbies, carolers, bell-ringing choirs, horse-drawn coaches, etc. The Budweiser Clydesdales also are part of this annual nineteenth-century event. (713) 280–3907 or (409) 280–3907.

Glow of Christmas at Ashton Villa. One of Galveston's grandest homes is at its best during this annual event. (409) 765–7921.

Griffin House Christmas Candlelight Tour in Tomball. The traditional songs and wassail of Christmas on the second weekend of the month. (713) 255–2148.

Heritage House Museum Candlelight Tour in Orange. You'll see Victorian Christmas touches in this nice old home, plus there's a gift shop full of Victorian toy replicas. (409) 883–3536.

International Holiday and Candlelight Promenade. Port Arthur lights up for this; call for details. (800) 235–7822.

Montgomery Candlelight Tours. Lovely homes dressed for the season. (409) 597–4155.